PARENTAL PIVOT

Thriving in Life and Career as You Transition to Parenthood

ANNA MINTO

Parental Pivot
Copyright ©2024 Anna Minto
Transformational Change, LLC
TrChange.com

All rights reserved. This book or any portion thereof may not be
reproduced or used in any manner whatsoever without the express
written permission of the publisher except for the use of brief quotations
in a book review. Please direct inquiries to AMinto@TrChange.com.

ISBN 979-8-9875587-2-0 (paperback)
ISBN 979-8-9875587-3-7 (ebook)

Book Design: Clarity Designworks

This book is dedicated to:

My clients, past, present and future,
who so vulnerably shared their journeys and experiences,
and have taught me so much to offer working parents
everywhere.

May you all thrive, not just survive!

"The privilege of a lifetime is to become who you truly are. Embrace your journey of self-discovery and growth, recognizing that each step brings you closer to your authentic self. This journey is not always easy, but it is the most rewarding path you can take."

—Carl Jung, Swiss psychiatrist and psychoanalyst

Contents

PART FOUR
TAKING YOUR LEAVE(S)

PART FIVE
PLANNING YOUR RETURN TO WORK

PART SIX
THE TRUTHS ABOUT RETURNING TO WORK

Why This Book Exists

Congratulations! As my children's paternal grandma, a very Zen, sage Japanese woman, once told me, "The Universe is about to shift. Imperceptibly, but definitively so." She couldn't have put it more succinctly. I wasn't quite sure what she meant at the time, but I quickly learned the wisdom in her words. The universe did indeed shift, and so did the complexity, chaos, and love in my life.

As a new parent, the transition can be overwhelming, filled with challenges and joys one never imagined. I read many pregnancy books, with my favorite being *What to Expect When You're Expecting* and had dozens of baby and parenting books. I felt totally prepared and informed to be pregnant and deliver a baby. I would even tell myself, *"You got this!"* But when my first child, Charlotte, arrived weeks early, I quickly realized that no amount of reading could have fully prepared me for the realities of motherhood.

Fortunately, I had the support of my family—my mum, Fran, who flew to London for the birth, and my dad, Clive, who was an exceptionally involved father to my sister and me in a time when many dads didn't "do diapers." My children's father was also a hands-on dad from the start. The initial phase of figuring out how to care for a tiny, wild, pink, screaming person was a steep learning curve, but I quickly found my footing and embraced the journey of motherhood.

But that was only one part of the story. The other piece of me— the driven-to-succeed, Type A, Harvard MBA, fast-track consultant at Boston Consulting Group—was completely in the dark about navigating my career post-baby. There were no books on "how to think about returning to work," and I oscillated between "I'm never going back to work" and "I need to work to be truly fulfilled." It was trial by fire.

Over the years, I balanced my career with motherhood, navigating various work arrangements and maternity leaves. I spent 17 years at Boston Consulting Group, eventually becoming a Managing Director and Partner. But looking back, I wish I had more guidance on managing it all.

Fast forward to more recent times, and I've had the privilege of coaching over 500 clients in more than 6,000 one-on-one sessions. Through these experiences, I've connected the dots, built up my knowledge, and learned invaluable lessons from the journeys of the incredible women and men I've coached. Their stories, challenges, and successes have informed, inspired, and enriched my approach, helping me to create frameworks and strategies that support new parents in this critical life transition.

This book is for executive leaders—both moms and dads—who are approaching or finishing up parental leave. It's not about *whether* to return to work but *how* to think about and prepare yourself to thrive.

The precursor book, "*Maternity Magic: Empower and Discover Yourself while Planning for and Returning from Maternity Leave,*" was written primarily for "mom," who typically gave birth and took extended maternity leave. The wonderful emergence of paternity leaves and the increased role of "dad" in parenting has shifted the dynamics, and leaves are more commonly referred to as "Parental Leaves," often distinguishing the birth-giver and the birth-partner. The complexities (and joys) of dual and differing combinations of parental leaves I saw with my clients sparked the genesis of this next edition—*Parental Pivot*—written for both "moms" and "dads" (please see my caveat about the use of this terminology below).

This book is not a "quick read" but rather an opportunity to reflect and explore. Many chapters have space for you to jot down your thoughts and decisions, making it more of an interactive exploration than a "how to" guide.

May you discover what works best for you, your partner, and your family!

Anna

Caveat About "Mom" and "Dad" Terminology

In this book, I frequently use the terms "mom" and "dad" (or "mother" and "father") to refer to the birth-giver and the non-birth-giver. I want to take a moment to acknowledge that these terms are simplifications and do not encompass the full spectrum of family structures, gender identities, and parenting roles.

Families come in many shapes and forms—single parents, same-sex couples, non-binary parents, adoptive families, surrogate families, and blended families, to name just a few. Each family brings its own unique experiences and perspectives to the journey of parenting. My use of "mom" and "dad" is intended to offer clarity and ease of understanding, but I fully recognize that not all parents fit neatly into these traditional roles.

Some people also distinguish "birth-giver" from "birth-partner," to clarify the person who also journeys through pregnancy, labor and delivery (typically) in addition to taking on parenting roles.

Whether you are a single parent, a member of the LGBTQ+ community, a grandparent raising a child, or part of any other family structure, the concepts and strategies discussed in this book are meant to be adaptable and inclusive. The core principles—navigating the challenges of parental leave, maintaining your career trajectory, and thriving in both your personal and professional life—apply to all parents, regardless of how you identify or how your family is structured.

My goal is to offer guidance and support that can be tailored to your unique situation. I encourage you to adapt the advice in this book to fit your own life and to consider the exercises and strategies as tools that can be customized to your personal journey as a parent.

Thank you for joining me on this journey, and I hope you find the insights in this book valuable, whatever your family looks like.

 **PLEASE NOTE!** 

Part One, *Know Who You Are*, and Part Two, *Know What You Want* are all about deepening your understanding of yourself.

I believe they are foundational precursors to navigating the journey of parental leave(s).

Therefore, I have put exploring these topics of self-discovery up-front.

If, however, you already know yourself very well and would prefer to jump straight in, please proceed directory to Part Three – *Planning your Leave(s)*.

KNOW WHO YOU ARE

Before diving into the practicalities of parental leave, it's crucial to take a step back and truly understand the person embarking on this journey—you. This isn't just about preparing for the physical and logistical aspects of becoming a parent but about grounding yourself in a deep understanding of your identity, values, and essential qualities. Knowing who you are, such as identifying the core values that drive your thoughts and behavior, is the foundation for making decisions that align with your true self, allowing you to navigate the challenges of parenthood with clarity and intention.

This process begins with self-reflection. Understanding your personality, your habitual patterns, and how you tend to behave under stress or in times of change is essential. Tools like the Enneagram offer invaluable insights to identify your personality type, helping you recognize your strengths and the areas where you might need to be more mindful. The Enneagram isn't just about labeling yourself; it's about understanding how your unique traits can influence your approach to parenting, work, and life. It's also about understanding tendencies to migrate in certain directions under environments of stress or, conversely, under environments of security.

Beyond understanding your personality, reflecting on your Core Values—the principles that guide your decisions and actions is equally important. Identifying these values will help you make choices that are not only practical but also deeply aligned with what matters most to you. In times of change, your values serve as an anchor, ensuring that your chosen path resonates with your authentic self.

Finally, consider the golden thread that weaves through your life—your Essential Positive Quality. This is the constant that has been present in your experiences, the core element that makes you uniquely "you." Recognizing this thread will provide you with a sense of continuity and purpose, even as you step into the new and often unpredictable world of parenthood.

Take your time with these three foundational elements, have a pen handy, take notes-to-self, and enjoy the exploration. By laying this groundwork, you will be better equipped to make decisions that are aligned with who you are, setting the stage for a parenting journey both intentional and fulfilling.

In this Part, we will explore these chapters:

1. Enneagram Type

2. Core Values

3. Essential Positive Quality

Enneagram Type

The Enneagram is used in the world of psychology, in similar ways as the Myers-Briggs (MBTI) is used in the world of business. Both tools are heavily validated and broadly used. In my opinion, the Enneagram has four key advantages over the MBTI because:

- It focuses on behavioral "whys" (the root cause of an action) rather than the behaviors themselves.

- There are paths to growth and development.

- It highlights how behaviors migrate under conditions of stress and security.

- It's simple—there are nine "Polarities," which are organized into three triads ("Pearls") grounded in the gut, heart, or head.

The following table summarizes how the tool is organized.

ENNEAGRAM OVERVIEW		
<u>RED PEARLS</u>	**GREEN PEARLS**	**BLUE PEARLS**
Gut, Instinct Reality, Impact Present Anger	Heart, Feeling Self, Seen Past Worth	Head, Thinking Separated, Security Future Fear
8: Challenger 9: Peacemaker 1: Reformer	2: Helper 3: Achiever 4: Individualist	5: Investigator 6: Thinker 7: Enthusiast

The characteristics typical of *red pearls* are driven from the gut. It's all about instinct and facing reality in the present. The people who identify most with these qualities look for how they are impacting the world and how the world impacts them. They operate on an "anger" continuum, which can be a mild grumbly "grrrr" in the belly or in the extreme, rage and fieriness.

The qualities that are typical of *green pearls* are driven from the heart. It's all about feeling and being seen by others. Projecting their self-image is important. People who resonate most with this type tend to spend considerable time thinking about the past. They operate on a "self-worth" continuum, which can be mildly expressed as feeling embarrassed or "less than," or in the extreme, can be pride, vanity, or shame.

People who resonate with *blue pearls* are driven by their thinking head. They separate and compartmentalize analytically. They want to feel safe and secure about the future. They operate on a "fear" continuum, which can be expressed in a mild form as anxiety, worry, and "think, think, think," and in the extreme as "Chicken Little."

We all have some red, green, and blue in us. Some of us are more anchored in one or two than others.

Which color(s) do you most resonate with? Which colors do not? Here's a worksheet that can help you discover whether you operate primarily from the gut, heart, or head (or a combination of them).

3 PEARLS SELF-AWARENESS WORKSHEET

Scale each item and reflect on the <u>overall</u> description of each TRIAD.

0 = Not true at all. 10 = Always true.

2 3 4

/10 HEART - I move and feel moved mostly by my feelings. When I walk into a room, I usually first emotionally connect with how I relate to others to determine my next action.

/10 SELF EXAGGERATION - If I reflect, I think I am unconsciously aware of how I am exaggerating aspects of myself and hiding others. I often have a heartfelt longing for my wholeness to be seen.

/10 HOW CAN I BE SEEN? If I reflect, I am often very aware of how I'm being seen by others. I tend to project a self-image to feel good about myself and get what I need from others.

/10 WORTH CONTINUUM - Under pressure, my default reaction is usually a mix of:
- At a softer volume it could express as feeling embarrassed, less than, or masked.
- At a louder volume it could manifest as pride, vanity, shame, or even self-contempt.

TOTAL

5 6 7

/10 HEAD - I move and feel moved mostly by my thinking. When I walk into a room, I usually first use my mind to consider things and determine my next move.

/10 PERCEPTION OF SEPARATENESS - If I reflect, I am aware of how I carry an unconscious perception of separateness. A clear type of mental dividing and polarizing. A categorizing and compartmentalizing of life.

/10 HOW CAN I BE SAFE AND SECURE? If I reflect, I am often unconsciously checking in with how secure I feel. My thoughts seek ways to manage this by searching for answers to calm my concerns.

/10 FEAR CONTINUUM - Under pressure, my default reaction is usually a mix of:
- At a softer volume it could express as anxiety, "think, think, think," and worry.
- At a louder volume it could manifest as dread, panic, "chicken little," horror or even terror.

TOTAL

8 9 1

/10 GUT - I move and feel moved mostly by a gut feel of things. When I walk into a room, I usually rely mostly on my instincts to determine my next action.

/10 RESISTING REALITY - If I reflect, I seem to have an underlying unconscious resistance to reality. An underlying "Grrr." An initial gut-based pushing back at life and my experiences.

/10 HOW CAN I IMPACT? If I reflect, I am often unconsciously aware of how I am being impacted and how I am impacting my world. I feel in in my body and its reaction to the situation.

/10 ANGER CONTINUUM - Under pressure, my default reaction is usually a mix of:
- At a softer volume it could express as irritation, grumpiness, or aggravation.
- At a louder volume it could manifest as passion, rage, wrath, or even fury.

TOTAL

Now on to the nine Polarities within those three colored triads, or Pearls.

The good news is that the Polarities (the nine "types") are easy to recognize and relate to. You will probably be able to identify different Polarities among your close friends, family, and colleagues. Don't put too much weight on the "name" of each Polarity—some sound loftier and more aspirational than others. For example, most people want to be helpers and achievers, but not all are fundamentally *driven* by this need. Some of my clients prefer to rename each of the Polarities as someone they are familiar with so they can really envision and remember it.

The bad news is that it can initially seem complex. The richness of information behind the arrows representing influence under conditions of security (the arrows pointing in both directions to/from the Polarity type) and under conditions of stress (the arrow pointing toward the Polarity type) can be confusing at first. For example, a 2 (Helper), incorporates the great characteristics of both 8 (Challenger) and 4 (individualist) under security, yet gets the not-so-great characteristics of the 8 (Challenger) under stress.

There are also "wings" on either side of a Polarity, one of which is typically more heavily weighted. For example, a 2 (Helper) might have a 1 (Reformer) or a 3 (Achiever) wing.

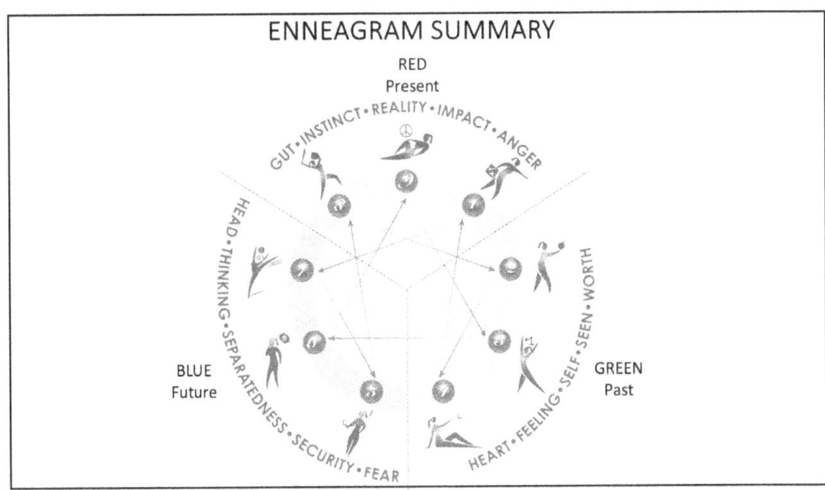

Just to add to the confusion: some individuals modulate their approaches and style as they grow, and some people (while in the moment of taking the assessment) can be primarily under conditions of stress or security. This can generate an assessment that suggests multiple possibilities for the individual's Polarity. At this point, it's tempting to think, "*Well, that doesn't enlighten me much!*" and throw the "results" in the trash bin. Take the time to explore it, even if it might seem useless at first.

The most enlightening approach to realizing the richness of the Enneagram is to explore it live with a Certified Enneagram Coach (which I am). But since we are not speaking live, I'll share my take on each Polarity as nine one-page descriptions (and for you logical types, don't ask me why the numbers start with two, with one at the end. I've often wondered about that and wanted to rotate the whole thing myself, but alas, that would totally confuse things!).

All pages are formatted the same and include:

- A figurine that captures the essence of the Polarity

- A list of descriptive words on the left (with the generally more appealing ones at the top and the generally less flattering ones below)

- A guide to other Polarities accessed under conditions of security or stress at the bottom.

- Remember that your "wing" lies on either side of your number (e.g., the number to the left or the right of you in the circle).

I realize it's less informative to read alone than to discuss, but hopefully, this gets you started. As they say at Nike, "*Just do it!*" (Learn and explore your Enneagram type.)

GREEN

I'm trying to be helpful

2 *The Helper*

Giving
Nurture
You
Love
Connect
Kind
Warm
Hero
Yes
Hostess
Charming
Pleasing
Proud
Sentimental
Flattery
Sensitive
Possessive
Martyr

You Are Possible

8 *The Challenger*

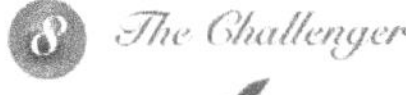

4 *The Individualist*

GREEN

*I'm trying to be the **best***

3 *The Achiever*

Success

Win, 1st

Action

Competitive

Faster

Visible

Star

Me

Network

Entrepreneurial

Yes

Outdo

Flattery

Entertain

Show-off

Vain

Self-promote

Self-serving

Arrogant

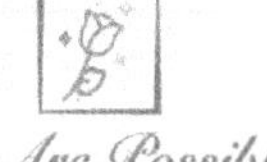

You Are Possible

9 *The Peacemaker*

6 *The Thinker*

GREEN

HEART • FEELING • SELF • SEEN • WORTH

*I'm trying to be **unique***

Different
Original
Unique
New
Me
Self-expression
Creative
Flair
Deep
Outsider
Feelings
Sensitive
Wounded
Strange
Moody
Drama
Dramatic

You Are Possible

STRESS & SECURE POINT

SECURE POINT

BLUE

I'm trying to
understand

Understand

Know

Learn

Observe

Focus

Watch

Detach

Intense

Alone

Isolated

Bookworm

Cool

Aloof

Ivory tower

Hermit

BLUE

I'm trying to feel **secure**

Question

Solve

Maybe

What if?

Diligent

Plan

Test

Check

Discern

Feedback

Defend

Support

Protect

Unsure

Cautious

Doubt

Worry

Chicken Little

You Are Possible

BLUE

HEAD • THINKING • SEPARATEDNESS • SECURITY • FEAR

I'm trying to be __happy__

Energy

Alive

Happy

Positive

Imagination

Dream

Freedom

Possibilities

Social

YOLO

Play

New

Adventure

Dare me

Scattered

Unfocused

FOMO

Wild

Unreliable

You Are Possible

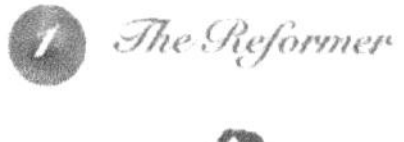

RED

I'm trying to be **strong**

Lead
Presence
Strategy
Focus
Resourceful
Now
Direct
Decisive
Respect
Power
Loyalty
My will
My way or highway
Command
Challenge
Revenge
War
Ruthless

You Are Possible

8 The Challenger

RED

*I'm trying to be **peaceful***

9 — *The Peacemaker*

Peace
Go with the flow
Patient
Self-effacing
Nice
Merge
Kind
Neutral
OK
Chilled
Dreamer
Invisible
Numb
Avoid
Not now
Tuned out
Slow
Denial
Boiling point

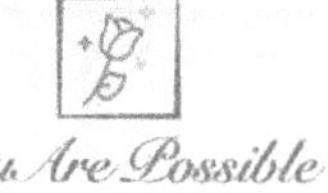

You Are Possible

6 — *The Thinker*

STRESS & SECURE POINT

3 — *The Achiever*

SECURE POINT

RED

GUT • INSTINCT • REALITY • IMPACT • ANGER

*I'm trying to be **good***

1 *The Reformer*

Right or wrong
Good or bad
Rules
Responsible
Standards
Morals
Structure
Fix
Ideas
Improve
Perfect
Correct
Should
Strict
Critic
Righteous

4 *The Individualist*

7 *The Enthusiast*

STRESS & SECURE POINT

SECURE POINT

You Are Possible

(There, see, Polarity 1 eventually shows up!)

If you are still struggling with discovering your type, here's a worksheet to help guide your thinking around which Polarity you are growing from. Have fun and explore! Even better, discuss the nuances with a Certified Enneagram Coach.

9 POLARITIES SELF-AWARENESS WORKSHEET

Scale each and reflect on the <u>overall</u> description of each POLARITY.

0 = Not true at all. 10 = Always true.

2	/10	I'm trying to be seen as <u>helpful</u>. I'm trying not to be seen as **selfish**.	*I am a <u>helper</u>. I place **your needs** above my needs. I do **a lot for others**, and I work hard to be seen as **kind** rather than unkind. I'm **proud** to be your ideal someone, instead of being humbly real. To **give** is easier than to receive, **even at my expense**. I can pretend "I'm okay" instead of being emotionally honest.*
3	/10	I'm trying to be seen as the <u>best</u>. I'm trying not to be seen as a **loser**.	*I am an <u>achiever</u>. By winning I avoid the pain of losing. I say "Yes I can" rather than admit "No I can't." Let's deliver results **fast** rather than slow. I can **wing it** and **make it happen** rather than engage in tedious learning. I can show a **facade of success** to hide fear of failure. Let's **show** that I can **solve** this problem **quick**. I can **burn out**.*
4	/10	I'm trying to be seen as <u>unique</u>. I'm trying not to be seen as **ordinary**.	*I am an <u>individualist</u>. I'd rather be a **dysfunctional outsider** than a functional sheep. **My emotional needs** are above your emotional needs. It's all about **me** not you. I feel things **deeply** rather than objectively. My **emotions** feel like facts. I prefer **drama** to reality.*
5	/10	I'm trying to <u>understand</u>. I'm trying not to lack **understanding**.	*I am an <u>investigator</u>. One can never have enough **knowledge** to remove ignorance. I feel **safer** when **isolated** rather than engaged. I can **hide in my mind** to avoid my heart. It's **easier to observe** than participate. I strive for **competency** in life and fear incompetence.*
6	/10	I'm trying to feel <u>secure</u>. I'm trying not to **lose support**.	*I am a <u>thinker</u>. I seek **information** and **truth** and ask a lot of **questions**. I'd rather **over-plan** than risk being under prepared. I fear deceit. Should I **trust or doubt**? **Fairness** is important and I speak bravely against **unfairness**. Am I with **us or them**? I'm sensitive to the **underdog** vs. aggressor.*
7	/10	I'm trying to be <u>happy</u>. I'm trying not to be **unhappy**.	*I am an <u>enthusiast</u>. I chase **fun** and fear boredom. I want **freedom** from feeling trapped. I keep **busy** to avoid stillness. I seek **pleasure** to run from pain. I keep many **possibilities** open to **avoid limitation**. I **dream** of a **happy future** rather than focus on the realities of the present.*
8	/10	I'm trying to be <u>strong</u>. I'm trying not to be **weak**.	*I am a <u>challenger</u>. I take **control** rather than submit. I choose **war** and I don't easily surrender. I want **power** to not feel powerless. It's **my way or the highway**. **Revenge** is better than forgiveness. **Honor me**, and never be disloyal to me. I **own** rather than share or give.*
9	/10	I'm trying to be <u>peaceful</u>. I'm trying not to disturb the **peace**.	*I am a <u>peacemaker</u>. It's often easier to **tune out** rather than be fully awake. I prefer to take my time **slowly** rather than be very dynamic. It's better to **avoid** rather than confront. I can **numb** instead of asserting myself. It's easier to **hide** than show up, **follow** than lead. **But when pushed, I pounce.***
1	/10	I'm trying to be <u>good</u>. I'm trying not to be **bad**.	*I am a <u>reformer</u>. I appreciate and **follow the rules**. There's only **right or wrong**. It's **black or white**; there is no gray. I'm striving for **perfect** and struggle with imperfection. I have very **high standards**, and don't tolerate low standards. I tend to be **hyper responsible**, not irresponsible. I expect others to follow the rules and **let them know it**.*

Multiple assessments are available online (of varying quality and cost). If you are still unclear, my recommendation is to go to the original Enneagram Institute source:

www.EnneagramInstitute.com

Take the "RHETI" assessment, which has 144 questions. The fee at the time of this writing is $15. It takes about 30 to 40 minutes to complete. It will then provide you with an output report and a more detailed description of the top couple of Polarities you identify with.

If you want to dig deeper, there is a ton of literature out there about the Enneagram. My personal favorites are:

- *The Wisdom of the Enneagram* by Don Richard Riso and Russ Hudson. It explores the nine personality types and their psychological and spiritual growth.

- *Understand Yourself, Understand Your Partner: The Essential Enneagram Guide to a Better Relationship* by Jennifer Schneider and Ron Corn. It describes the relationship dynamics between pairings and can provide invaluable insight into any co-parenting relationship as you enter a new phase of your partnership.

My Enneagram Type:

____

My Stress Point:

____

My Secure Points:

____

My Wing(s):

____

Core Values

Values aren't chosen. They evolve and emerge with life experiences, wisdom, and time. They are a central part of who we are at our core. They highlight what we stand for—our personal code of conduct. Identifying those values can make our lives more consistent and fulfilling. If we don't, our behaviors can be inconsistent and lack cohesion. That makes us grumpy—and others around us grumpy.

Here's an approach to identifying your own personal core values, adapted from Scott Jeffrey's "7 Steps to Discovering Your Core Values," www.ScottJeffrey.com.

1. *Put yourself in a space of open-mindedness*—a mindset where we are unlocked for learning. Create a place for quiet reflection and contemplation and grab a pen and some paper.

2. *Glance over some ideas of what personal core values can be.* There are plenty of lists of core values online. Some of them have as many as several hundred listed. Following are a little over 200 suggestions for getting your brain warmed up. But don't limit yourself to these. Just use it as potential thought starters.

CATEGORIES OF CORE VALUES...A STARTER LIST OF IDEAS

ACHIEVEMENT
Accomplishment
Ambition
Capable
Challenge
Competence
Credibility
Determination
Development
Drive
Effectiveness
Empower
Endurance
Excellence
Famous
Greatness
Growth
Hard work
Improvement
Influence
Intensity
Leadership
Mastery
Motivation
Performance
Persistence
Potential
Power
Productivity
Professionalism
Prosperity
Recognition
Results-oriented
Risk
Significance
Skill
Skillfulness
Status
Success
Talent
Victory
Wealth
Winning

COURAGE
Bravery
Conviction
Fearless
Valor

CREATIVITY
Creation
Curiosity
Discovery
Exploration
Expressive
Imagination
Innovation
Inquisitive
Intuitive
Openness
Originality
Uniqueness
Wonder

ENJOYMENT
Amusement
Enthusiasm
Experience
Fun
Playfulness
Recreation
Spontaneous
Surprise

FREEDOM
Independence
Individuality
Liberty

HEALTH
Body image
Calm
Energy
Fitness
Strength
Vitality

INTEGRITY
Accountability
Candor
Commitment
Dependability
Dignity
Honesty
Honor
Responsibility
Sincerity
Transparency
Trust

Trustworthy
Truth

INTELLIGENCE
Brilliance
Clever
Common sense
Decisiveness
Foresight
Genius
Insightful
Knowledge
Learning
Logic
Openness
Realistic
Reason
Reflective
Smart
Thoughtful
Understanding
Vision
Wisdom

FEELINGS
Acceptance
Comfort
Compassion
Contentment
Empathy
Grace
Gratitude
Happiness
Hope
Inspiring
Irreverent
Joy
Kindness
Love
Optimism
Passion
Peace
Poise
Respect
Reverence
Satisfaction
Serenity
Thankful
Tranquility
Welcoming

ORDER
Accuracy
Careful
Certainty
Cleanliness
Consistency
Control
Decisive
Economy
Justice
Lawful
Moderation
Organization
Security
Stability
Structure
Thorough
Timeliness

PRESENCE
Alertness
Attentive
Awareness
Beauty
Calm
Clear
Concentration
Focus
Silence
Simplicity
Solitude

SPIRITUALITY
Adaptability
Altruism
Balance
Charity
Communication
Community
Connection
Consciousness
Contribution
Cooperation
Courtesy
Devotion
Equality
Ethical
Fairness
Family
Fidelity

Friendship
Generosity
Giving
Goodness
Harmony
Humility
Loyalty
Maturity
Meaning
Selfless
Sensitivity
Service
Sharing
Spirit
Stewardship
Support
Sustainability
Teamwork
Tolerance
Unity

STRENGTH
Assertiveness
Boldness
Confidence
Dedication
Discipline
Ferocious
Fortitude
Persistence
Power
Restraint
Rigor
Self-reliance
Temperance
Toughness
Vigor
Will

3. *Start writing your list.* Just write what comes to mind. If you get stuck (and yes, most of us do!), try these three approaches that can help unveil your values:

   a. *Best experiences.* Think of a meaningful experience that stands °ut for you in a positive way. Ask yourself: *What was going on? What made it so special? What values were you honoring at that time?*

   b. *Worst experiences.* Go to the opposite extreme and think of an experience that made you mad, frustrated, or sad. Ask yourself: *What was going on? What were you feeling? What values were you suppressing at that time?*

   c. *Code of conduct.* Think about what is most important for you to have in your life (beyond meeting basic needs and surviving). Ask yourself: *What must you have to be fulfilled? What gives you energy and pleasure?*

4. *Group like things together.* Look for common themes, such as the categories in the example value lists above (achievement, courage, creativity, etc.). Within each group, highlight the most important by circling them. Minimize the less important by bracketing them. You should now have a messy piece of paper with lots of notes, scratch-outs, and chaos.

5. *Prioritize and zoom in.* From the messy paper in step 4, consider taking a fresh piece of paper and prioritizing those that really (really) resonate with you. Too few, and you won't really capture the integral you. Too many, and you won't be likely to remember them all. Most clients settle in on a half dozen to a dozen or so.

6. *Expand.* Not the list of values but the description or color behind them. It's hard to remember a generic laundry list of

values, and adding descriptors or emotional context can help clarify things. For example, "*I value honesty because it lets me have a clear conscience, which helps me feel free to be me.*"

7. *Revise.* Not immediately. Give yourself a break. Come back to your list of core values every couple of days for as often as you like, refining the list to ensure that they:
   - Inspire you
   - Reflect the true you
   - Trigger an emotional feeling
   - Are consistent
   - Play to your strengths
   - Are meaningful and memorable
   - Are prioritized

8. *Rate yourself.* Give yourself a score on a scale of 1–10 for each, and notice where you are today in living your personal core values. Where you rate yourself low, decide what you are going to do to change that. Where they are high, keep doing what you are doing.

As you move forward into planning and returning from your leave, these crystal-clear thoughts about values will guide clarity in the decisions you will be making. Keep it close at hand!

Essential Positive Quality

An essential positive quality (or EPQ) is a term that describes a core virtue or essence you embody, which has remained with you throughout life, like a golden thread weaving your path. It's a quality that embodies the deepest part of you, and a value or virtue that you hold dear. Sure, there are lots of nice things you can say about yourself. But the EPQ gets to the heart of the matter and shines through us always (well, almost always).

Stop and think about yours for a moment. What might it be? What's the short list? What would your friends and family say? What did you already discover about your values in Chapter 2?

Following is a (not exhaustive) list of some EPQs you might highlight or consider. Circle those that MOST represent you, then keep narrowing it down. What's the short list? Perhaps your words aren't even on the list! What's the word or two that is you?

ESSENTIAL POSITIVE QUALITIES...A STARTER LIST

Analytical	Devotion	Honesty	Passionate	Stability
Appreciative	Dignity	Humility	Patience	Steadfastness
Balanced	Driven	Innocence	Perseverance	Strength
Calm	Enduring	Insightful	Persistence	Soft
Caring	Energy	Integrity	Playful	Tenacity
Champion	Enthusiasm	Intentional	Power	Tender
Clarity	Faith	Joyful	Preparedness	Transparency
Compassion	Fierce	Justice	Protective	Trustworthy
Courageous	Flexible	Kindness	Purity	Understanding
Creativity	Generosity	Love	Purposeful	Warmth
Curiosity	Generous heart	Loyalty	Regal	Welcoming
Decisive	Graciousness	Majesty	Resilience	Wisdom
Deep	Gratitude	Mysterious	Responsible	Wonder
Defender	Grounded	Nobility	Self-awareness	
Determined	Helpfulness	Openness	Selflessness	

Now that you (hopefully) have one or a couple in mind, reflect on it. Where has it shone through? Where has it carried you through? How has it evolved? Why is it such a part of you?

Hold it tight! It reflects the essence of "you"!

My EPQ:

PART TWO

KNOW WHAT YOU WANT

As you navigate the journey of balancing parenthood and your professional life, it's essential to take a step back and truly understand what you want to get out of life. Part Two, "Know What You Want," is dedicated to helping you explore and define your deepest desires, aspirations, and sense of purpose. This section is about clarifying your personal and professional goals so that you can make intentional choices that align with who you are and what you value most.

The first chapter, **"Why Am I Here?"** encourages you to revisit your sense of purpose. This is not just about what you do for a living but about understanding what drives you. Whether through examining **Your Purpose**, exploring your **Ikigai** (the Japanese concept of finding the intersection between what you love, what you're good at, what the world needs, and what you can be paid for), or creating **Vision/Dream Boards** that visually map out your aspirations, this chapter helps you connect with the deeper meaning behind your daily actions. Knowing why you're here gives you a foundation to build on, guiding your decisions and helping you prioritize what truly matters.

The second chapter, **"How Am I Doing?"** focuses on reflection and self-assessment. It's easy to get caught up in the everyday without pausing to evaluate where you are. This chapter introduces several tools to help you take stock of your life and progress. Concepts like **4,680 Weeks** (a reflection on the brevity of life), the **Lifetime Lifeline** (a visual representation of your life's journey), and metaphors such as **Jet Ski, Canoe, Catamaran** (which explore different approaches to navigating life's challenges) offer unique perspectives on how you're doing. You'll also explore strategies for **Protecting the Rocks** (prioritizing what's most important), assess yourself with the **Performance/Potential Matrix**, and consider **A Note on Being Selfish**, which encourages you to embrace self-care as a vital part of your overall well-being.

Together, these chapters provide a comprehensive framework for understanding what you want out of life and how you can align your actions and decisions to achieve those desires. By taking the time to explore these ideas, you're investing in a clearer, more intentional path forward—one that honors both your ambitions and your well-being.

No human being is the same as another human being, just like no two snowflakes are identical. Some people are more like others, and some people are less like others. I think of it like a garden. Each plant is unique and special in its own beautiful way. However, each one seeks different sources of energy, nutrients in the soil, levels of moisture, and amounts of sunshine. Like plants in a garden, each of us humans have different needs in order to best thrive.

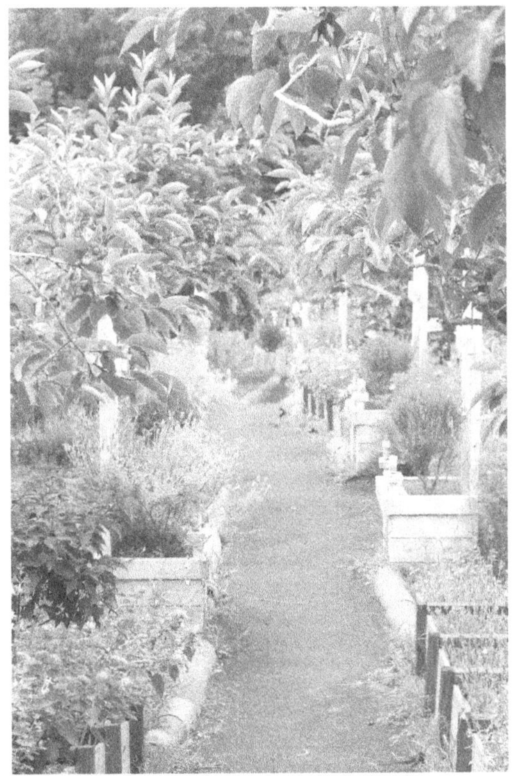

Photo credit: Jade Seok, Unsplash.com

In this Part, we will explore these chapters:

4. Why Am I here?

5. How Am I doing?

4

Why Am I Here?

Discovering your purpose in life is crucial in guiding your journey, especially as you prepare for the profound experience of parenthood. In this chapter, we'll explore three interconnected elements that help you define your "why." First, we'll delve into the concept of **Your Purpose**, the core driver that gives your life meaning and direction. Next, we'll introduce "**Ikigai**," a Japanese framework that finds the sweet spot between what you love, what you're good at, what the world needs, and what you can be paid for. Finally, we'll discuss the creation of a **Vision/Dream Board**, a tangible representation of your goals and aspirations. This board is a daily reminder of where you want to go and why it's worth the effort. By exploring these three elements, you'll gain clarity on why you're here and how to align your life with your deepest passions and talents.

In this chapter, we will explore these concepts:

A. Your Purpose

B. Ikigai

C. Vision/Dream Boards

A. YOUR PURPOSE

Everyone has a "Purpose" in life. Few of us actually ever articulate it. While almost every company, organization, and group define theirs, we rarely define ours. If we are the "CEO of Me," then we should probably be clear on what "me" is here to do.

A Personal Purpose Statement is a simple sentence that captures what one believes they are here on earth to do and be. For example, my (ever emerging) Purpose is:

"I empower people to thrive in the kaleidoscope of life"

Other examples from my clients include:

- *"I create bold communities by connecting the dots"*

- *"I make the world a safer place"*

- *"I shine a light so others can see"*

- *"I support the communities I live in to be more harmonious"*

You get the drift. So, what's your Purpose? What's your magical power?

I suggest setting aside some uninterrupted quiet time (say 30 minutes once a week) for a few weeks to give yourself the mind-space to reflect. Here's some space for you to iterate and explore.

Initial Thoughts: "My Purpose in Life is to …"

Next Week Thoughts: "My Purpose in Life is to …"

Later Weeks Thoughts: "My Purpose in Life is to …"

Final Thoughts (for now!): "My Purpose in Life is to ..."

____

____

____

____

____

It looks super simple once you've developed something that resonates with you, yet it takes a lot of time and reflection to really crisp up your Purpose.

If you're having difficulty, pick a sentence that roughly describes yourself and iterate on that idea as the weeks go by. The shorter, simpler, and more visual you can be, the better. It's hard to remember a whole paragraph about your Purpose. A single sentence can distill it into something memorable.

B. IKIGAI

生き甲斐

(OK, I am trusting that the Japanese symbols above do indeed translate to the word "Ikigai"!)

Ikigai is a Japanese concept about being. There isn't a good translation of the word into English or Western languages. It describes the balance between:

1. What you love and are good at (passions and talents); and

2. What the world (or organization) needs and is willing to pay for

I suggest sitting in a quiet place for 15 minutes, once a week for a couple of weeks. Put it on your calendar (or it is unlikely to happen) and commit to it. (It's only 15 minutes, after all.) Grab paper and pen(s), and make yourself comfortable in a special, quiet place. You might even play soft music or light a candle, perhaps with a calming aromatherapy scent. Do whatever pleases you. Shut the door and ask not to be interrupted. (Almost *anything* can wait 15 minutes, can't it? OK, well, maybe not a fire, but that's pretty unlikely to happen.)

Begin by taking a deep, cleansing breath. Then sit quietly and contemplate:

- *How does this apply in your life today?*

- *How does this framework pertain to your upcoming new parenting role or life phase?*

- *At what intersection(s) have you resided in the past?*

- *Where do you eventually want to be, and when?*

Jot down your thoughts here over the next couple of weeks. Have fun. Iterate. Think deep. Here's some space for you:

C. VISION/DREAM BOARDS

Knowing your Purpose in life is a foundational starting point, but what does it mean? How does it look? What does it feel like? That's where Vision/Dream Boards come in. They translate the "why" (Purpose) to the "what" (Vision). They look forward to the next 1–5 years to show the kinds of things you "do" or "feel" that bring your Purpose to life.

They make it real. And they will evolve.

Some clients revisit their Vision Boards every year as circumstances shift and new experiences and opportunities emerge.

Here's how to create one:

- Set aside 15 minutes in your calendar outside of work hours. Sit in a quiet, uninterrupted place.

- Settle yourself in

- You can get started in many different ways:

  » *Draw (as in the old-fashioned kind of approach).* Take a fresh, crisp blank piece of paper and some colored pens and pencils. Draw symbols and words and ideas about what matters most to you. Doodle. Get creative, use sparkles. Cut and paste images like you did in kindergarten! Whatever sings from your heart and soul. There's no right or wrong answer!

  » *Find inspiration in pictures and images.* Start with a blank PowerPoint slide. Gather stock images from places like Unsplash.com (which has a broad array of free downloadable photos), Pinterest, or Google images or quotes. Pour through your own photo album.

» *Consider Open AI.* Several of my clients have created a first pass by feeding ChatGPT (or other platforms) with key phrases and words about what they envision, asking for a visual representation to be created. Most report that it was a decent first attempt, though no one has told me it created the perfect picture from the start, and all have added to it with their own images and personal photos.

» *Draw upon reflections made in your journal* if you keep one.

- After your first pass, set a (calendared) time each week to revisit it and either add to it, edit it, or completely restart it. Each time, expand and refine what that looks and feels like. Make it yours and in your style.

Here are some examples of how different and unique they can be:

If you are in a partnership, it can be very interesting to both create your own Vision/Dream board and share them in a quiet moment. Key here is NOT to create yours, stick it under your partner's nose and ask them what they think about it or how they would modify it. Coming together with each of your drafts allows you to share and create a family Vision/Dream depiction that is co-created and co-owned by both of you.

How Am I Doing?

As we navigate the whirlwind of life, it's easy to lose sight of the big picture—especially in the face of daily demands and responsibilities. The constant push and pull of work, family, and personal obligations can make it difficult to pause and reflect on where you truly stand in your journey. However, taking stock of where you are and how you're doing is crucial, not just for your personal growth but for ensuring that your priorities remain intact. This chapter invites you to step back from the daily grind and assess your life with intention and clarity.

Here, we will confront the reality of our limited time on earth and the importance of living intentionally at every stage of life. The concept of **4,680 Weeks** serves as a stark reminder of the finite nature of our time, urging us to make every moment count. We'll also explore the **Lifetime Line**, a visual tool to help you map out your past, present, and future, giving you a clearer perspective on your journey and the choices that lie ahead.

To navigate life's challenges, we'll introduce the metaphor of **Jet Ski, Canoe, Catamaran**—different phases in the currents of life. Protecting what matters most is essential, and **Protecting the Rocks** will guide you in safeguarding your top priorities amidst the chaos.

Beyond work, it's enlightening to evaluate your performance in all aspects of life. The **Performance/Potential Matrix** offers a framework to assess how you're doing, not just in your career but in your relationships, health, and personal growth. Finally, we'll touch on **A Note on Being Selfish**, emphasizing the importance of self-care and why prioritizing yourself is not only okay but necessary for a fulfilling life.

Regularly evaluating how you're doing in these areas will help you stay aligned with your true self, making the journey ahead more meaningful and fulfilling. By taking the time to reflect, you'll be better equipped to navigate the challenges and opportunities that life (and parenthood) present, ensuring that you're living with purpose and intention at every step.

Concepts:

     A.　4,680 Weeks

     B.　Lifetime Line

     C.　Jet Ski, Canoe, Catamaran

     D.　Protecting the Rocks

     E.　Performance/Potential Matrix

     F.　A Note on Being Selfish

A. 4,680 WEEKS

Our human lives are actually quite short.

Here is a 90-year lifespan in years, with each row representing a decade:

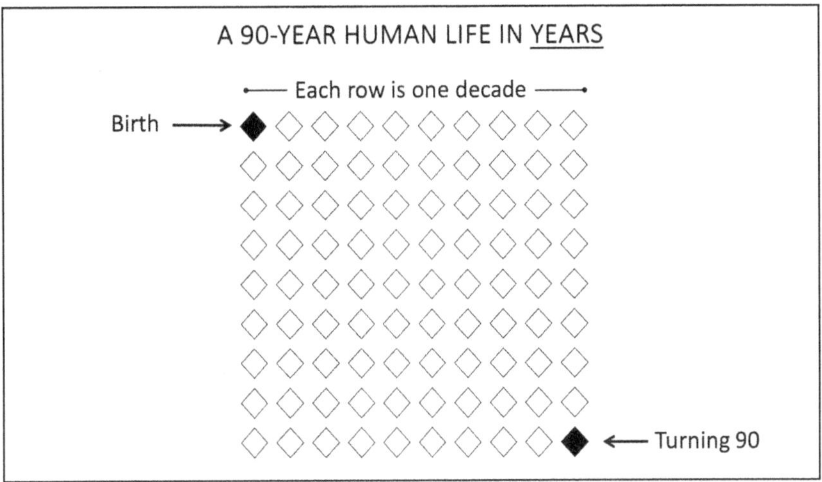

And here it is in months, with each row representing three years for a total of 1,080 months:

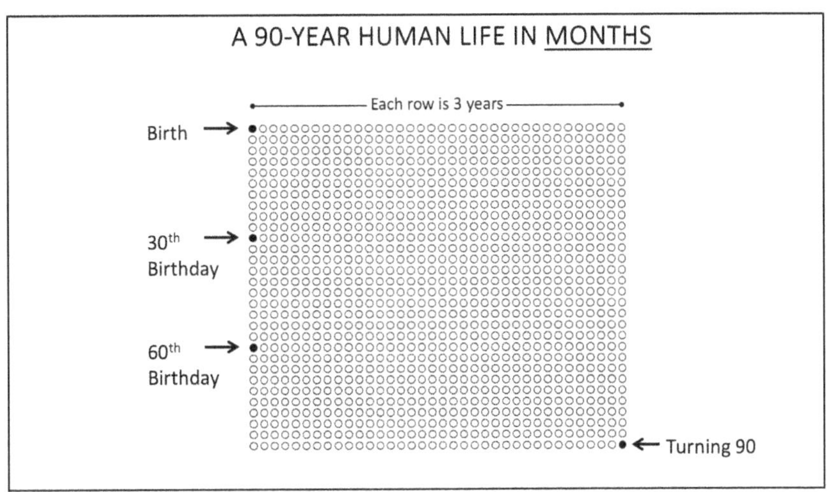

And finally, in weeks, with each row representing a year for a total of 4,680 weeks:

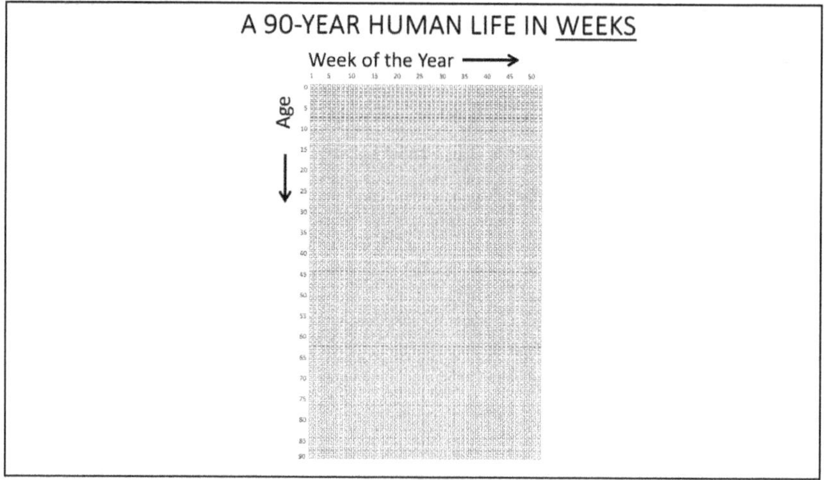

Maybe it's just me, but it doesn't sound like a lot of time. Some weeks seem to just fly by, especially as we get older. On the other hand, that's a lot of dots, and you're not even halfway through them (unless, of course, you get hit by a bus tomorrow, but that may be even less likely than winning the lottery).

B. LIFETIME LIFELINE

Now, let's pull it all back from the generic 4,680 weeks to the perspective of "you."

Take a piece of paper and put a "0" on the left side of the page. The zero represents the start of your life when you were born. Now, make a guess at how long you will live and write it down on the right side of the page. (Yes, I know we're getting a bit morbid here.) Draw a line between your birth and death. This is your life timeline. Mark your current age with a big star.

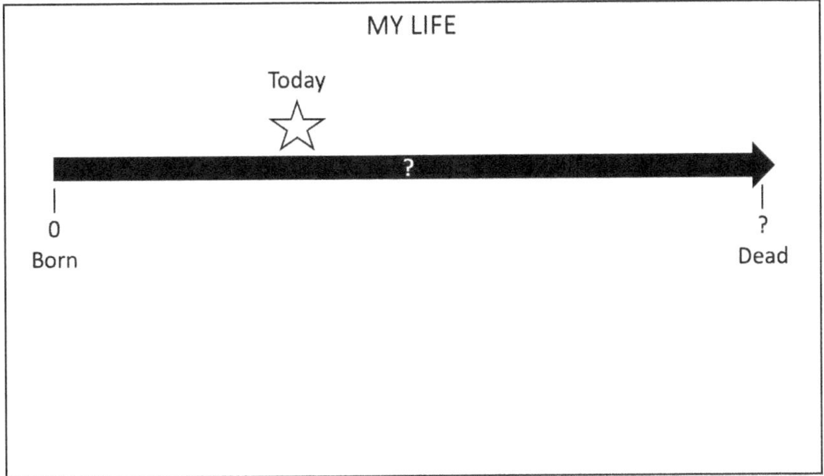

Now, let's divide that line into a half dozen or so "life segments," drawing dividing lines at the roughly correct spot on the timeline.

The early segments (say, childhood, teen, and college years) are what I call the "*should*" years. There are a lot of things we really "should" do, such as: becoming potty-trained, learning to tie our shoes, and getting a degree if we wish to go into business.

After the early *should* years, there are the "*my choice*" years where we choose what to do and how we want to do it. Notable events might include marriage(s), child(ren), retirement (active), and retirement (fully nursing home supported).

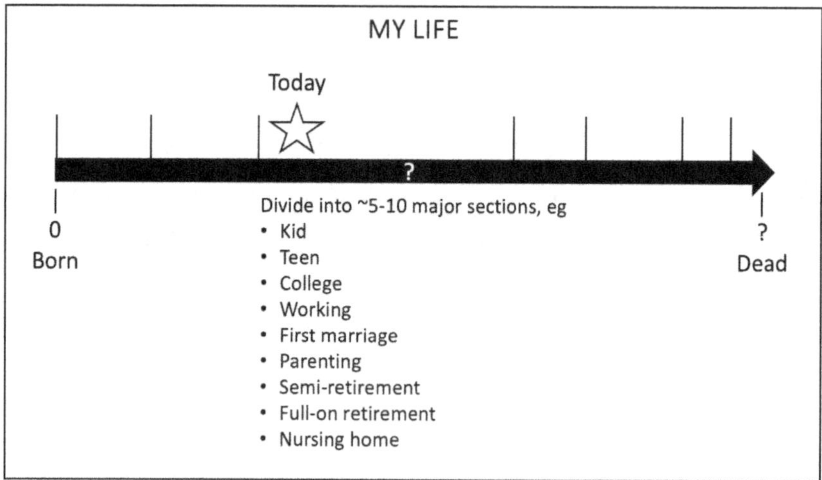

Sitting and reflecting on their life on one page, my clients are often surprised by what they see. In particular, they note how long the "working" stage often is and how relatively early on they are in their lifetime career. The point here is to think about where you are in life—where you've been and where you might go. This exercise puts your about-to-be-parent milestone, its (never-ending) parenting phase, and its overlay with career choices into perspective.

Here's a space for you to noodle on:

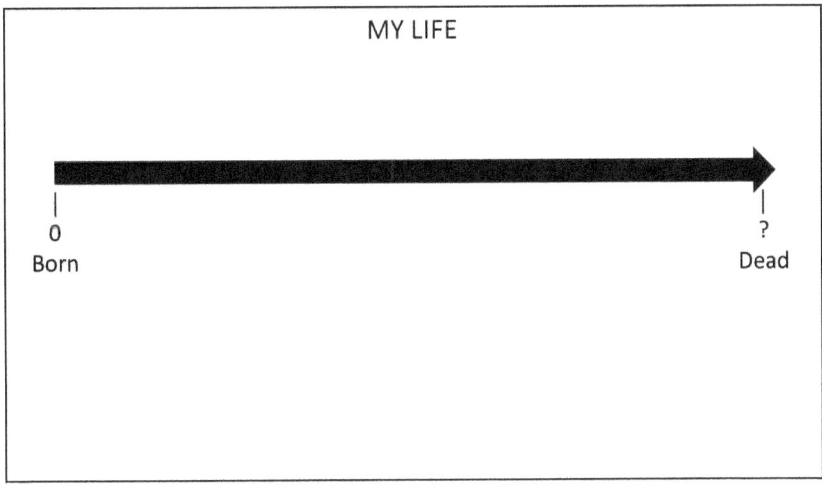

If you are in a partnership, it can be very interesting to each independently create a Lifetime Lifeline and share them in a quiet moment. Key here is NOT to create yours, stick it under your partner's nose and ask them what they think about it or how they would modify it. Coming together with each of your drafts allows you to share and create a family Lifetime Lifeline that is co-created and co-owned by both of you. Here are some possible discussion starters when you share and compare:

- *What are the big chapters of your lives?*

- *What "phase" are you in now, and how long will it be?*

- *What "aha's" emerge?*

- *What sits well with you, and what doesn't?*

Enjoy exploring!

C. JET SKI®, CANOE, CATAMARAN

Here's another way of thinking about life stages, using a boat analogy.

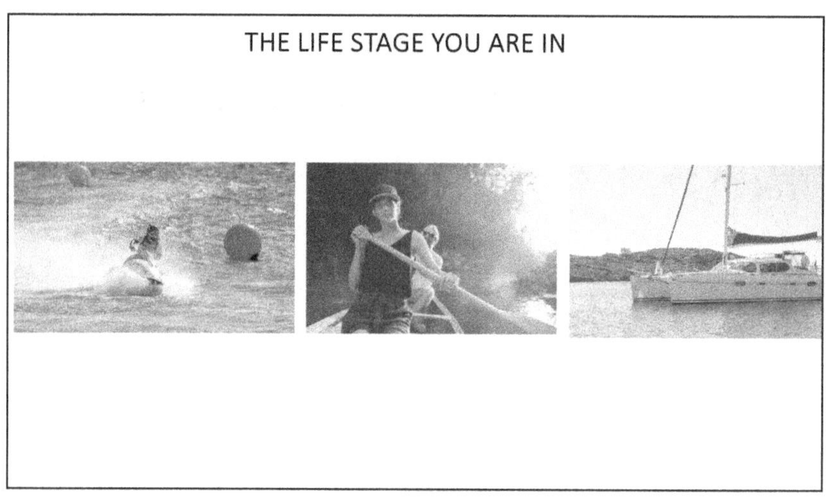

*Photo credits: Jet Ski – Alice Challies; Canoe – Getty Images;
Catamaran – Miquel Gelabert, Unsplash.com*

Life's journey can be compared to different modes of travel, each reflecting the various stages we navigate as we grow, evolve, and occasionally question our life choices. Think of it as a progression from the wild, carefree days of a Jet Ski to the teamwork (and potential bickering) required in a Canoe, and eventually to the more stable, slightly less thrilling—but often most enjoyable—ride on a Catamaran. Let's break it down and have a little fun with it.

Jet Ski®: The Early Years

Ah, the Jet Ski® phase. Remember when life was all about you? No kids, no real responsibilities, just you zipping around, exploring the world with the wind in your hair, and the only worry being whether or not you applied enough sunscreen. This is the phase where you're the captain of your ship, with little concern for what tomorrow brings! You're focused on having fun, meeting people (sometimes quite literally, by nearly running them over), and doing what you want when you want. Sometimes, that independence might even make you a little reckless. But who cares? You're young and free; the world is your oyster, or at least your personal water park. Occasionally, you might invite someone to hop on the back and join you for the ride, but they know it's your show, and they're just along for the thrill.

Canoe: The Middle Years

Then comes the Canoe stage. This is where life gets interesting—and by interesting, I mean you've added a partner to your journey, and the smooth waters of your Jet Ski days start to look like white-water rapids. Canoeing requires coordination, teamwork, and a good sense of humor (especially when you're trying to paddle through life with a baby on board). You quickly learn that if one person rocks the boat—intentionally or not—you both get soaked and possibly tipped over. You have to work together to steer through the obstacles that come your way, whether navigating through the demands of parenting or just trying to agree on what's for dinner. And adding a kid (or two) to the mix is like trying to paddle while juggling flaming torches. It's unpredictable, chaotic, and somehow, still kind of fun. Just remember, in the canoe, communication is key—unless you want to end up swimming for shore while your partner yells, *"I told you to steer left!"*

Catamaran: The Later Years

Finally, we reach the Catamaran phase. This is the stage where you've probably seen and done a lot and are ready to sail smoothly for a while. The Catamaran is stable, comfortable, and a bit more leisurely. You're no longer battling rapids or worrying about capsizing every five minutes. Instead, you're enjoying a more relaxed pace of life—maybe the kids are grown, or you've simply learned that not every wave needs to be conquered at top speed. Sure, one person can still throw things off course, but it's a lot harder to tip a Catamaran. This is the time to enjoy the journey, reflect on where you've been, and maybe even let the autopilot take over now and then. It's not as fast paced as the Jet Ski® or as intense as the Canoe, but that's kind of the point. You've earned the right to sit back, sip a cold drink, and enjoy the ride.

Embrace Your Current Stage

So here you are, likely in the Canoe phase, paddling like mad and wondering how you got here. With a baby on board or one on the way, you're gearing up for some serious turbulence. But don't worry—you've got this. The trick is to recognize where you are, laugh at the absurdity of it all, and keep paddling. Embrace the chaos, lean into the unpredictability, and remember, the journey is just as important as the destination. And who knows? Maybe one day, you'll look back on these rapids with a smile—right before you pour yourself a well-deserved drink on your Catamaran.

D. PROTECTING THE ROCKS

Ah, priorities! The word alone is enough to make even the most organized person break into a cold sweat.

We all know the importance of prioritizing, but how often do we let the little things take over, leaving the big, important stuff scrambling for space? Enter the age-old (but still pretty awesome) experiment with a jar, some rocks, pebbles, and sand to drive the point home.

Picture this: You've got a mason jar (or any container, really) and a bunch of rocks, pebbles, and sand. The goal is to get everything to fit neatly into the jar. Easy, right? Well, let's see.

- *Method 1:* You start by pouring in the sand. It fills up the jar pretty quickly—maybe halfway. Next, you add the pebbles. There's some jostling, but they mostly squeeze in there. Finally, you try to place the rocks on top. But uh-oh, the rocks are sitting awkwardly on the top, towering above the rim. When you try to put the lid on, it's like trying to close an overstuffed suitcase.

- *Method 2:* Now, let's try it differently. This time, you start with the rocks—plop them right into the bottom of the jar. Next, you add the pebbles. They slip in nicely around the rocks. Finally, you pour in the sand. The tiny grains sift between the pebbles and rocks, filling in the gaps. You put the lid on, and voilà—it all fits perfectly! The jar is full, but everything's in there. Everything is as snug as a bug.

So, what's the deal with this experiment? The moral of the story is about how we prioritize our time and energy. The rocks represent your biggest, most important priorities—things that matter, like family, health, and personal goals. The pebbles are the less critical but still important things—maybe work projects, paying bills, or household chores. And then there's the sand, which is all the little, pesky stuff that clutters up your day—emails, social media, that never-ending laundry pile.

If you start by filling your jar (your day, your life) with sand, you're going to run out of room for the rocks. The important stuff gets squeezed out, sitting awkwardly on top, not fitting in, just like those poor rocks in Method 1. But if you start with the rocks, making sure your top priorities get prime real estate, everything else falls into place. The pebbles can find their way in, and the sand—the little stuff—just fills in the cracks.

And we all know that the sand will always be there, demanding your attention with its annoyingly persistent "must-do" vibe. But it's the rocks that need to go in first if you're going to live a balanced, meaningful life, and not like you're constantly trying to jam an over-stuffed lid onto your day.

So, next time you're staring at your to-do list with the same dread as a kid staring at a plate of broccoli, remember the jar experiment. Prioritize the rocks—those big, beautiful priorities that give your life meaning. The rest? It'll either fit in, or you'll realize it wasn't that important after all.

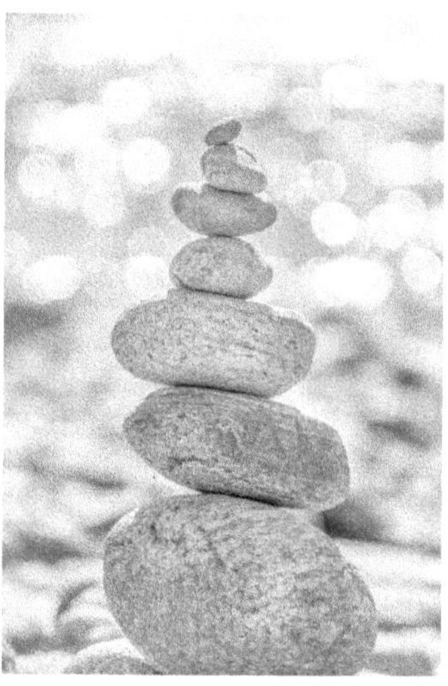

Photo credit: Deniz Altindas, Unsplash.com

Your Rocks:

____

____

____

____

Your Pebbles:

____

____

____

____

Your Sand:

____

____

____

____

E. PERFORMANCE/POTENTIAL MATRIX

Many companies use a "Performance/Potential" matrix to evaluate the career development of their leadership pipeline. "Performance" is how you are perceived to be doing today in your current role. "Potential" is how you are perceived to be able to grow into a new or elevated role with time and/or focused effort. Often, the Performance/Potential matrix is called the "nine box." If you're unfamiliar with it, here's how it is laid out.

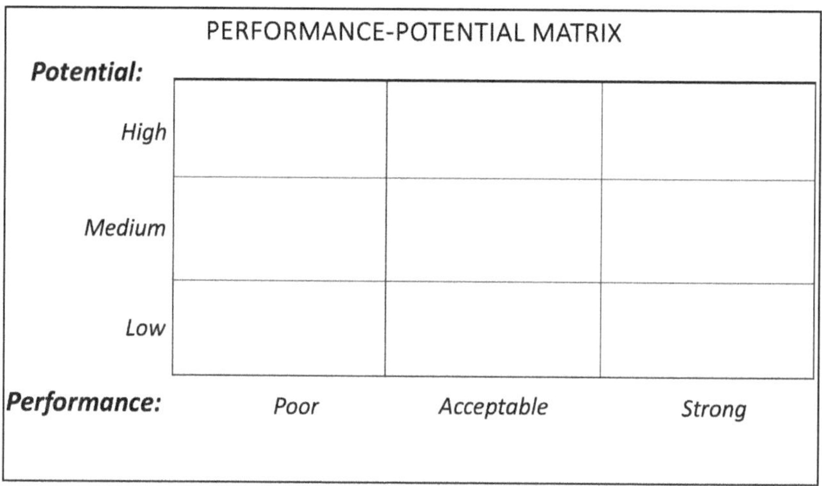

You can layer in color coding (red-orange-yellow-green) to make it visual or use black and white (from dark to light). In general:

- People falling into the *red (black)* box find themselves on an exit plan.

- Those in the *orange (dark gray)* find themselves on some form of PIP (Performance Incentive Plan).

- Those in the *yellow (light gray)* are likely on some form of PDP (Personal Development Plan).

- And those in the *green (white)* are very well positioned. They get the big bonus and incentive payouts, and everyone pays a lot of attention to how to develop and retain them. These are often called "HiPos" (High Performance/High Potential).

Most of us who reach leadership positions have a good track record of performance and potential (white or light gray) and are currently in those three boxes of the upper-right corner.

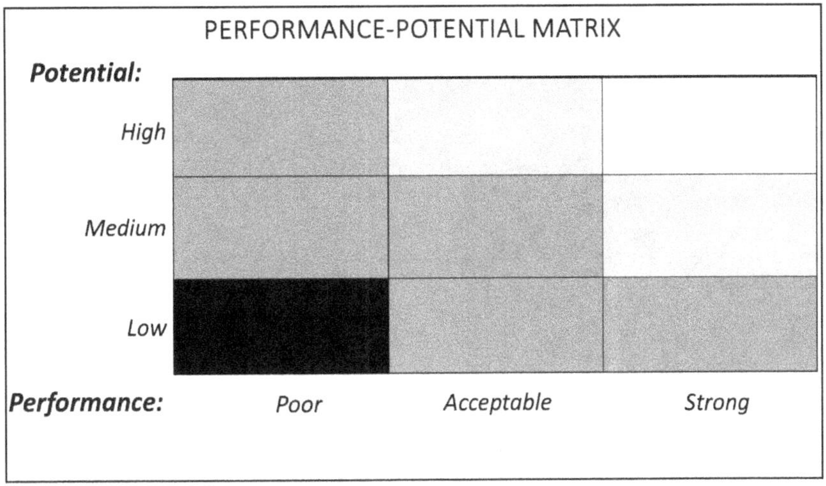

You are likely familiar with this thinking from a career perspective, either conceptually or in practice at review time. I have two important questions for you to consider regarding the Performance/Potential (nine-box) framework.

1. *Have you thought about this for yourself outside of the work context?* At work, we typically get annual or semiannual performance reviews, including some form of assessment on

performance potential. Yet, as the "CEO of you," have you ever taken stock of how you're doing on your nonwork priorities (your life!)? How are you doing in other areas of your life (as a partner, a friend, a daughter, a son, or a member of your community)? Not to mention "you" – for example, your needs to be quiet, exercise, relax, and have alone time? It might be worth some consideration. Placing your key priorities or roles on the matrix above can be quite enlightening.

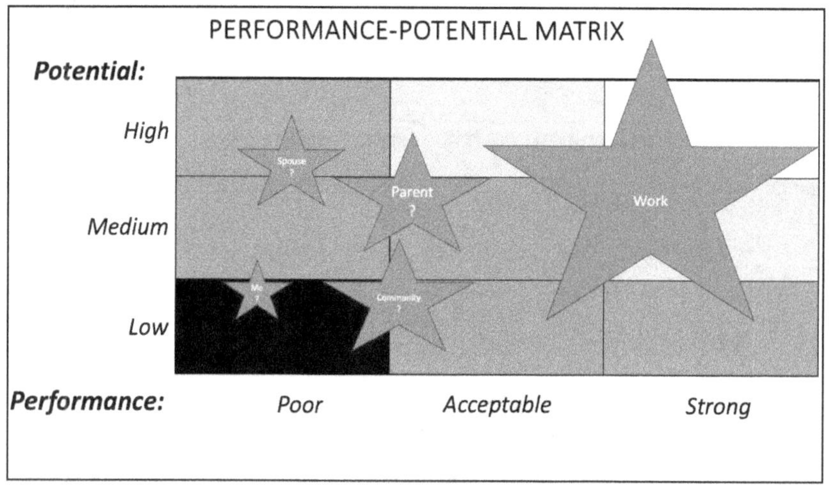

2. *Do you want to be upper-upper right-right box in anything you do?* Most aspiring leaders expect to be in the upper-right (white) box. And we can become pretty unmotivated if we are not—arguing about it, becoming upset about it. Which I believe has often led to companies refining and dividing the green (white) box even further: to "very high," "very-very high," and even "exceptional" segments. A disproportionate percentage of the leadership population is often classified into the upper-right (white) box. Many green (white)-box leaders, not wanting to be anything less than the best (and

not accustomed to being anything less than #1), then strive to achieve the elusive topmost spot, where the North Star lies.

3. Consider this: Getting into and staying in that elusive North Star box takes an inordinate amount of dedication, focus, time, and energy. And you cannot be a North Star in everything you do. So, consider asking yourself whether your current career, in the context of other current or imminent priorities, is something you really want to aspire to be at the top of? This is likely a foreign concept for many readers. Just think for now about whether being "very good" is better than "outstandingly, untouchable, exceptional" in the relative scheme of things. It's not that you wouldn't be able to reprioritize at a future moment in time as life's journey unfolds.

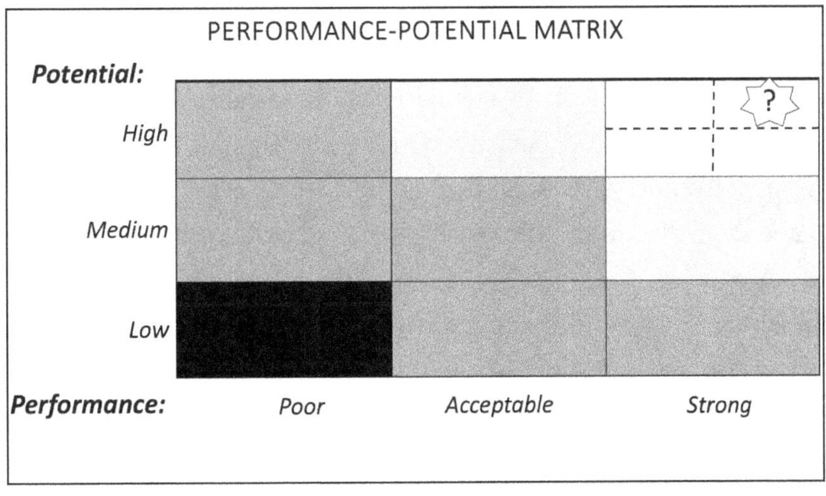

F. A NOTE ON BEING SELFISH

Parenthood is a wild ride. It's eye-opening, awe-inspiring, incredible, and exciting. But let's not kid ourselves—it's also new, unknown, mysterious, mistake-laden, unpredictable, scary, exhausting, and often filled with fear of failure, uncertainty, imposter syndrome, and anxiety.

It's like being handed the keys to a rollercoaster that never stops, and you're expected to hang on, throw your hands in the air, and enjoy the ride, all while smiling deeply. Overwhelming? Absolutely. And that's just the "parenting" side of the equation. Don't forget the rest of life—work, relationships, keeping the household running, and the odd attempt to maintain some semblance of a social life. As a friend of mine says, when *"life gets lifey,"* it's easy to get lost in the shuffle.

Pre-baby, it's all too easy to get lost in work, and post-baby, it's just as easy to get lost in new parenthood. The demands are endless: taking care of the baby, the family, the partner, the friends, the community, and, oh yes, all those other people who suddenly seem to need you even more now that you're a parent. Somehow, amid all this caregiving, we forget to take care of the most important person— ourselves. If we're not happy, growing, living, and thriving, well… let's just say we might not be the most pleasant people to be around. When self-care takes a backseat, we're not being self-ish enough, and that's where things start to unravel.

"Selfish" tends to get a bad rap, like it's synonymous with "greedy" or "inconsiderate." The word implies, incorrectly, that taking care of yourself means taking away from someone else—like there's only so much happiness, energy, or joy to go around, and if you take more, someone else gets less. It's the old "if there's a finite number of coconuts on a deserted island, and I take one extra, someone else gets one less" scenario. Sure, we live in a world of finite resources: finite energy, time, water, and food, for example. But here's where things get interesting—self-care and "selfishness" actually belong in the world of the infinite.

In the world of the infinite, things like love, creativity, and passion are limitless. Taking time to boost yourself up doesn't rob others of their energy or joy—it actually has the opposite effect. When you invest in your well-being, you're not just filling your cup—you're ensuring you have more to give to others. Self-care isn't about being selfish in the negative sense; it's about being *self-ish*—taking care of "me" so that "we" can thrive. When you're in a good place, you're better equipped to be a supportive partner, an engaged parent, and a more effective leader in both your personal and professional life. Being self-ish, in this way, is a win-win.

Let's break it down:

- **Self** (noun): A person's essential being that distinguishes them from others, especially considered as the object of introspection or reflexive action.

- **Ish** (adverb): To some extent.

So, being self-ish means taking care of your essential self to some extent. I think we could all be a little more self-ish.

Have you considered scheduling an exquisite weekly self-care "hour of indulgence" with your self-ish self? Imagine taking that luxurious bubble bath without the guilt, singing in the shower like no one's listening, dancing in the rain just because you can, or digging your hands into the garden and reconnecting with nature. Or maybe it's just sitting in silence, savoring a cup of coffee, or doing whatever it is that brings you joy. Whatever it is, do it—and do it for you.

Indulging your self-ish self isn't just good for you—it's good for everyone around you. When you take care of yourself, you bring your best self to the table, whether in your relationships, work, or parenting. And yes, even indulging in reading this book in a quiet spot, with a little "me-time" to learn and explore, is an investment in yourself. The investment in you is always worth it.

So, go ahead—light the candles, run the bath, and let yourself relax. Bubble bath, anyone?

Source: Shutterstock.com

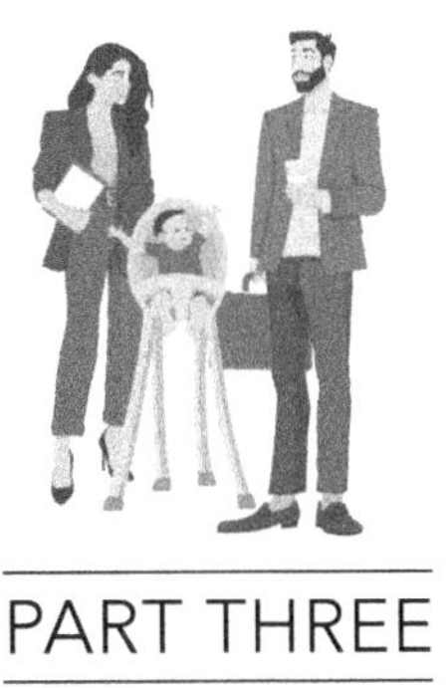

PART THREE

PLANNING YOUR LEAVE(S)

Preparing for parental leave is about much more than simply marking dates on a calendar. It's an opportunity to thoughtfully plan how you'll balance your roles as a parent and a professional, ensuring that your time away from work supports both your family's needs and your needs and career aspirations. In this section, we delve into the emotional, practical, and strategic aspects of planning your leave, providing insights and tools to help you navigate this significant life transition with intention and confidence.

In this Part we will explore these chapters:

6. **Give Yourself Grace:** The journey into parenthood is filled with unknowns. This chapter encourages you to be kind to yourself during this life-changing time, recognizing that perfection isn't the goal—self-compassion is.

7. **Expectant Moms: Growing Your Baby is Job 1:** A reminder to pregnant moms that the most important task at hand

is nurturing the life growing within you. Everything else, including work, comes second.

8. **Expectant Dads: Embracing Your Role and Preparing for the Journey Ahead:** Dads-to-be have their own important role to play. This chapter helps expectant fathers prepare for the emotional and practical journey ahead.

9. **Countdown To Baby To Dos:** There seems to be so much to do leading up to the birth! This chapter will share critical items and provide a checklist to assign responsibilities to mom, dad, or both.

10. **Understanding and Navigating Paternity Leave Bias:** This chapter addresses the biases that fathers may face when taking paternity leave, offering strategies to navigate these challenges and advocate for your role as a parent.

11. **Coordinating Dual Parental Leaves:** When both parents take leave, timing and coordination are key. This chapter explores different approaches and helps you decide what's best for your family.

12. **Scrutinize The HR Policy, Then Think Beyond:** Understanding your company's leave policy is just the first step. This chapter encourages you to think creatively about how to make the most of your leave.

13. **Check The Law:** It's essential to know your legal rights when it comes to parental leave. This chapter provides an overview of relevant laws and how they might apply to you.

14. **Work Approaches:** This chapter offers practical advice on how to manage your work responsibilities leading up to your

leave, including whether to stay connected and how to handle the handoff of your duties.

15. **Work Tactics:** When it comes to preparing for leave, the devil is in the details. This chapter covers everything from crafting the perfect out-of-office message to planning your baby's big debut.

16. **Claws And Fur:** This chapter emphasizes the importance of self-care—down to the seemingly trivial details—because how you feel about yourself matters, especially during such a transformative time.

17. **Support Approaches:** Your support network is crucial during parental leave. This chapter offers guidance on timing grandparental visits, putting them to work, considering a night nurse, and getting a jump-start on hiring a nanny or securing daycare.

This part of the book is designed to equip you with the knowledge and strategies you need to make informed decisions, allowing you to approach your leave with confidence and clarity. Whether you're a mom, dad, or a couple navigating this journey together, these chapters provide a comprehensive guide to planning a leave that works for you and your family. And don't miss out on Chapter 15—it's a super easy but mission-critical piece of advice before delivery!

Give Yourself Grace

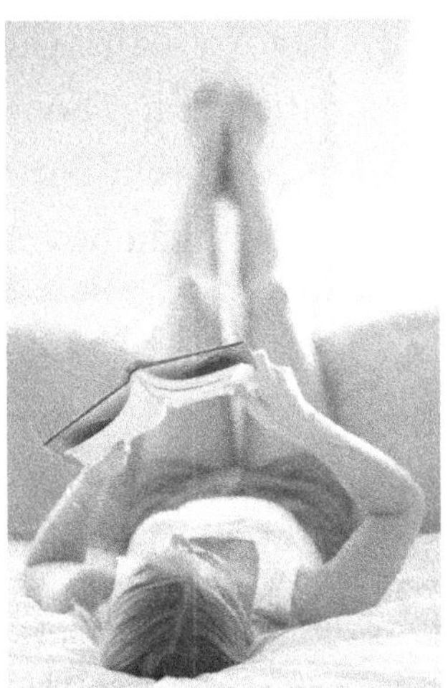

Photo credit: Amanda Vickers, Unsplash.com

Before we dive into the nitty-gritty of planning, exploring, and taking action, let's hit the pause button and talk about something critical—giving yourself grace. As the due date approaches, there's often a frantic drive to "get it all done" before your leave starts. You might find yourself trying to tie up every loose end, clear every to-do list, get every home maintenance item fixed and ensure that everything is perfectly in place. But let's be realistic: your leave could start anytime, and guess what? You'll survive (and thrive) even if every item on your list isn't crossed off.

Consider this your permission slip to take a break. Like right now. How about a nap? A long walk? A bubble bath? One of those heavenly pregnancy or couples' massages? This book, and everything else, can wait until you're done just "being" instead of "doing." Because let's face it, pregnancy comes with its own set of challenges—not just the obvious physical ones, but emotional, relational, mental, and spiritual ones as well—and for both parents. It's a lot, and while it's tempting to power through, now is the perfect time to dial it back a notch.

Here's the thing: we live in a world that glorifies busyness, where being constantly "on" and getting things done is seen as a badge of honor. But pregnancy is your, and your partner's time to embrace the art of slowing down. Yes, you might be tempted to channel your inner superhero and conquer every task, but consider these alternative approaches instead:

- *Stop trying to do it all:* Seriously, nobody's handing out awards for most completed tasks. Sometimes, less is more.

- *Make "slow down" your motto:* Life isn't a race. Take your time, enjoy the moments, and remember that rest is productive too.

- *Let go of absolutes:* Life is full of gray areas, and that's okay. Flexibility is your friend.

- *Learn to set boundaries:* Saying "no" isn't just okay—it's necessary. Protect your energy.

- *Look for compromises:* Not everything needs to be perfect. Good enough is often just right.

- *Lean on dear friends and colleagues:* Trust me, they want to help. So let them.

- *Practice saying no:* It really is a complete sentence. No guilt required.

There's a delicate balance between doing and being; and pregnancy is the perfect time to master this. Just "being" might sound counterproductive in our "always-on" culture, but it's actually a crucial part of this journey. When you give yourself permission to just be—to rest, relax, and recharge—you're actually doing something incredibly important: taking care of yourself, your baby, and your partner. And when you take care of yourself, you're better equipped to take care of everyone else.

Once the baby is here, you're going to have days where things don't go as planned. Maybe the baby's onesie is on backward, or you realize you've been wearing mismatched socks all day, haven't brushed your hair since yesterday, or haven't shaved for a week. And you know what? That's okay. Laugh it off, shrug it off, and move on. Nobody has it all together, no matter what Instagram says. The truth is, everyone is just winging it, hoping for the best.

So, practice giving yourself grace. Learn how to embrace messiness, imperfection, and chaos. Take that bubble bath, indulge in that nap, and let go of the idea that you have to do it all. Because the truth is, you're doing just fine—even when it doesn't feel like it. And remember, no one's going to grade you on the completion of your to-do list. You've got this, and you're doing an amazing job, just as you are.

Expectant Moms:
Growing Your Baby Is Job 1

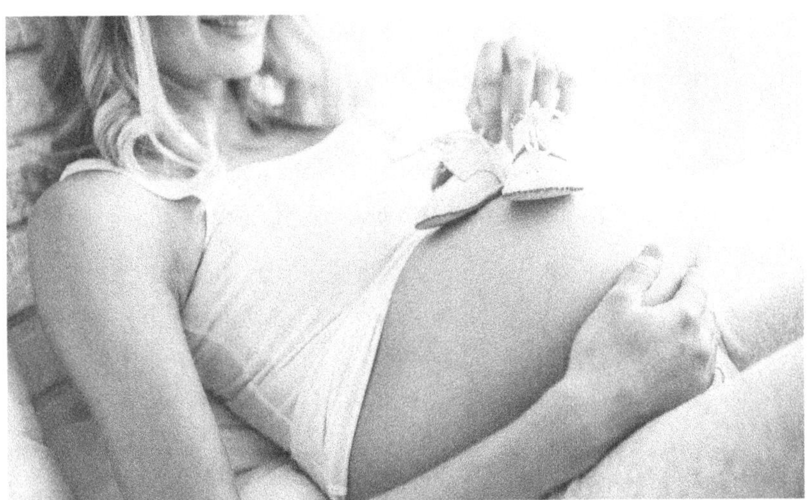

Photo credit: Getty Images, Unsplash.com

Pregnancy is an incredible journey that profoundly transforms your body, mind, and life. But growing a baby is no small feat. It's not business as usual; it's a monumental task that demands your time, energy, and focus. As exciting as this time is, it's also physically exhausting, emotionally intense, and can bring new challenges to your relationships. It's important for moms-to-be to recognize that pregnancy is "Job 1" and to give themselves the grace to not be 110% in every other area of their lives, because let's face it—growing a baby is hard work!

The Physical Demands of Pregnancy

From the moment you see those two lines on the pregnancy test, your body begins an incredible transformation. Your baby starts as a tiny cluster of cells and, over the course of nine months, grows into a fully formed human being—all thanks to the hard work your body is doing around the clock.

- *Morning Sickness, Fatigue, and More:*
  - » Many women experience nausea, commonly known as morning sickness, during the first trimester. It's not just inconvenient; it can be debilitating. Even when the nausea subsides, pregnancy often brings fatigue that can make it difficult to keep up with your usual pace.
  - » Your body is working overtime to support your growing baby—producing extra blood, managing hormonal changes, and preparing for childbirth. This physical demand can leave you feeling exhausted, even after a full night's sleep.

- *Physical Changes and Discomfort:*
  - As your baby grows, your body undergoes significant changes. From weight gain to swollen feet to back pain and shortness of breath, these physical shifts are your body's way of making room for your baby. But they also mean that everyday activities, like walking or even sitting comfortably, can become challenging.

- Don't forget the emotional roller coaster. Hormones are surging, and with them come mood swings, anxiety, and even moments of doubt. All of this is a normal part of the process, but it's a lot to handle on top of everything else.

- *The Emotional and Mental Load.* Pregnancy isn't just about physical changes; it's also an emotional and mental journey that can be both exhilarating and overwhelming. You're preparing to welcome a new life into the world, which brings a host of new responsibilities, fears, and dreams.

- *Emotional Ups and Downs:* Hormonal changes during pregnancy can lead to intense emotions. One minute you might be overjoyed; the next, you're in tears over something seemingly trivial. These emotional swings are normal but can be exhausting.

- *Mental Load of Preparation:* You're not just growing a baby but also mentally preparing for the enormous life changes that are coming. Whether it's planning for the birth, thinking about how to balance work and parenting, or simply processing the idea of becoming a parent, your mind is constantly working through these big questions.

- *Relationship Dynamics:* Pregnancy can also bring changes to your relationships. Whether it's navigating the shift in dynamics with your partner, dealing with well-meaning but unsolicited advice from family and friends, or balancing work relationships, these changes can add another layer of stress.

Recognizing Pregnancy as "Job 1"

Given all that pregnancy entails, it's crucial to recognize that this is your most important job right now. Growing a baby isn't just something happening in the background while you go about your usual routine—it's a full-time job. And like any demanding job, it requires your focus, energy, and dedication.

- *Give Yourself Grace:* A reminder from the last chapter!

  » It's easy to feel like you need to keep up with everything else at the same pace you did before pregnancy. But it's important to give yourself grace and acknowledge that slowing down is okay. You don't have to be 110% in every other area of your life right now.

  » If you need to take more breaks, cut back on your workload, or even delegate tasks you'd normally handle yourself, that's okay. Your body and mind are doing something extraordinary—growing a new life. That deserves recognition and respect.

- *Prioritize Self-Care:*

  » Taking care of yourself during pregnancy isn't a luxury; it's a necessity. Self-care should be a priority whether it's getting extra rest, eating well, exercising (within the limits of what's comfortable and safe), or finding time to relax.

  » Listen to your body. If you're tired, rest. If you're feeling overwhelmed, take a step back. It's okay to say no to extra commitments or to ask for help when you need it.

- *Focus on What Matters:* As much as possible, try to focus on what truly matters during this time. Your health and your baby's health are top priorities. Everything else can be managed, adjusted, or postponed if necessary.

Pregnancy is one of the most significant and challenging jobs you'll ever have. It's a time of incredible change, growth, and preparation. While it's easy to get caught up in "keeping up" with your usual responsibilities, it's essential to remember that growing a baby is your most important job right now. Give yourself the grace to step back from being 110% in every other area of your life. You are doing something amazing—nurturing and growing a new life. That's hard work, and it deserves all the recognition, support, and self-care you can give yourself.

Expectant Dads: Embracing Your Role and Preparing for the Journey

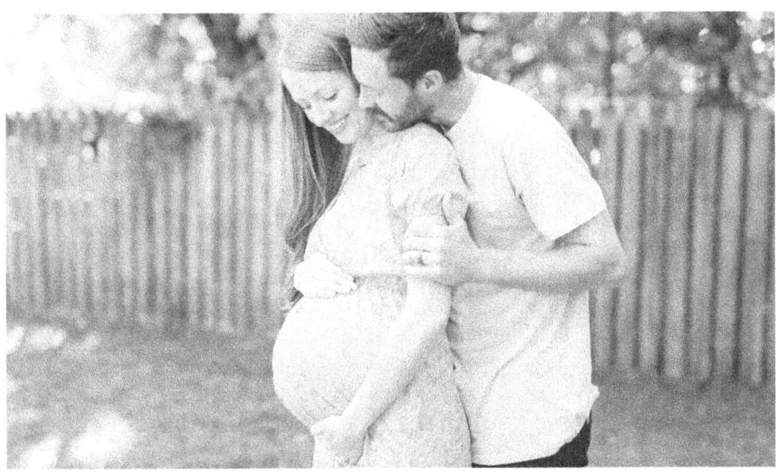

Photo credit: Brooke Cagle, Unsplash.com

While the physical work of pregnancy is carried by the mother, expectant dads have their own unique and important role to play in the journey to parenthood. The experience of becoming a dad comes with its own set of challenges, responsibilities, and emotional shifts. While you may not be the one physically growing the baby, your role is crucial in supporting your partner, preparing for the new arrival, and navigating the changes that are coming your way. This chapter is about recognizing the significance of your role as an expectant dad and giving yourself permission to prioritize this monumental transition.

The Emotional and Mental Load of Expectant Dads

Pregnancy doesn't just transform the mother; it's a life-changing event for dads as well. As you prepare to become a father, you're likely experiencing a wide range of emotions—from excitement and joy to anxiety and uncertainty.

- *Emotional Shifts:* As an expectant dad, you might feel a mix of emotions that can change from day to day. There's the excitement of meeting your child but also the weight of the responsibilities that lie ahead. It's natural to feel anxious about becoming a parent, especially if this is your first time. These emotional shifts are a normal part of the process, and it's important to acknowledge and process them.

- *Mental Preparation:* While your partner is busy growing the baby, your mind is likely buzzing with thoughts about what kind of father you want to be, how you'll balance work and family, and how your life is about to change. You're also likely thinking about the practical aspects—preparing the nursery, learning about baby care, and supporting your partner through her pregnancy.

- *Relationship Dynamics:* Pregnancy can bring changes to your relationship with your partner. As you both prepare for parenthood, there may be new challenges to navigate, such as differing opinions on parenting or the added stress of the upcoming changes. Your role as a supportive partner is vital during this time, and open communication is key.

Recognizing Your Role as "Job 1"

Just as growing a baby is the mother's primary focus during pregnancy, your primary role is to support, prepare, and engage in the journey to becoming a dad. This is "Job 1" for you right now, and it's a role that deserves your full attention and effort. Here are some suggestions to think about:

- *Support Your Partner:*
  - » One of your most important jobs during pregnancy is to support your partner. This includes being there for her emotionally, helping with physical tasks as her body changes, and being involved in the pregnancy journey— attending doctor's appointments, learning about the stages of pregnancy, and preparing for labor and delivery.

  - » It's also important to recognize that your partner is doing incredibly hard work. Acknowledge her efforts, listen to her needs, and be ready to step in whenever she needs help, whether that's taking on more household responsibilities or simply being a source of comfort and encouragement.

- *Prepare for Fatherhood:*
  - » Preparing to become a father involves more than just assembling cribs and stocking up on diapers. It's about mentally and emotionally readying yourself for the changes that are coming. Take time to educate yourself about newborn care, read up on parenting strategies, and discuss your hopes and fears with your partner.

> » You might also consider talking to other dads about their experiences. Hearing firsthand what to expect can help you feel more prepared and less anxious about the unknown.

- *Balance Work and Family Preparation:*

  > » While work remains an important part of your life, it's okay to recognize that your priorities are shifting. As the due date approaches, you might find it harder to focus 100% on your job, and that's perfectly normal. This is a time when your role as an expectant dad is just as important as your professional responsibilities.

  > » If possible, start planning your work/life balance now. Discuss your upcoming parental leave with your employer, set boundaries where needed, and begin thinking about how you'll manage your time once the baby arrives. Remember, your presence and involvement in your family's life are invaluable.

- *Give Yourself Grace.* It's easy to feel like you need to have everything figured out before the baby arrives, but giving yourself some grace is important. You're entering uncharted territory, and it's okay not to have all the answers right away.

- *Embrace the Learning Curve:* Becoming a dad is a learning experience, and it's okay not to be perfect. You'll make mistakes, you'll learn on the job, and that's all part of the process. Give yourself permission to grow into your role as a father over time.

- *Take Care of Your Well-Being:* Just as you're focused on supporting your partner, don't forget to take care of yourself as well. Pregnancy can be a stressful time, and it's important to manage your own stress levels. Make time for activities that help you relax and recharge, whether that's exercise, hobbies, or spending time with friends.

- *Be Present:* Finally, be present in the moment. This is a special time in your life, and being fully engaged is important. Whether it's feeling your baby kick for the first time, attending childbirth classes, or just having heart-to-heart conversations with your partner, these are moments that will stay with you forever.

As an expectant dad, you have a big job ahead of you—one that's just as important as the physical work of pregnancy. Your role involves supporting your partner, preparing for fatherhood, and navigating the emotional and mental shifts that come with this life-changing event. By recognizing that this is "Job 1" and giving yourself the grace to focus on this new chapter, you're setting yourself up to be the best dad and partner you can be. Remember, growing into fatherhood is a journey, and it deserves your full attention, effort, and care.

Countdown to Baby To Dos

Sometimes, the list of things to do before the big arrival can feel daunting. So, while you're glowing (or maybe it's just the sweat from trying to tie your shoes or from surfing the emotional swings of expectant parents), it's time to face the challenge: prepping for your little one's arrival. Don't worry. This isn't like trying to assemble an IKEA crib without instructions (though that may be on the list too). Think of this as your "baby prep boot camp,"—except with more diaper shopping and fewer burpee drills.

Now, before you go into full nesting overdrive and start color-coding your baby socks, take a deep breath. You've got this! Yes, there are a lot of things to do, but we're breaking it down into bite-sized chunks. Consider this your "21-gun-salute" personal guide to staying sane amidst the whirlwind of planning, pediatrician interviews, and figuring out exactly how to install that car seat without wanting to scream. Because, trust me, the car seat will win at least the first round. But just like you'll soon become a diaper-changing ninja, you'll crush this list in no time. Ready? Let's do this!

1. *Announcement*—Create, decide the medium (social media, email, in-person), and execute a birth announcement plan to share the exciting news with family and friends.

2. *Birthing Classes*—Research and decide on a birthing approach and classes that would help prepare you both.

3. *Birth Plan*—Create a birth plan outlining your preferences for labor and delivery, choose the birth location (hospital, home, birthing center), and discuss your plan with your medical team.

4. *Clothing and Diapering* – Figure out what to dress the little one in and purchase (with a word of caution that almost all new parents buy too many little things that baby grows out of before sometimes even wearing). Figure out and purchase what kind of diapers (again, a word of caution to start with smaller packs, possibly from multiple brands, so you can find out what best suits you and your baby and can change your mind without a stockpile of less-than-ideal tiny diapers).

5. *Documenting Memories*—Plan how to capture the early moments, whether it's through baby journals, photography, or digital memory-keeping apps. Some parents even employ an in-hospital and/or first-days professional photographer (my client's results have been stunningly beautiful).

6. *Equipment*—Research, order, and assemble essential baby gear like car seats, strollers, cribs, and safety equipment, ensuring everything is set up before the baby arrives. Hope that it's easier to do than assembling an outdoor grill (you know what I mean if you've ever attempted that).

7. *Family*—Coordinate family visits, set schedules, and communicate expectations for when and how family members can offer support after the baby's arrival.

8. *Feeding*—Decide whether you'll breastfeed or formula-feed, and source the necessary supplies like breast pumps, bottles, formula brands, nipple treatments, and soothers.

9. *Financial Planning*—Review your budget for baby-related expenses (diapers, formula, childcare), set up savings accounts or college funds (it's never too early!), and explore any available tax deductions for dependents.

10. *Grow the Baby*—Keep yourself healthy and attend regular prenatal appointments to monitor the baby's growth and development. Clearly, Mom is the only one taking the lead on this ;-). Dads, don't forget it really is a big job (no pun intended).

11. *Healthcare Coverage*—Ensure health insurance is updated to cover the baby, review benefits, and make necessary medical preparations.

12. *Legal Documents*—Update or create important legal documents, including wills, guardianship designations, and medical directives related to the baby's future. Learn the process for obtaining birth certificates and passports (which may have to be started soon after birth if you plan to travel soon and show off the new addition).

13. *Mental and Emotional Support*—Identify postpartum support groups, therapists, breastfeeding support coaches, or parenting classes to help manage the mental and emotional challenges that come with new parenthood.

14. *Nanny/Daycare*—Pre-plan and research nannies or daycare options, apply early and schedule interviews to secure

childcare for when you return to work. You'll probably be surprised how long some of these processes and waitlists are!

15. *Nursery*—Design and create a calming and functional nursery space by purchasing and assembling furniture and décor items for the baby's room. If you are not a handyman pro (and don't want to start training for it), consider a professional assembler.

16. *Parental Leave(s) Strategy*—Particularly for dual working parents, it's time to take a look at the timing of those leaves, and for many support partners with some form of paternity leave, when to plan on taking it (at birth, during mom's leave, after mom's leave).

17. *Pediatrician*—Research pediatricians, schedule consultations if needed, and engage one as your baby's healthcare provider early on to ensure readiness.

18. *Postpartum Recovery*—Prepare for the mother›s recovery by gathering postpartum care items such as comfortable clothing, breastfeeding bras, perineal care products, and pain relief essentials.

19. *Siblings' Care*—Make arrangements for the care and attention of older siblings during labor, the hospital stay, and after bringing the baby home.

20. *Support (Night Nurse, Friends, Family)*—Consider engaging a night nurse if desired, and establish a support network of friends and family who can assist you during the newborn stage.

21. *Vaccination and Health Planning*—Research and prepare for the baby's vaccination schedule and plan early pediatric appointments to monitor the baby's health. Learn where you may have options (such as for immunizations and circumcisions).

Here's a worksheet for this prep list to help identify who is going to be on-point for what—mom, dad, or both (though if you choose both, be clear about what that means about the division of to-dos!). Add to it or expand it as suits your situation.

COUNTDOWN TO BABY RESPONSIBILITIES

	Mom	Dad
Announcement	☐	☐
Birthing Classes	☐	☐
Birth Plan	☐	☐
Clothing and Diapering	☐	☐
Documenting Memories	☐	☐
Equipment	☐	☐
Family	☐	☐
Feeding	☐	☐
Financial Planning	☐	☐
Grow the Baby ;-)	☐	☐
Healthcare Coverage	☒	☐
Legal Documents	☐	☐
Mental and Emotional Support	☐	☐
Nanny/Daycare	☐	☐
Nursery	☐	☐
Parental Leave(s) Strategy	☐	☐
Pediatrician	☐	☐
Post-Partum Recovery	☐	☐
Siblings Care	☐	☐
Support (Night Nurse, Friends, Family)	☐	☐
Vaccination and Health Planning	☐	☐
???		
?	☐	☐
?	☐	☐
?	☐	☐

10

Understanding and Navigating Paternity Leave Bias

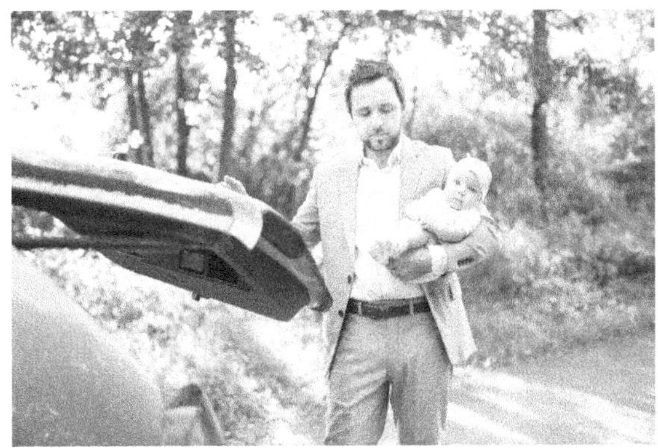

Photo credit: Getty Images, Unsplash.com

While maternity leave has become more accepted and expected in most workplaces, paternity leave is still battling a significant bias in many sectors. Parental leave bias, particularly paternity leave bias, refers to the prejudices and misconceptions that some employers and colleagues may hold toward fathers who take time off to care for their newborns and postpartum partners. Unlike maternity leave, which is widely recognized as essential, paternity leave is sometimes seen as a luxury or even unnecessary. For fathers, this bias can manifest in several ways—from being viewed as less committed to their jobs to facing pressure to "make up" for the time they took off to being seen as having been given the "gift" of an extended and rejuvenating vacation.

Paternity leave bias stems from outdated gender roles and stereotypes that view men primarily as breadwinners rather than active participants in parenting. While progressive companies are beginning to recognize the importance of paternity leave, many organizations and individuals still harbor misconceptions about its value.

This chapter will explore the different types of paternity leave biases, how they can impact your career, and strategies for mitigating these biases while emphasizing the importance of your role as a new parent.

Types of Paternity Leave Bias

- *The "Luxury" Bias:*
  This bias arises when paternity leave is viewed as an optional luxury rather than a necessity. Colleagues or employers might see your time off as a "break" rather than a vital period for bonding with your newborn and supporting your partner.

- *The "Vacation" Bias:*
  Some people may equate paternity leave with a vacation, assuming that time away from work means relaxation rather than the reality of sleepless nights, diaper changes, and the intense demands of caring for a newborn.

- *The "Career Impact" Bias:*
  This bias reflects the assumption that taking paternity leave shows a lack of commitment to your career. Some might believe that by taking time off, you're not as dedicated to your job, which can lead to concerns about your future career advancement or job security.

- *The "Make-Up Work" Bias:*
  Upon returning to work, some dads face pressure to "make up" for the time they were away. This can result in unrealistic expectations to work longer hours, take on extra projects, or prove their worth to colleagues and supervisors who may view their leave as a disruption to the team.

Strategies to Mitigate Paternity Leave Bias

While you can't entirely control others' perceptions, there are strategies you can use to mitigate the impact of paternity leave bias and emphasize the importance of your role as a new parent.

- *Frame Your Leave as a Parenting Responsibility:*

  » When discussing your paternity leave, focus on the responsibilities you'll be taking on—such as supporting your partner's recovery, bonding with your baby, and helping to manage the household. This helps to frame your leave as a necessary and responsible decision rather than a luxury or vacation.

  » Use language that underscores the importance of your role, such as "I'll be taking paternity leave to support my partner and to ensure that our family has a strong start during this critical time."

- *Educate Your Colleagues:*

  » Sometimes, bias stems from a lack of understanding. Take the opportunity to educate your colleagues about the realities of paternity leave. You might share insights about the challenges of newborn care, the need for parental bonding, and the importance of shared parenting responsibilities.

> » If your company offers information sessions or training on parental leave, encourage colleagues to attend. Awareness and education can help shift perceptions over time.

- *Set Clear Expectations Before and After Your Leave:*

  > » Before going on leave, communicate with your team and supervisors about how your responsibilities will be managed in your absence. Reassure them that you've put a plan in place to ensure a smooth transition and that you'll be fully engaged upon your return.

  > » Upon returning, avoid trying to "make up" for your time away. Instead, focus on reintegrating smoothly, catching up where necessary, and resuming your responsibilities with the same level of commitment you had before your leave.

- *Highlight the Long-Term Benefits:*

  > » Emphasize the long-term benefits of paternity leave, both for your family and the organization. Studies have shown that involved fathers contribute to healthier family dynamics (which contribute to strong work performance) and that supportive parental leave policies can improve employee morale and retention. *"Happy wife, happy life,"* as the saying goes – but what about *"Happy life, better work"*?

  > » When discussing your leave, consider framing it as an investment in your long-term well-being and productivity, which ultimately benefits the company.

- *Be Confident and Assertive:*

  > » Approach your paternity leave with confidence. Understand that you have a right to take this leave and that it's an important aspect of modern parenting.

» If you encounter pushback or negative comments, address them directly but diplomatically. For example, you might say, "I understand this is a new experience for our team, but taking this leave is important for my family and for me as a father."

- *Avoid Comparisons with Traditional Vacations:*

  » It can be tempting to share stories about memorable moments during your leave but be mindful of how these are framed. While sharing the joys of parenting is fine, avoid discussing your leave in a way that could reinforce the "vacation" bias. Instead, consider focusing on the responsibilities and challenges you faced, which help underline the seriousness of paternity leave.

Paternity leave bias is a real challenge that many dads face, but by understanding the different types of bias and using strategies to mitigate them, you can help shift perceptions in your workplace. Remember, taking paternity leave is not only your right—it's a vital step in supporting your family and fulfilling your role as a parent. By framing your leave as an essential parenting responsibility, educating your colleagues, setting clear expectations, and approaching your leave with confidence, you can help combat paternity leave bias and pave the way for a more inclusive and supportive work environment for all parents.

11

Coordinating Dual Parental Leaves

Photo credit: Kelly Sikkema, Unsplash.com

In today's evolving workplace, many progressive companies are offering generous parental leave policies for both birth-givers and birth-partners. Often referred to as "Parental Leave," these policies recognize the critical role that both parents play in the early stages of a child's life. While the birth-giver may receive an extended leave period (often up to six months), birth-partners typically have options ranging from one to three months. These leaves can often be taken all at once, in intervals, starting from the date of birth, or spread out over the first year.

With so many choices, it's important to consider the pros and cons of each option to determine what will work best for your family. This chapter explores the various approaches to taking partner leave and how to make an informed decision supporting your family's needs and your career.

Option 1: Taking Leave Immediately After Birth

Pros:

- *Immediate Bonding*: Taking leave right after the birth allows you to bond with your newborn from day one. This is a crucial time for building emotional connections and getting involved in daily caregiving tasks.

- *Supporting the Birth-Giver*: The first few weeks postpartum can be physically and emotionally challenging for the birth-giver. Being home during this time means you can provide essential support, help with household tasks, and share in the responsibilities of newborn care.

- *Navigating the Transition Together*: The early days of parenthood are full of adjustments. Taking leave right away allows you and your partner to navigate this new chapter together, building a strong foundation as a parenting team.

Cons:

- *Potential Overlap*: If both parents take leave simultaneously, there might be less overall time spent with the baby at home before returning to work. This could lead to a shorter period where one parent is always home with the baby.

- *Returning to Work Sooner:* If you take your full leave immediately, you'll be back at work sooner, which might feel rushed as you're still adapting to parenthood.

Option 2: Taking Leave After the Birth-Giver Returns to Work

Pros:

- *Extended Time at Home*: Staggering your leave so that you take it after the birth-giver returns to work ensures that your baby has a parent at home for longer. This can ease the transition to external childcare and reduce the need for full-time childcare right away.

- *Solo Bonding Time*: Being the primary caregiver while your partner is back at work allows you to build a strong, independent bond with your baby. This solo time can also boost your confidence in being a parent and building your relationship with your child.

- *Supporting Your Partner's Transition Back to Work*: By taking leave when your partner returns to work, you can help ease their transition back into the workforce, knowing that the baby is in good hands at home.

Cons:

- *Delayed Support:* Not taking leave immediately after birth means your partner might have to navigate the early postpartum period without as much hands-on support.

- *Missed Early Milestones:* Depending on the length of your delayed leave, you might miss out on some of the early milestones, such as the first smiles or the first time the baby rolls over.

Option 3: Splitting Leave into Multiple Intervals

Pros:

- *Flexibility:* Splitting your leave into multiple intervals allows you to be present at key moments throughout the baby's first year. This could include the first few weeks after birth, the transition to solid foods, or the early stages of crawling and walking.

- *Ongoing Support:* By spacing out your leave, you can provide ongoing support to your partner and your baby as they hit different stages of development.

- *Balancing Work and Family:* This approach allows you to balance your professional responsibilities with your desire to be involved in your baby's early life. It can also help manage work commitments during busy periods.

Cons:

- *Potential for Disruption:* Splitting leave can create disruptions at work, as you'll be in and out of the office multiple times. This could make it harder to maintain continuity on projects or with clients.

- *Adjustment Periods:* Each time you return to work, you'll need to readjust to your professional routine, which can be challenging. Similarly, your baby might need to readjust to changes in caregiving.

Option 4: A Hybrid Approach—Taking Some Leave Immediately and Some Later

Pros:

- *Best of Both Worlds:* A hybrid approach allows you to be there for the crucial early days right after birth while also saving some of your leave for later on. This can maximize your time with your baby across different stages of development.

- *Continuous Support:* You can provide ongoing support to your partner during the immediate postpartum period and their return to work.

- *Flexibility to Adapt:* This approach gives you the flexibility to adapt your leave based on your family's evolving needs, whether it's dealing with sleep regressions, introducing new foods, or managing the baby's first illness.

Cons:

- *Complex Planning:* A hybrid approach requires careful planning to coordinate with your partner's leave, work commitments, and the baby's needs. It may also involve negotiating with your employer to ensure you can take leave in this way.

- *Multiple Adjustments:* Like splitting leave, a hybrid approach involves multiple transitions back to work, which can be challenging for both you and your employer.

Making the Decision

When deciding how to take your partner leave, consider the following factors:

- *Your Family's Needs:* Think about what will best support your partner and baby during the early months. Discuss with your partner how you can share responsibilities and provide the most effective support.

- *Your Work Commitments:* Consider your professional responsibilities and how taking leave at different times might impact your work. Talk to your employer about your options and how to balance your leave with ongoing projects or deadlines.

- *Your Personal Preferences:* Reflect on how you want to experience your baby's first year. Do you want to be there for the very beginning, spread out your time, or support your partner's return to work?

- *Company Policy:* Review your company's parental leave policy to understand your options. Some companies may have specific rules about how leave can be taken, so make sure you're clear on the details.

Choosing when and how to take partner parental leave is a significant decision that can shape your experience of your baby's first year. Whether you choose to take leave immediately after birth, stagger it for later, split it into intervals, or combine approaches, the most important thing is to make a choice that works best for your family's unique needs. By considering the pros and cons of each option, discussing your plans with your partner and employer, and reflecting on your preferences, you can create a leave plan that supports your role as a parent and professional.

Scrutinize Your HR Policy, Then Think Beyond

Photo credit: Tim Gouw, Unsplash.com

When planning your parental leave, whether you're an expectant mom or dad, it's crucial to fully understand what your employer offers and think strategically about how to make the most of it. The first step? Dive into your company's leave policies. Whether you've already glanced at the handbook or had a chat with HR, now's the time to get all the details in writing and make sure you know exactly what to expect.

Start by reviewing the key components:

- *Length of Leave:* Maternity leave typically ranges from 6 to 26 weeks in the U.S., while paternity leave might be shorter, often between 2 to 12 weeks. It's crucial to know how long you're entitled to be away from work. If you're based outside the U.S., you might find that leave can extend significantly—up to 12 months in Europe or even 18 months in Canada, though some caveats are usually involved.

- *Extension of Leave:* Some companies allow you to add vacation days or take an unpaid leave of absence to extend your time off. This is often more flexible for maternity leaves but can sometimes be negotiated for paternity leaves as well. Make sure to clarify these options with your HR department.

- *Compensation:* Understand how your pay will be handled during leave. Typically, you might receive full base salary, but policies on bonuses or incentive compensation can vary. Ensure you know what's covered and what's not and how it applies to maternity and paternity leave.

- *Health Care Benefits:* Health care benefits are critical for moms and dads. Most plans cover prenatal, delivery, and postpartum care, but the specifics can vary. Some employers offer extremely generous benefits—one client of mine even referred to her company's plan as the "$5 baby policy" because the only out-of-pocket expense was the initial maternity visit copay. Others might have more complex processes, with varying out-of-pocket costs depending on how closely you follow the plan's guidelines. Be sure to enroll your newborn in your health insurance plan as soon as possible to avoid any surprises.

These policies are the baseline—the "table stakes"—and often have little room for negotiation. However, there's usually some wiggle room in how you manage the specifics of your leave, especially when it comes to the informal aspects.

Beyond the formal policy, consider the unwritten rules and the conversations that can offer flexibility:

- *Starting Leave Early:* Whether you're preparing for maternity or paternity leave, think about when you might want to start it. Maybe your baby arrives early, or perhaps you want to take some time off before the due date to prepare. How does this impact your leave?

- *Working During Leave:* Sometimes, a quick check-in or small task during leave can feel necessary. How does this work with your company's policy, and how might it affect your return? This is particularly relevant for shorter paternity leaves, where staying connected might ease the transition back to work.

- *Managing Communication:* The emails won't stop, and clients might still reach out. Whether you're a mom or dad, how will you handle communication during your leave? What's the best way to set up your out-of-office message to maintain professionalism while setting clear boundaries?

- *Out-of-Office Messages:* Crafting the right message is key (see Chapter 14). It's about setting expectations without overcommitting and making sure that colleagues and clients know how to proceed in your absence.

These conversations are crucial for both moms and dads. While some aspects might keep you up at night, most situations are manageable with a good employer-employee relationship. And remember, it's okay to ask for forgiveness rather than permission sometimes—life doesn't always go according to plan, and that's perfectly fine.

It's also a good idea to ask around and learn from others who've been through this process. What strategies worked for them? What challenges did they face? By gathering insights, you can make informed decisions and avoid common pitfalls.

Ultimately, planning your leave—maternity or paternity—requires a balance of understanding the formal policies and navigating the informal nuances. Go with the flow, ride the wave, and trust that you'll find a rhythm that works for you and your family. The key is to stay flexible and open-minded, knowing that life will continue, and so will your career

Check the Law

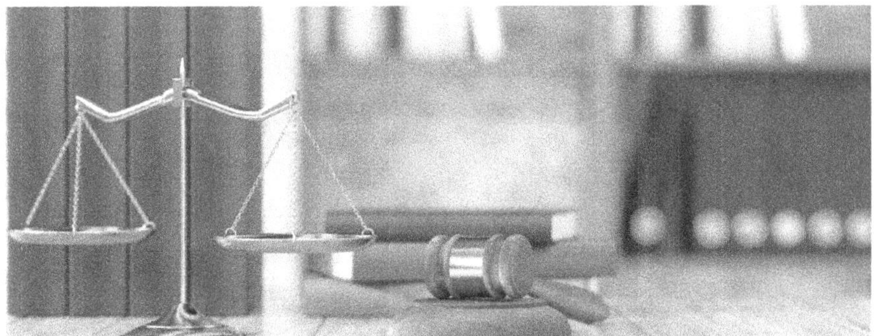

Photo credit: Getty Images, Unsplash.com

Several states in the U.S. have enacted laws mandating paid family and medical leave (PFML), which often include provisions for both maternity and paternity leave. These laws are designed to provide financial support and job protection for employees taking time off to bond with a new child, whether through birth, adoption, or foster placement.

It is important to note that I am not an attorney, and the details of these laws can change over time. Therefore, I strongly recommend that you research or consult legal professionals to clarify and confirm the most current information and any updates.

Here's an overview of some key states with PFML laws:

- *California:* California offers up to 12 weeks of paid leave for new parents. Employees receive 60-70% of their wages, paid by the state through its disability insurance program, not directly by the employer. However, job protection is only provided if the employee is also covered under the federal Family and Medical Leave Act (FMLA) or the California Family Rights Act (CFRA). **Leave can be taken any time within the first 12 months after the child's birth or placement for adoption or foster care.**

- *Colorado:* Starting January 1, 2024, Colorado's Family and Medical Leave Insurance (FAMLI) program allows eligible employees to take up to 12 weeks of paid leave. Benefits are paid by the state through a payroll deduction system that both employers and employees contribute to. The leave is job-protected for employees who have been with their employer for at least 180 days. **Leave can be taken any time within the first 12 months after the child's birth or placement for adoption or foster care.**

- *Massachusetts:* Massachusetts provides up to 12 weeks of paid family leave, with job protection. The benefits are paid through a state-administered insurance program funded by employee and employer payroll contributions. **Employees can take this leave any time within the first year after the child's birth, adoption, or foster placement.**

- *New Jersey:* New Jersey's Family Leave Insurance (FLI) program provides up to 12 weeks of paid leave at 85% of the employee's average weekly wage, capped at $903 per week. The state pays these benefits through an insurance fund supported by payroll contributions. **Leave can be taken continuously or intermittently during the first year after the child's birth or placement for adoption or foster care.**

- *New York:* New York offers up to 12 weeks of paid family leave, with benefits set at 67% of the employee's average weekly wage, up to a maximum of $971.61 per week. The benefits are paid by the state's insurance fund, with employee contributions. **New York's program allows leave to be taken at any time within the first 12 months following the birth or placement of a child.**

- *Connecticut:* Connecticut's Paid Leave Authority provides up to 12 weeks of paid leave, with benefits paid by the state through a payroll deduction system. Employees receive up to 95% of their average weekly wage, with job protection included. **The leave can be taken at any time within the first year of the child's birth, adoption, or foster placement.**

- *Washington:* Washington State's paid family leave program offers up to 12 weeks of paid leave, with benefits paid by the state. Employees receive up to 90% of their weekly wage, with a cap of $1,206 per week. **Leave can be taken continuously or intermittently within the first 12 months after the birth or placement of a child for adoption or foster care.**

In these states, the paid leave benefits are typically administered through a state insurance fund funded by payroll contributions from employees, employers, or both. The specific rules regarding when the leave can be taken (e.g., immediately after birth or at any time during the first year) provide flexibility for parents to use the leave in a way that best suits their family's needs.

Again, please ensure that you verify this information with up-to-date resources or legal counsel, as state laws can evolve, and the specifics may change.

Work Approaches

Deciding how to handle work during parental leave is a deeply personal choice, shaped by your career goals, family needs, and personal values. For some, fully disconnecting might seem like a dream, while others may feel the pull to stay partially engaged with their work. There's no one-size-fits-all answer, but there are plenty of strategies to help you navigate this important decision.

In this chapter, we'll explore various approaches to managing work while on leave, offering guidance on completely disconnecting or maintaining some level of involvement. From deciding when and how to hand off responsibilities, to contemplating the advice to shut down the laptop, to making those crucial decisions in the final weeks before leave begins, we'll cover practical strategies to help you strike a balance between your professional commitments and your new role as a parent.

Whether you're leaning towards staying connected, stepping away entirely, or finding a middle ground, this chapter provides the insights you need to create a plan that aligns with your goals and supports a smooth transition into parenthood.

Here, we'll delve into key considerations:

A. **Reconsider Shutting Down The Laptop**: We'll explore the pros and cons of staying connected, helping you decide if a complete shutdown is the right choice or if there's value in keeping a foot in the door.

B. **Yes, No – And Maybe:** Learn how to set boundaries and make decisions about what you will and won't take on during your leave, ensuring you protect your time while still feeling in control.

C. **The Handoff:** Discover best practices for handing off your responsibilities so you can leave knowing your work is in good hands and return without a mountain of chaos waiting for you.

D. **The Last Long Weeks – To Stop Or Not?:** As you approach your leave, we'll help you weigh the options of winding down early or pushing through until the last possible moment.

E. **Note To Dads On Nesting:** For expectant dads, we'll provide some insights into the nesting instinct and how you can support your partner (and yourself) during this busy, emotional time.

By the end of this chapter, you'll clearly understand the work approaches that best fit your situation, empowering you to make decisions that support your career and your growing family.

A. RECONSIDER SHUTTING DOWN THE LAPTOP

Photo credit: James McKinven, Unsplash.com

Conventional wisdom, along with many well-meaning colleagues, friends, and that one overly enthusiastic HR person, will likely tell you to "Shut down your laptop" and "fully disconnect—take advantage of your leave!" It sounds like a dream, right? Two months (or more) of pure baby bliss with zero work distractions. And yes, in the short term, this advice is golden. But let's face it: we're not living in a perfect world where babies sleep through the night and your work email stays miraculously empty.

Let's get real for a second. Is it truly realistic to shut down your laptop, toss it into a drawer, and dust it off a few months later as if nothing happened? We live in a world of constant connectivity—Slack, Chat, WhatsApp, Teams, LinkedIn, Zoom, voicemail, and the never-ending pings of whatever else you habitually use. Even if you manage to disconnect, how many times have you heard of someone who genuinely, completely "shut everything off"? It's rarer than finding a unicorn in your backyard.

So, here's the reality check: shutting down might sound like the ultimate escape, but it could also lead to the not-so-glamorous re-entry experience where you spend your first few days back drowning in a digital avalanche. Consider how you'll handle this before you hit the power button for the last time.

Then, there's the question of practicality and wisdom. Some of us are lucky enough to have jobs that allow us to walk away for an extended period and simply pick back up on our return—no harm, no foul. If that's you, congratulations! You've won the work-life balance lottery. But for the rest of us mere mortals working in fields where continuity and relationships are key (think professional services like consulting, financial advising, advertising, legal, etc.), going AWOL for months might not be the best career move.

In these industries, relationships don't just pause because you're on leave. They're like slow-cooking stews—requiring consistent attention, occasional stirring, and just the right amount of seasoning over time. A few months of complete silence might lead to a well-intentioned colleague stepping in temporarily but finding it hard to let go when you return. Or worse, that key client might have moved on to someone else who was just a little more available.

This isn't to say there's a one-size-fits-all answer here. As always, you have to weigh the pros and cons and decide what's best for you. But it's worth considering whether some interim (often low effort) involvement could benefit YOU. Maybe there's a key proposal you want to stay looped into, a high-visibility meeting you don't want to miss, or a quick reach-out to a key customer that could make all the difference when you're back in the saddle. And what about those people you sponsor? Are you committed to attending annual performance and bonus meetings? A little strategic engagement might just keep those relationships warm without pulling you away from baby snuggles.

Which brings me to another point—what's in your yes/no/maybe buckets? For that, let's move on to the next section, where we'll discuss prioritizing your engagements during leave.

B. YES, NO AND MAYBE

Let's get into the nitty-gritty of decision-making during parental leave with a little something I like to call the *"Hell, No!"* vs. *"Oh, Yes!"* Venn diagram. Picture two overlapping circles: one labeled *"Hell, No!"* (where all the things you absolutely do NOT want to deal with during your leave reside) and the other labeled *"Oh, Yes!"* (where all the things you'd actually enjoy or see value in doing). The sweet spot in the middle, where the circles overlap, is your *"Maybe"*—those work roles or tasks that might warrant a bit of extra thought before you fully commit or decline.

Now, I know what you're thinking: *"Do I really need to draw a Venn diagram just to plan my leave?"* Well, hear me out. This isn't just about being detail-oriented; it's about giving yourself a clear framework to help you navigate the murky waters of work commitments during leave. And, okay, maybe it's also a fun excuse to whip out some colored markers and get a little creative—who doesn't love a good diagram?

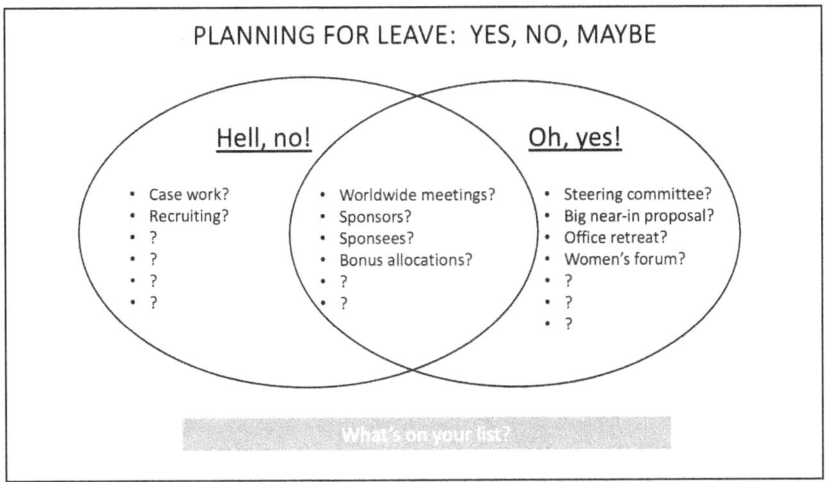

Start by populating the "Hell, No!" circle. This is where you put all the things that make you cringe at the mere thought of dealing with while you're knee-deep in diapers and baby bliss. Maybe it's that quarterly budget review that feels like pulling teeth or the company-wide Zoom calls that always seem to happen right when the baby decides to cry as if it's the end of the world. Whatever it is, if the idea of doing it during your leave makes you want to throw your laptop out the window, it goes in this circle.

Then there's the "Oh, Yes!" circle. This is where you put the tasks that you might actually look forward to—a quick check-in with a favorite client, a key strategy session that could shape your career trajectory, or even attending that worldwide practice meeting you secretly love because it's a chance to flex those brain muscles. Think of these as your little breathers, where stepping away from the baby zone for a hot minute might actually feel invigorating. Plus, if you decide to pop in, you can always figure out the logistical details later—like how to justify your appearance at the meeting without anyone realizing you're still in pajama bottoms.

And then there's the "Maybe" zone—the space where the circles overlap. This is where you put the tasks that aren't a definite yes or no. Maybe it's a meeting that's important but not mission-critical or a project update you could handle in a half-hour while the baby naps. The beauty of the "*Maybe*" zone is that it gives you flexibility. It allows you to consider each task on a case-by-case basis and decide what's worth your time and energy without feeling locked into a binary yes/no mindset.

Now, here's where you get to think outside the box. Just because something lands in your "*Hell, No!*" circle doesn't mean it's off the table forever. Maybe there's room for negotiation or flexibility. Could you attend that dreaded meeting but delegate the prep work to someone else? Or perhaps you can set boundaries—like committing to be there for the first half, but no one bats an eye when you mysteriously vanish right before the Q&A.

On the flip side, just because something lands in your *"Oh, Yes!"* circle doesn't mean you have to do it. Choosing rest over work is perfectly okay, even if the task seems enjoyable or beneficial. Remember, the goal is to balance your professional commitments with your new role as a parent in a way that feels right for you.

So, grab those markers, draw those circles, and start plotting below. Whether you find this exercise amusing, therapeutic, or just plain helpful, the important thing is that it gives you clarity. And hey, who knew that a Venn diagram could be such a lifesaver when planning parental leave?

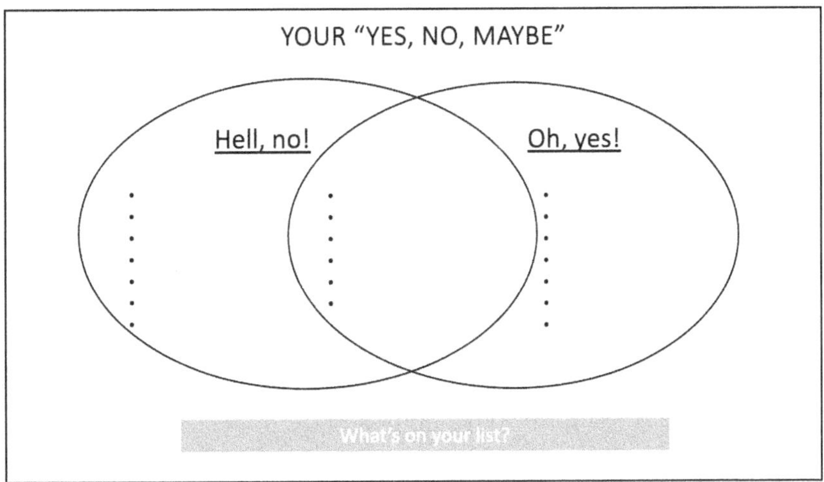

C. THE HANDOFF

Oh my gosh! I've seen and heard it all. While ambitious, successful senior women executive leaders share so many common characteristics, their approaches to handing off work responsibilities cover the spectrum of possibilities. Perhaps some are driven by the unpredictability of the timing of the arrival, and some are driven by physical, mental, and emotional overload. But it starts well before that—like in months 7 or 8. Here are the stereotypes I have observed:

- *The Ostrich.* The Ostrich carries on with life as usual. She acts as though she is seven months pregnant (even though she feels like she is ten months pregnant) and just carries on doing what she is doing. For this type, the possibility of the baby arriving early really doesn't enter her consciousness. She just keeps doing her best today, and she doesn't worry about tomorrow, next week, or next month. After all, she'll be on leave, and it will become someone else's problem. Right? If you do not intend to return to work, and the exit is anything but graceful (either through your actions or the baby's early arrival), then being an Ostrich is not a bad strategy. But if you are like this, you may leave your colleagues in the lurch. You may be obliging people you don't want to be bothered with in the early days of leave to call/email/Slack you with "just one small but very urgent question" or "just a super quick call to…?" It's kind of a setup for angst—for you as well as your colleagues.

- *The Slave.* Now, the Slave takes a polar opposite approach. She wants to transition with perfection (think Enneagram Type 3 Achievers) and be of great help to those she leaves behind (think Enneagram Type 2 Helpers). The problem is, not only does she not have to do it all right up until the end, but she's also probably not actually (ahem…) capable of doing it all. Her body and emotions remind her that she cannot pull all-nighters at this stage in her journey. She enters labor unbelievably sleep-deprived and wiped out. And she typically makes her swansong exit at the most inopportune time. I made mine for my second child with waters breaking at a Senior Leadership Steering Committee meeting, which was, as I now admit, on the eve of my due date. But I kept thinking *"Hey, I got this!"* Save yourself the hassle. Admit that there is a ramp-down to entering the likely birth date. Don't try to get everything you possibly can accomplished with the belief that you will be making it easier on others and helping them out. (Can we say, "a little impending leave guilt"?).

- *The Relay Runner.* Ah, this one I like. She is slow, thoughtful, planned, and realistic. She allows herself to let go with appropriate forewarning. Her process is smoother, easier, and more efficient. However, she can also create a little anxiety as she thinks *"Well, I've handed off a lot of stuff, so now I don't have as much work to do as usual"*. Geez, what a problem to have! While your work effort is moving down, your body and emotional needs are ramping up. And that's perfectly fine. Most of your coworkers are, have been, or will be in similar situations, or at least have extended family who are, have been, or will be. Most of them have empathy and are supportive (let's hope so!). It's perfectly fine not to be too busy in those last weeks. In fact, that may be the best thing to do for your organization and colleagues over the transition phase.

Clearly, I have an opinion about which are the preferable modes of operation. (At times, I have been told that I am not subtle.) Yup, Relay Runner!

Clearly, everyone makes their own choices.

I simply suggest that you become aware of your choices and the implications for how you will go into your leave!

"Just a thought!" (as my mother would say when giving clear advice while not wanting to appear that she was). And she was almost always right!

Photo source: Getty Images/Unsplash.com

D. THE LAST LONG WEEKS–TO STOP OR NOT?

As you inch closer to the finish line of pregnancy (and your belly inches further and further out), those final weeks can feel like an eternity. Sure, everyone knows that pregnancy doesn't last forever, but when you're in week 39 (or, yikes, week 41), it can certainly *feel* like you've been pregnant forever. Around this time, I get a flood of questions from expectant moms wondering whether they should keep working or start their leave a little early.

Let's talk numbers for a second. About two-thirds of all births happen in weeks 38, 39, and 40. That's a decent spread of unpredictability—enough to keep you on your toes (assuming you can still see your toes at this point). Whether you're someone who's been powering through like a warrior or feeling more like an ostrich with your head in the sand, the last few weeks can be a mental and physical rollercoaster.

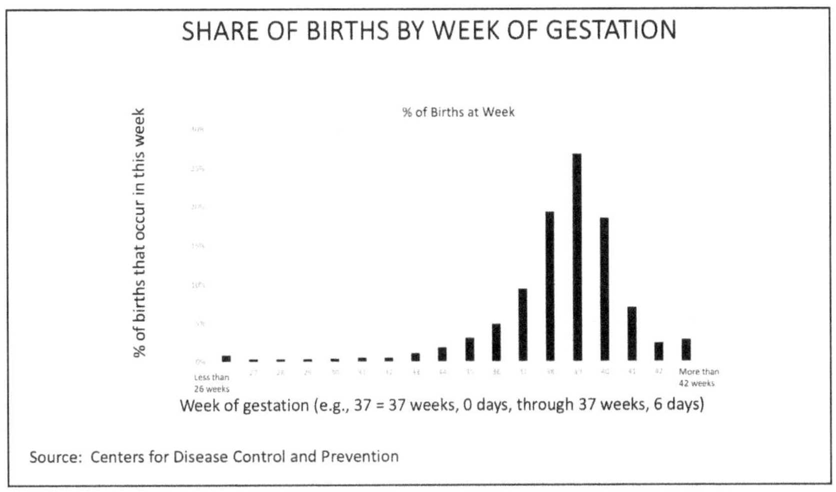

The reality of the last month, especially those final weeks, is that the glow of pregnancy often starts to fade—if it ever existed. Most moms-to-be aren't exactly basking in the joy of it all at this stage. Instead, I hear a lot more of *"How much longer until this baby arrives?!"* and a lot less of *"I'm loving every minute of this pregnancy!"*

So, here's the big question that often comes up: *"I'm exhausted, I'm over it, and I'm fed up. Should I go on leave early?"* Let me start by saying, it's not about what *I* think—it's about what *you* think. Or even more importantly, how you *feel*. Sure, you could make a pros and cons list, but at the end of the day, the decision really comes down to what feels right for you.

Let's put this in perspective. A year from now, you'll probably not remember that you took an extra week of leave (paid or unpaid). In the grand scheme of your life, career, and finances, those few extra days aren't going to make or break anything. What matters is how you feel in the moment. If your body and mind are screaming for a break, listening to them is okay.

And most people know better than to argue with a super-pregnant woman. Telling a very pregnant person that she's wrong about anything is a fast track to the doghouse (or worse). So, do what feels best for you and your baby. Whether you decide to power through those last weeks or kick back and start your leave early, the important thing is that you're taking care of yourself. After all, this is your journey; only you know what's best for you.

E. NOTE TO DADS ON NESTING

Photo credit: Margaret Jaszowska, Unsplash.com

As the delivery countdown begins, you might notice some changes in the mother of your child that seem to defy logic—or at least your previous experience. Suddenly, the woman who used to be perfectly content with a relaxed evening on the couch is now on a mission, as if preparing for an Olympic event. Don't be surprised if you come home to find her scrubbing the baseboards, reorganizing the pantry, or, yes, meticulously cleaning the dust off the top of the refrigerator (which, let's be honest, hasn't seen the light of day since you moved in). This is nesting in full swing, and it's driven by a powerful combination of hormones, anxiety, and the primal urge to prepare for the baby's arrival.

Alongside this cleaning frenzy, you might also notice a few other quirks. Perhaps she suddenly decides that every single onesie needs to be washed, ironed, and folded *just so,* even though the baby won't care if they come out of the laundry basket a little wrinkled. Or maybe she develops a newfound obsession with rearranging the furniture—for the fifth time this week—because the baby absolutely needs to have the perfect feng shui in the nursery. These are all normal, if somewhat bewildering, behaviors that come with the territory of late pregnancy.

As these last few weeks bring hormonal shifts, heightened anxiety, and the undeniable nesting instinct, it's a good time to support your partner in dialing back from work. Encouraging her to focus on self-care and rest instead of that last big project can help ease the transition into motherhood. After all, preparing for a baby is a full-time job, and she'll need all the energy she can muster for the big day ahead. So, when you see her making a beeline for the vacuum cleaner at 10 p.m., gently remind her that it's okay to let a few things go—and that you're there to help pick up the slack, both now and once the baby arrives. Plus, you might even score some extra points by tackling that dust on top of the fridge yourself!

Work Tactics

Preparing for parental leave involves more than just marking your out-of-office dates on the calendar—it's about ensuring that your professional responsibilities are handled smoothly in your absence so you can fully focus on your new role as a parent. In this chapter, we'll delve into the essential work tactics to help you transition seamlessly from the office to your home life, setting you and your team up for success.

First, we'll explore "**The Art Of The Hand-Off**," covering the importance of documenting your roles and delegating tasks effectively. This isn't just about handing over a to-do list; it's about ensuring that your responsibilities are clearly defined and that your colleagues are fully prepared. Next, we'll guide you through crafting "**The Perfect OOO Message**." While it may seem like a straightforward task, an out-of-office message is your first line of communication during your leave and requires careful thought to convey the right information and set the right expectations.

"**Your EA**" reinforces that Executive Assistants can be your ultimate ally during this time, keeping everything on track while you're away. We'll discuss how to leverage your EA's skills to manage communications, prioritize tasks, and ensure that nothing falls through the cracks. Finally, we'll cover how to "**Announce Like A Pro**" when it comes to sharing your exciting news with colleagues and clients. Whether you opt for a formal email or a more personal approach, we'll provide tips on how to plan your baby's debut to keep your professional relationships strong and supportive.

Finally, we'll address "**Nuances With Paternity Leaves**," which often differ from maternity leaves in duration and flexibility. We'll explore how dads can navigate these shorter or fragmented leaves while still applying the work tactics discussed in this chapter. Understanding these nuances will help you make informed decisions aligning with your professional and personal goals.

By mastering these work tactics, you'll be able to step away from your desk with confidence, knowing that your responsibilities are in good hands and that you've laid the groundwork for a smooth transition back to work when the time comes.

In this chapter, we will explore:

A. *The Art Of The Hand-Off:* Documenting and delegating your roles.

B. *The Perfect OOO Message:* It's not that simple.

C. *Your EA:* The ultimate air traffic control.

D. *Announce Like a Pro:* Planning your baby's debut.

E. *Nuances with Paternity Leaves:* There are some substantial differences.

A. THE ART OF THE HANDOFF: DOCUMENTING AND DELEGATING YOUR ROLES

Photo credit: Curated Lifestyle-RG, Unsplash.com

As you prepare for parental leave, one of the most important tasks you need to tackle is the hand-off of your various roles within your organization. While your official job description might outline your primary responsibilities, the reality is that your role likely extends far beyond that. From recruiting and interviewing to marketing, mentoring, and other key functions, it's essential to document all the hats you wear and ensure that each one is assigned to a capable "volun-told" point person.

Documenting, assigning, and communicating are Crucial. Leaving your organization without a clear understanding of is a recipe for confusion and potential disruption.

1. *Identifying All Your Roles.* By documenting all of your official and unofficial roles, you provide a roadmap for your colleagues to follow, ensuring that nothing falls through the

cracks. This helps maintain the smooth operation of your organization and gives you peace of mind, knowing that your work is in good hands. Start by taking a comprehensive inventory of everything you do within your organization. This includes your primary job responsibilities and any additional roles you've taken on over time. Consider the following areas:

- *Core Job Functions:*
  These are the tasks directly related to your job description, such as managing projects, leading teams, or overseeing operations.

- *Recruiting and Interviewing:*
  If you're involved in hiring, make sure to document your role in the recruiting process, including any specific strategies or interview techniques you use.

- *Marketing and Public Relations:*
  Outline any responsibilities related to promoting your organization, whether it's managing social media accounts, writing content, or representing the company at events.

- *Mentoring and Coaching:*
  If you mentor junior employees or provide coaching, document your approach, the individuals you work with, and any ongoing initiatives.

- *Committee Work and Special Projects:*
  List any committees you serve on or special projects you're involved in, including your role, responsibilities, and the current status of each.

- *Networking and Relationship Management:*
  If you manage key relationships with clients, partners, or stakeholders, document these connections and outline any regular communications or ongoing commitments.

2. *Assign Point Person(s) for Each Role.* Once you've identified all of your roles, the next step is to assign a point person for each one. This is where the concept of being "volun-told" comes into play—sometimes, people need a little nudge (or strong suggestion) to step up. Here's how to approach it:

   - *Match Skills with Responsibilities:*
     Choose point people based on their skills and experience. Assign tasks to those best suited to handle them, even if it means stretching their current role a bit. For example, if you mentor junior employees, consider passing this role to someone with strong leadership and interpersonal skills.

   - *Communicate Clearly and Early:*
     Have one-on-one meetings with each person you're delegating responsibilities to. Clearly explain the role, why you've chosen them, and your expectations. Be upfront that these roles are crucial to the organization's success during your absence.

   - *Provide Documentation:*
     Give each point person detailed documentation of their assigned role. This should include step-by-step instructions, key contacts, deadlines, and any other relevant information. The more comprehensive the documentation, the easier it will be for them to step in seamlessly.

- *Set Expectations for Reporting and Communication:*
  Make sure each point person knows how often they should report back to you (if at all) and what level of communication is expected. Establishing clear lines of communication will help prevent any issues from escalating unnoticed.

- *Empower Them to Make Decisions:*
  Encourage your point people to take ownership of their new roles. Empower them to make decisions within the scope of their responsibilities and let them know that you trust their judgment.

3. *Communicate the Hand-Off.* Once you've assigned your roles and briefed your point people, it's time to communicate the hand-off to the broader team or organization. Here's how to do it effectively:

- *Announce the Transition:*
  Send an email or hold a meeting to inform your team or organization about the temporary transition of responsibilities. Be clear about who takes over each role and how to contact them.

- *Express Confidence in Your Team:*
  Highlight your confidence in the point people you've chosen. This reassures your team and reinforces your trust in those taking on the roles.

- *Offer a Transition Period:*
  If possible, offer a short transition period where you can be available to answer questions or provide guidance as your point people get up to speed. This can help smooth the transition and build their confidence.

- *Encourage Collaboration:*
  Remind your team that they're all in this together. Encourage collaboration and open communication among the point people to support each other and share insights.

Documenting your roles and assigning them to trusted point people before you go on parental leave is essential for maintaining the continuity and success of your organization. By being explicit about what you do, choosing the right people to take over, and clearly communicating the hand-off, you can confidently step away, knowing that everything is under control. Remember, your colleagues might joke about being "volun-told," but in reality, they're stepping up to ensure that your organization continues to thrive while you focus on your new role as a parent.

B. THE PERFECT OUT-OF-OFFICE (OOO) MESSAGE: IT'S NOT THAT SIMPLE

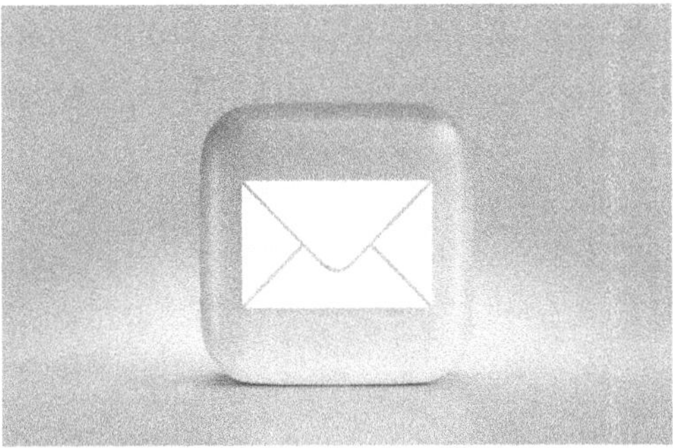

Photo credit: Maria Shalabaieva, Unsplash.com

When the time finally comes to step away from work and dive into the incredible (and exhausting) world of parenthood, one of the most important tasks you need to complete is setting up your out-of-office

(OOO) message. A well-crafted OOO message does more than just inform people of your absence; it sets expectations, directs them to the right resources, and helps maintain your professional relationships while you focus on your new baby. In this chapter, we'll explore the different options for writing an OOO message, what to consider, and how to ensure it's activated at the right time.

Your OOO Message Matters. It's your first line of communication with anyone who tries to reach you during your leave. It's important because it informs them that you're unavailable and provides guidance on what they should do in your absence. A clear and well-thought-out OOO message can prevent confusion, ensure that important matters are handled, and give you peace of mind knowing that your work is under control while you're away. Here, we'll explore three considerations in creating a strong OOO message: approaches to crafting, key message elements, and enabling delivery.

1. *Approaches to Crafting Your OOO Message.* When writing your OOO message, there are several factors to consider, including how much information you want to share, who your audience is, and what kind of access (if any) you'll have to your email during leave. Here are some options to consider:

   - *The Brief and Simple Approach:*
     » *Example:* "Thank you for your email. I am currently on parental leave and will not be checking emails regularly. I will return on [date]. For urgent matters, please contact [backup person] at [contact information]."

     » *When to Use:* This approach is best if you want to keep things straightforward and avoid sharing too much detail. It's ideal for those who plan to fully disconnect during their leave and prefer to limit access to their time.

- *The Detailed and Informative Approach:*

  » *Example:* "Thank you for your message. I am on parental leave until [return date]. During this time, I will be checking emails [insert frequency, e.g., once a week, only in emergencies, etc.]. For assistance with [specific issues], please contact [backup person] at [contact information]. For [other matters], please reach out to [another contact]. I appreciate your understanding during this time."

  » *When to Use:* This option works well if you need to provide specific instructions for different types of inquiries. It's useful for professionals with ongoing projects, clients, or responsibilities that require continuity in their absence.

- *The Personalized Approach:*

  » *Example:* "Thank you for your email. I'm currently on parental leave enjoying time with my new baby and will be away from the office until [date]. I'll check emails occasionally, but please contact [backup person] for immediate assistance. I look forward to reconnecting with you when I return."

  » *When to Use:* This approach is great if you want to add a personal touch to your OOO message, perhaps for clients or colleagues with whom you have close relationships. It balances professionalism with a bit of warmth and personality.

- *The Hybrid Approach:*
  - » *Example:* "Hello, and thank you for your email. I am currently on parental leave and will return on [date]. During this time, I will not be checking emails regularly. For immediate assistance, please contact [backup person] for [specific matters] or [another contact] for [other issues]. I will be available via email on [specific dates] for urgent matters only."
  - » *When to Use:* This option is ideal if you need to stay partially connected but want to set clear boundaries. It provides a mix of details and allows you to specify when you'll be reachable.

2. *Key Elements to Include in Your OOO Message.* No matter which style of OOO message you choose, certain elements are essential to include:

- *Your Return Date:* Clearly state when you will be back, so people know when to expect a response.

- *Alternative Contacts:* Provide contact information for colleagues or teams who can handle specific inquiries in your absence.

- *Frequency of Email Checks (if any):* If you plan to check your email occasionally, indicate how often and for what types of matters.

- *Acknowledgment and Appreciation:* A polite thank you or acknowledgment of the email shows professionalism and respect.

- *Clear Instructions:* If you're directing people to another person or resource, make sure the instructions are straightforward and easy to follow.

3. *Enabling the OOO.* Timing is crucial when activating your OOO message. Ideally, you should enable it just before you start your leave. However, if you're unexpectedly away (such as an early delivery), you should have a plan in place for someone to activate it on your behalf. Here's how to approach it:

   - *Set It Up in Advance:* Draft your OOO message well before your due date. If you're using an email platform that allows you to schedule when an OOO message goes live, take advantage of this feature to ensure it's activated at the right time.

   - *Designate a Backup:* If your leave starts unexpectedly, your Executive Assistant or a trusted colleague should be tasked with enabling your OOO message. Make sure they have access to your email settings or know where your draft is saved.

   - *Coordinate with IT:* If your organization has specific protocols for OOO messages, coordinate with your IT department to ensure everything is set up correctly. This is particularly important if you need to give them access to your email settings.

   - *Consider a Staggered Approach:* If your leave date is flexible, consider setting an initial OOO message that indicates you are preparing for leave and then updating it to the full leave message once the baby arrives.

Setting up your Out of Office message is critical in preparing for parental leave. It's your way of maintaining professionalism, setting boundaries, and ensuring that your work and relationships continue to run smoothly while you focus on your new baby. By carefully considering your options, crafting a message that fits your needs, and ensuring it's activated at the right time, you can confidently step away from work, knowing that everything is under control. Remember, this is your time to focus on your family, and a well-thought-out OOO message helps you do just that.

C. YOUR EA: THE ULTIMATE AIR TRAFFIC CONTROL

Photo credit: Getty Images, Unsplash.com

As an executive, your role involves juggling numerous responsibilities, managing key relationships, and ensuring that everything in your organization runs smoothly—even when you're on parental leave. Enter your Executive Assistant (EA), the unsung hero who can act as your air traffic control during this time. By setting clear rules of engagement and leveraging your EA's skills, you can ensure that your work continues seamlessly and that you stay connected in a prioritized, efficient way.

Your EA is one of your best assets during leave. Your EA knows your schedule, your priorities, and how you like things done. They are your right hand, and during your leave, they can be the linchpin that keeps everything moving smoothly. From managing client communications to filtering urgent matters, your EA can ensure you remain informed without being overwhelmed. The key is to establish a clear plan for how you'll work together during this time. There are three key elements: setting up rules of engagement, staying connected without being overwhelmed, and maintaining customer service excellence.

1. *Set Up Rules of Engagement.* Before you head off on parental leave, it's crucial to sit down with your EA and establish rules of engagement. This ensures that both of you are on the same page about what's expected and how to handle various situations. Here are some suggestions for laying out these rules:

   - *Prioritize Communication Channels:*
     » *Email:* Decide how you want your EA to handle your inbox. Will they manage it entirely, forwarding only critical messages, or will they summarize key points in a daily or weekly update? Establish criteria for a "must-see" email versus what can wait.

     » *Phone Calls:* Determine if there are specific people or types of calls that should be immediately routed to you. For other calls, provide guidelines on how your EA should handle them—whether it's taking a message, setting up a follow-up, or redirecting the caller to someone else.

» *Text Messages:* If texting is part of your usual workflow, decide whether you want to be copied on texts or if your EA should manage them independently.

- *Client and Stakeholder Communication:*

  » *Proactive Updates:* Your EA can send out scheduled updates to key clients and stakeholders, informing them of your availability and who they can contact in your absence. This helps manage expectations and ensures that no one feels neglected.

  » *Escalation Process:* Establish a clear process for escalation. Define which issues require immediate attention and which your EA can handle or delegate to other team members. This ensures that only the most critical matters reach you while everything else is managed smoothly.

- *Calendar Management:*

  » *Blocking Out Time:* Make sure your EA knows which periods are strictly off-limits for work-related matters, such as feeding times or family activities. Conversely, identify times when you're open to being contacted if necessary.

  » *Meeting Management:* Your EA should be able to reschedule, cancel, or delegate meetings as needed. They can also take notes on your behalf or arrange for a trusted colleague to cover key meetings during your absence.

- *Task Delegation:*

  » *Delegating Responsibilities:* Work with your EA to identify which of your tasks can be delegated to others in your team. This could involve temporary reassignment of projects or simply allowing your EA to handle more of your day-to-day responsibilities.

  » *Tracking Progress:* Your EA can also keep track of ongoing projects, ensuring that deadlines are met and that you're regularly updated on progress.

- *Crisis Management:*

  » *Defining a Crisis:* Clarify what qualifies as a crisis that warrants immediate contact. This could include things like major client issues, significant organizational changes, or personal emergencies.

  » *Action Plan:* Develop a clear action plan for handling crises, including who should be contacted first and what steps should be taken before escalating the issue to you.

2. *Stay Connected Without Being Overwhelmed.* You want to stay connected during your leave without being constantly pulled back into work. Here's how your EA can help you achieve that balance:

- *Daily or Weekly Summaries:*
  Instead of being bombarded with individual messages, ask your EA to compile a daily or weekly summary of key updates, decisions that need your input, and any other important information. This allows you to stay informed without feeling overwhelmed.

- *Pre-Scheduled Check-Ins:*
  Schedule brief check-ins with your EA at regular intervals. These can be quick, 10–15-minute calls where your EA brings you up to speed on essential matters and you provide any necessary direction. This ensures you're always in the loop without being constantly on call.

- *Manage Expectations with Clients and Colleagues:*
  Your EA can send out a pre-leave announcement to clients and colleagues, letting them know about your upcoming leave, how long you'll be away, and who they should contact in your absence. This helps manage expectations and reduces the likelihood of people reaching out to you directly.

- *Create a "No-Contact" Buffer:*
  Establish specific times when your EA knows not to contact you unless it's an absolute emergency. This buffer gives you time to focus on your family without worrying about work interruptions.

3. *Maintain Customer Service Excellence.* Your clients and colleagues rely on you, and you want to ensure they feel supported even when you're not fully available. Here's how your EA can help maintain high standards of customer service during your leave:

- *Personalized Responses:*
  Work with your EA to create personalized responses for different types of inquiries. For instance, a trusted client might receive a warm, personalized message letting them know who will be handling their account while you're on

leave, while routine inquiries might get a standard response with contact information for your backup.

- *Client Follow-Up:*
  Your EA can take on the role of following up with clients after meetings, ensuring that any action items are completed, and that the client feels attended to. They can also schedule follow-up meetings for when you return.

- *Monitoring for Red Flags:*
  Ask your EA to keep an eye out for any signs of dissatisfaction or urgent issues from clients or stakeholders. This allows you to address potential problems proactively rather than dealing with fallout after you return.

- *Regular Updates to Clients:*
  Set up a system where your EA sends out regular updates to key clients, letting them know about any progress on projects or changes in timelines. This helps keep the lines of communication open and ensures that clients don't feel neglected.

Leveraging your Executive Assistant as your air traffic control during parental leave is one of the smartest moves you can make to ensure that your work and responsibilities continue seamlessly. You can stay connected without being overwhelmed by setting clear rules of engagement, delegating tasks effectively, and maintaining open communication. Your EA is there to support you, allowing you to focus on your new role as a parent while still keeping your finger on the pulse of your professional world. With the right plan in place, you can enjoy your leave, knowing that everything is under control.

D. ANNOUNCE LIKE A PRO: PLANNING YOUR BABY'S BIG DEBUT

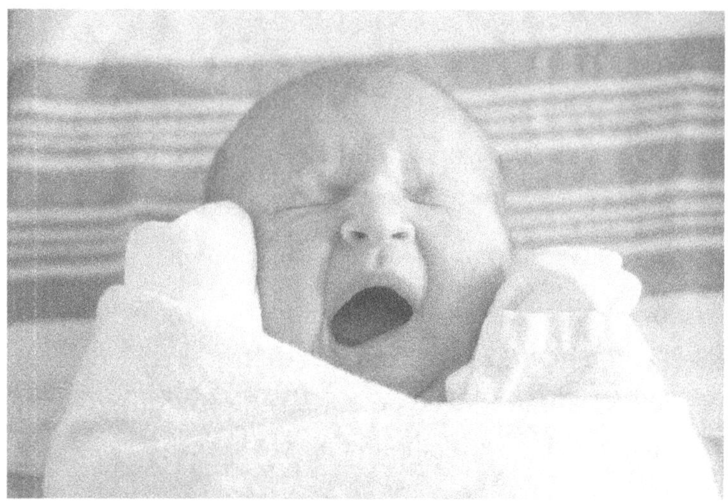

Photo credit: Tim Bish, Unsplash.com

Amidst all the excitement of preparing for your baby's arrival, one crucial detail often gets overlooked until it's too late: how you're going to announce the big news. The moment your little one arrives, you'll be swept up in a whirlwind of emotions, sleepless nights, and adjusting to your new life. The last thing you'll want to do is scramble to figure out how to share the news with everyone. That's why it's so important to have a solid announcement plan in place *before* the big day.

Planning Ahead Matters—once your baby arrives, your brain will be functioning on about two hours of sleep, and your priorities will revolve around keeping a tiny human alive. Deciding who to tell, how to tell them, and when to do it will not be at the forefront of your mind. That's why having a plan in place is crucial. With a little forethought about choosing your media, who you want to include, and who is designated to send the message(s), you can ensure that everyone who matters gets the news in a way that's timely, thoughtful, and stress-free.

1. *Choose Your Announcement Media.* In today's digital age, there are countless ways to announce the arrival of your little one. Here's a breakdown of the most common options:

   - *Email:*

     » **Pros:** Email allows you to craft a personalized message and send it to a select group of people. It's perfect for family members and close friends who deserve a more intimate announcement.

     » **Cons:** Depending on how many people you want to include, drafting and sending individual emails can be time-consuming.

   - *Social Media (Facebook, Instagram, etc.):*

     » **Pros:** Social media is ideal for reaching a large audience quickly. It's a great way to share your joy with extended family, friends, and acquaintances who may not be in your inner circle but still want to celebrate with you.

     » **Cons:** Once it's out there, it's out there. Be prepared for a flood of comments, likes, and messages. Also, consider your privacy settings if you don't want the world to know every detail.

   - *Text Message or Group Chat:*

     » **Pros:** Texts are immediate and personal, making them a good choice for sharing the news with your closest circle. Group chats can also help you quickly spread the word to a select group.

» **Cons:** Not everyone may be in the same time zone, so be mindful of when you hit "send." Also, group chats can spiral out of control quickly, with everyone chiming in.

- *Traditional Mail:*

  » **Pros:** A printed announcement is a lovely keepsake, especially for older relatives who might appreciate something tangible. Plus, it feels more personal and special.

  » **Cons:** It's not exactly immediate. You'll need to prepare these in advance, and they'll likely be sent out after the baby arrives.

- *Workplace Communication:*

  » **Pros:** Emailing your colleagues and clients is a professional way to keep them informed, especially if your leave will affect them. It's also a nice way to maintain connections while you're out.

  » **Cons:** You'll need to be clear about your boundaries—what information you want to share and what you want to keep private.

2. *Decide Who to Include in Your Announcement Plan.* When planning your announcement, think about all the different groups in your life:

- *Family:*
  Your immediate family will likely want to know as soon as possible. Plan for how you'll inform parents, siblings, and close relatives—whether it's a phone call, a group text, or a personal email.

- *Close Friends:*
  Your best friends will want to celebrate with you right away. Consider sending them a quick text or a more detailed email, depending on your relationship.

- *Work Colleagues and Clients:*
  It's important to notify your workplace, especially if you have ongoing projects or clients who need to be informed of your leave. A pre-drafted email can be sent by you *or someone you designate.*

- *Social Media Followers:*

- For everyone else, a social media post can efficiently spread the word. Just make sure you've shared the news with those closest to you before broadcasting it to the wider world.

3. Designate *a "Sender."* You probably won't want to be fumbling with your phone right after giving birth, so consider designating someone you trust to send out the announcements on your behalf. This could be your partner, a close friend, or even a family member. Here's how to make it work:

   - *Create Drafts in Advance:*
     Write out your announcements before the big day. Craft an email template, draft a text message, and pre-write your social media post. That way, when the time comes, your designated sender can simply hit "send" on your behalf.

   - *Assign Specific Tasks:*
     Make it clear who is responsible for notifying which group. For example, your partner might send texts to close family while a friend posts a social media update.

- *Provide Contact Information:*
  Make sure your designated sender has all the contact information they need—email addresses, phone numbers, and social media handles. This will save time and avoid any last-minute scrambling.

- *Communicate Your Preferences:*
  Be specific about the timing and content of the announcements. If you want to wait a few hours after the birth to share the news, make that clear. Also, let them know if there's anything you don't want included, such as certain details or photos.

Planning your baby's announcement might not be at the top of your to-do list, but it's an important detail that can make the early days of parenthood a little less stressful. By deciding on your announcement approach ahead of time and designating someone to handle the logistics, you can ensure that everyone who matters gets the news in a way that's thoughtful and timely. And most importantly, you can focus on soaking up every precious moment with your new bundle of joy, knowing that the word has been spread exactly how you wanted it to be.

E. NUANCES WITH PATERNITY LEAVES: THERE ARE SOME SUBSTANTIAL DIFFERENCES

Photo Getty Images, Unsplash.com

While maternity leaves often come with an extended period away from work to accommodate both the physical recovery from childbirth and the early stages of bonding with the baby, paternity leaves typically look different. They tend to be shorter or taken in multiple intervals, offering unique challenges and opportunities. Understanding these nuances can help fathers make the most of their time away from work while ensuring their professional responsibilities are managed effectively. Here are six tips to consider:

1. *Fragmented or Short-Term Leave: Planning Ahead.* For many fathers, paternity leave might involve a few weeks off immediately after the birth, or it could be split into shorter intervals taken over the first year. This structure requires careful planning to ensure your work responsibilities are adequately covered during each absence. Unlike a longer maternity leave, where tasks can be handed off entirely, paternity leave might require more frequent touchpoints or a phased hand-off of

duties. It's crucial to communicate clearly with your team about your planned leave dates and ensure that everyone is aware of when you'll be out and when you'll return.

2. *Adjusting the Hand-Off: Strategic Delegation.* When preparing for shorter or fragmented paternity leave, the art of the hand-off becomes more about strategic delegation rather than a full transfer of duties. You might need to delegate specific tasks temporarily while maintaining responsibility for others that can be managed remotely or upon your return. For instance, instead of handing off an entire project, consider breaking down responsibilities so that you retain oversight of critical decisions while delegating day-to-day management to a trusted colleague. This approach ensures continuity while allowing you to stay connected with your work in a manageable way.

3. *Crafting the OOO Message: Tailoring Your Communication.* For shorter paternity leaves, your out-of-office (OOO) message may need to be more dynamic, reflecting the specific nature of your leave. If your leave is split into intervals, your OOO message can inform colleagues and clients about the exact dates you'll be unavailable, who to contact in your absence, and when they can expect a response. This level of detail helps manage expectations and reduces the likelihood of urgent matters piling up while you're away.

4. *Leveraging Your EA: Keeping the Lines of Communication Open.* Your Executive Assistant (EA) can be a valuable resource even during a short leave. Use your EA to keep track of ongoing projects, prioritize messages, and filter what needs your attention when you return. If your leave is fragmented,

your EA can also help manage the transitions between your time off and your time at work, ensuring that nothing falls through the cracks during these shifts.

5. *Announcing Your Leave: Balancing Professionalism with Personal Joy.* When planning your announcement, consider the shorter nature of paternity leave and how that might impact your communication. You might share your plans more casually, especially if your leave is brief or broken up. However, it's still important to convey the significance of this time in your life and to ensure that your colleagues and clients understand that while your leave may be short, it's a meaningful period for you and your family.

6. *Returning to Work: Easing Back In.* With paternity leave being shorter, the transition back to work might feel more abrupt. To ease this transition, consider scheduling a debrief with your team shortly after your return to catch up on developments. This will help you regain your footing without feeling overwhelmed. Additionally, allow yourself some flexibility in the first few days back, understanding that it may take a little time to fully shift back into work mode.

Paternity leave, though often shorter and potentially fragmented, plays a crucial role in supporting your partner and bonding with your newborn. By adapting the strategies typically associated with longer maternity leaves to fit the nuances of paternity leave, you can ensure that your time away from work is both fulfilling and professionally manageable. Whether taking a few weeks off or breaking your leave into intervals, careful planning, strategic delegation, and clear communication will help you make the most of this special time while maintaining your professional responsibilities.

Claws and Fur

Photo credit: Erop Kamelev, Unsplash.com

As your due date approaches, your mind is likely consumed with thoughts of the big day—what to pack in your hospital bag, how to handle contractions, and the excitement of finally meeting your little one. But let's not forget one important, albeit often overlooked, aspect of your pre-baby preparation: your beauty routine! Yes, I'm talking about those pedicures, leg shaves, or waxing sessions. Trust me, no one wants to star in a birth video with toes that look like they belong in a horror movie or legs that rival a grizzly bear.

The Case for the Pre-Baby Pedicure

Let's start with the toes. I get it—by the time you're in the final weeks of pregnancy, seeing your feet is a challenge, let alone reaching them. But picture this: you're in the delivery room, the camera's rolling (or maybe just your own eyes), and there they are—your toenails, looking more like talons than anything resembling human digits. The last thing you need is for your labor nurse to look down and wonder if you've been secretly training as a raptor.

A fresh pedicure is not only a treat for yourself but also a little bit of self-care that you deserve. Plus, those photos of tiny newborn toes next to yours will be much cuter if your toes aren't starring in a low-budget horror film. So, treat yourself to that pedicure—go for a fun color, maybe even something to match your baby's nursery theme. And if you can't reach, no worries. That's what the professionals are for!

Taming the Wild: The Case for Shaving or Waxing

Now, let's talk legs. We know shaving or waxing may be the last thing on your mind as you waddle through those final days of pregnancy but think of it as a courtesy to yourself—and anyone who might be in the delivery room. You've been growing a baby for nine months; you don't need to also grow a winter coat!

Imagine the moment you're in the hospital bed, legs propped up, ready to bring new life into the world. Do you really want your medical team wondering if they've wandered into a wildlife documentary? Let's face it: while labor is unpredictable, the one thing you can control is whether your legs are smooth enough not to frighten small children or make the nurses wonder if they need to call animal control.

Making It Fun: A Pre-Baby Beauty Day

Why not turn this necessary evil into a fun pre-baby ritual? Invite a friend or your partner for a spa day, or just take a few hours to pamper yourself. Go all out—get the pedicure, shave or wax those legs, maybe even throw in a massage or a facial. This may be your last hurrah before the baby arrives, so enjoy it!

Plus, it's a great way to relax and unwind before the big day. Consider it your final act of self-care before diaper changes and midnight feedings dominate your life. You'll thank yourself later when you look back at those birth photos and see smooth legs and perfectly polished toes instead of what could easily pass for Bigfoot sightings.

In the grand scheme of things, your toes and legs might seem like small details, but sometimes the little things make a big difference. A quick pedicure or leg shave isn't just about vanity; it's about feeling confident and ready as you head into one of the most important days of your life.

So, don't skip the pre-baby beauty prep. Because when the time comes, you want to be focused on the amazing moment ahead, not worrying if your feet are ready for their close-up or if your legs could use a weed-whacker.

And if you are the birth partner, not the birth giver, consider a surprise spa touch-up treat. After all, she has been putting in a lot of hard work growing your baby!

Support Approaches

Navigating parental leave is a unique journey and having the right support system can make all the difference. In this chapter, we'll explore various approaches to enlisting and managing support during this critical time, ensuring that you and your baby are well cared for.

First, we'll look at the **Timing and Length of Grandparental Visits**. While the idea of having grandparents around can be comforting, it's essential to plan these visits thoughtfully. We'll discuss how to time these visits so they're truly helpful—whether it's having them come right after birth to assist with those first few chaotic days or scheduling visits a bit later when you've found your rhythm but could use extra hands. The length of their stay is just as crucial; too short, and they might not be as helpful as you'd hoped; too long, and you might start to feel overwhelmed or lose precious bonding time with your baby.

Next, we'll cover **Putting Grandparents to Work**. Eager grandparents often want to help, but their idea of "helping" might differ from yours. We'll explore ways to channel their enthusiasm into tasks that genuinely lighten your load. Whether it's handling laundry, preparing meals, or running errands, clear communication about what you need will ensure that their presence is a blessing rather than a source of stress.

We'll also explore the benefits of hiring **The Night Nurse: A Game Changer?** For many sleep-deprived parents, a night nurse can be the difference between exhaustion and sanity. We'll discuss what a night nurse does, how to find one, and how this support can allow you to rest and recharge, making you a more present and engaged parent during the day.

Finally, we'll offer tips on **Getting a Jump-Start on Hiring a Nanny or Applying for Daycare**. The demand for quality childcare can be fierce, and in some places, securing a spot in a daycare center or finding the right nanny requires starting the process well before your baby is born. We'll guide you through the steps to get ahead of the curve, ensuring that when the time comes, you have reliable childcare, allowing you to return to work with peace of mind.

By thoughtfully considering these support approaches, you can create a smoother, more enjoyable experience during parental leave. This careful planning will allow you to focus on what truly matters: bonding with your baby and adjusting to your new life as a parent.

In this chapter, we'll explore:

A. Timing and Length of Grandparental Visits

B. Putting Grandparents to Work

C. The Night Nurse: A Game Changer?

D. Getting a Jump-Start on Hiring a Nanny or Applying for Daycare

A. TIMING AND LENGTH OF GRANDPARENTAL VISITS

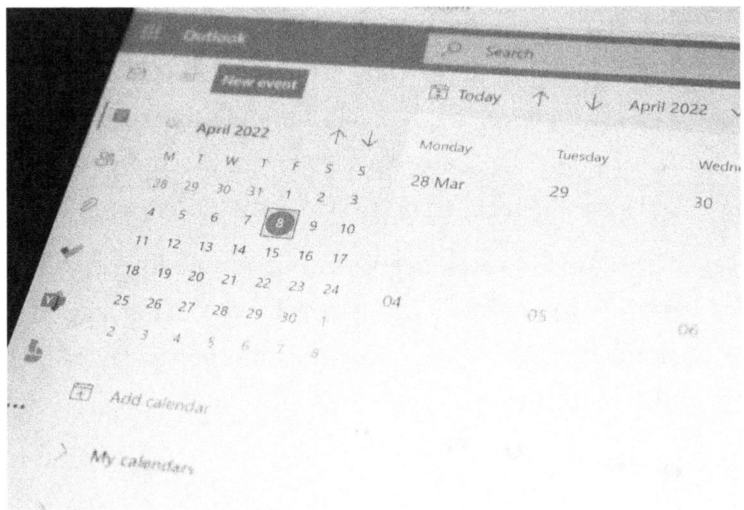

Photo credit: Ed Hardie, Unsplash.com

One of the joys of welcoming a new baby is the outpouring of love and support from family, especially from the grandmas and grandads. Whether it's your own parents or your partner's, grandparents often want to be a big part of this special time, and they can be an invaluable source of help and wisdom. However, balancing their desire to be involved with your need for space and establishing your own routines can be challenging. This chapter explores how to make the most of grandma and grandad visits during parental leave, including options for timing, length of stay, and setting boundaries.

Timing the Visit: What Works Best for You

When deciding when grandparents should visit, there's no one-size-fits-all answer. The right timing depends on your family's dynamics, the support you need, and how comfortable you are with having someone else around during those early days. Here are a few options to consider:

- *Immediately After Birth:*
  - » *Pros:* Grandparents can provide immediate help with household tasks, cooking, and even taking care of the baby while you rest. Their experience can be comforting as you navigate the initial days of parenthood.
  - » *Cons:* This is also a deeply intimate time for you and your partner to bond with your new baby. Having a guest, even someone as close as a mother or mother-in-law might feel like an intrusion.

- *After the First Few Weeks:*
  - » *Pros:* By this time, you'll have established some routines and might feel more comfortable with your new role. A grandparent's visit can be a welcome relief as the adrenaline wears off and exhaustion sets in.
  - » *Cons:* Waiting a few weeks means you might miss out on immediate help when it could be most beneficial.

- *Staggered Visits:*
  - » *Pros:* If you have multiple grandparents or a long leave, staggering their visits can provide you with continuous support over a longer period. It also gives each grandparent their own special time with the baby.
  - » *Cons:* This can extend the period during which your household feels less private, potentially leading to feelings of overwhelm.

- *Later in the Leave:*

  » *Pros:* This allows you to fully settle into your parenting role before welcoming a visitor. By then, you may be more confident and ready to accept help in specific areas, like transitioning back to work or establishing a sleep schedule.

  » *Cons:* Grandparents might feel left out of the early days, and they may push for an earlier visit.

Length of Stay: Finding the Right Balance

Determining how long grandparents should stay is another important consideration. Here are a few factors to weigh:

- *Short Visits (A Few Days):*

  » *Pros:* Short visits can provide just enough support without disrupting your new family dynamics. They're a great option if you value privacy and independence.

  » *Cons:* The visit might feel too short, especially if grandma and grandad are traveling a long distance or if you need extended help.

- *Moderate Visits (One to Two Weeks):*

  » *Pros:* A week or two can offer a good balance, giving grandma or grandad enough time to help out and bond with the baby without overstaying their welcome. This timeframe allows them to settle in and be genuinely helpful.

  » *Cons:* As the visit stretches beyond a few days, you might start feeling the need for your space, especially if you and the grandparents have different views on parenting.

- *Extended Visits (Three Weeks or More):*

  » *Pros:* Extended visits can be a lifesaver if you need ongoing help and have a particularly close relationship with your parents or parents-in-law. It's also beneficial if grandparents live far away and visit infrequently.

  » *Cons:* Long visits can lead to tension, especially with differing opinions on baby care or household management. It's crucial to set clear boundaries to avoid feeling overwhelmed.

Setting Boundaries and Managing Expectations

To ensure that grandparent's visit is positive for everyone, it's essential to set boundaries and manage expectations upfront:

- *Communicate Your Needs:* Be clear about what kind of help you're looking for, whether it's cooking, cleaning, or simply holding the baby while you nap. Grandparents often want to help but may not know the best way to do so.

- *Establish Ground Rules:* If there are certain things you prefer to handle yourself—like feeding or bedtime routines—communicate this early on. Setting these expectations can prevent misunderstandings and hurt feelings.

- *Balance Time Together and Apart:* It's important to spend quality time with your parents and ensure you have time alone with your partner and baby. Encourage grandparents to take breaks, enjoy the local area, or catch up with other family and friends.

- *Be Honest About Your Emotions:* If you're feeling overwhelmed, it's okay to say so. Grandparents are often understanding and may appreciate knowing how they can best support you.

Grandma and Grandad's visit during parental leave can be a wonderful opportunity to bond and receive much-needed support, but it's important to plan carefully to ensure it's a positive experience for everyone. By thoughtfully considering the timing and length of their stay, setting clear boundaries, and managing expectations, you can make the most of their visit while maintaining the harmony and privacy of your new family. Remember, this is your time to adjust to parenthood, and it's okay to prioritize what works best for you and your baby.

B. PUTTING GRANDPARENTS TO WORK

Photo credit: Getty Images, Unsplash.com

Grandparents can be a tremendous source of support during the early days of parenthood, but their role needs to be carefully considered and communicated. While they may be eager to bond with the new baby, it's essential to ensure that their presence enhances the well-being of the entire family, particularly the new parents. The key to a successful visit lies in assigning specific roles and tasks that align with your needs and setting clear expectations before the baby arrives.

Grandparents as Support, Not Distractions

It's natural for grandparents to want to spend time with the new baby, but it's crucial to remember that their primary role during these visits should be to support you—the parents. A new mom, especially, needs time to recover, rest, and adjust to her new role. Grandparents can play a pivotal role in this process by focusing on tasks that alleviate the daily pressures on new parents, allowing them to spend quality time with their baby.

Identifying What You Need

Before the baby arrives, take some time to consider what kinds of support you'll need most. This could be anything from household chores to meal preparation or even caring for older siblings. Being specific about your needs will make it easier to ask for help and ensure that grandparents feel useful and appreciated.

Here are some common areas where grandparents can be a big help:

- *Meal Preparation:*
  - » *Task:* Grandparents can be responsible for cooking meals, whether preparing a few freezer-friendly dishes before the baby arrives or cooking fresh meals during their stay.
  - » *Benefit:* This frees up time and energy for the new parents to focus on caring for the baby and themselves without worrying about what's for dinner.

- *Household Chores:*

  » *Task:* Assign grandparents to handle routine household chores like washing dishes, doing laundry, or tidying up the living spaces.

  » *Benefit:* Keeping the home environment clean and organized reduces stress and creates a more peaceful atmosphere.

- *Running Errands:*

  » *Task:* Grandparents can run errands such as grocery shopping, picking up prescriptions, or buying any last-minute baby supplies.

  » *Benefit:* This keeps you from having to leave the house for non-essential outings, giving you more time to rest and recover.

- *Taking Care of Older Children:*

  » *Task:* If you have older children, grandparents can take on the role of entertaining them, helping with homework, or even taking them on outings to give you some quiet time.

  » *Benefit:* This helps maintain a sense of normalcy for older siblings and ensures they still get plenty of attention while you focus on the new baby.

- *Providing Emotional Support:*

  » *Task:* Sometimes, the most valuable thing a grandparent can offer is a listening ear and emotional support. Encourage them to spend time with you, talking, listening, and offering advice or comfort when needed.

  » *Benefit:* This helps new parents feel less isolated and overwhelmed, providing a sense of reassurance during a time of great change.

Making the Ask Before the Baby Arrives

To ensure everyone is on the same page, having these conversations before the baby arrives is important. This gives grandparents time to prepare mentally and practically for their visit and helps to avoid any misunderstandings or disappointments. Here's how you can approach this conversation:

- *Be Clear and Specific:* Don't assume that grandparents will know what you need. Be explicit about the tasks you would like them to take on. For example, "Mom, it would be really helpful if you could handle the laundry and make dinner while you're here."

- *Set Boundaries Early:* If there are certain things you prefer to do yourself—like feeding the baby or putting them to bed— let grandparents know in advance. This prevents any awkwardness or hurt feelings later on.

- *Express Gratitude:* Frame your requests positively, emphasizing how much their help means to you. *"We're so grateful for your support,"* and *"it would make a huge difference if you could help us with these tasks."*

- *Plan Together:* Involve grandparents in the planning process by asking for their input on how they'd like to help. This makes them feel valued and respected and ensures their contributions align with your needs.

Grandparents can be a wonderful asset during parental leave, but to make the most of their visit, assigning them roles that truly support the family is crucial. By being clear about what you need, setting expectations before the baby arrives, and focusing on tasks that lighten your load, you can ensure that everyone has a positive and fulfilling experience. Remember, the goal is to create an environment where both the new parents and the grandparents feel valued, respected, and connected—without sacrificing the new family's needs.

B. THE NIGHT NURSE: A GAME CHANGER?

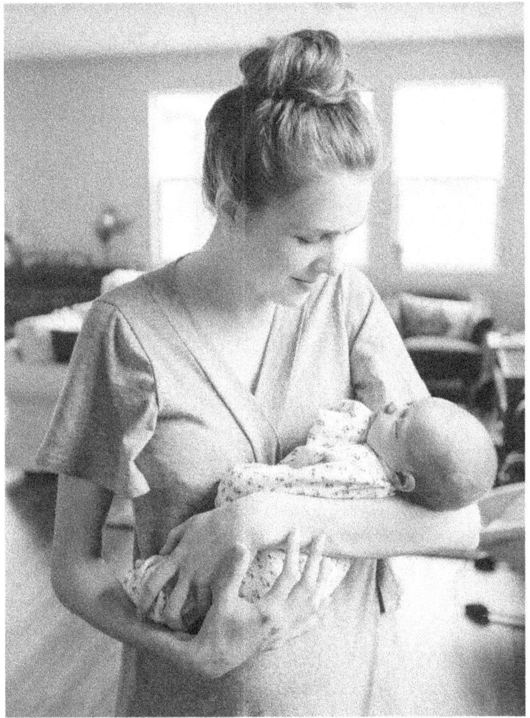

Photo credit: Wesley Tingey, Unsplash.com

The arrival of a new baby brings immense joy, but it also ushers in sleepless nights and overwhelming fatigue. For many new parents, the constant demands of night feedings, diaper changes, and soothing a restless baby can be exhausting. This is where a night nurse or newborn care specialist can be a game-changer. In this chapter, we'll explore what a night nurse does, the benefits they offer, and how to decide if hiring one is the right choice for your family.

What Is a Night Nurse?

A night nurse is a professional specializing in newborn care, particularly during the night hours. They are trained to handle all nighttime baby care, allowing parents to get much-needed rest. While the specific duties of a night nurse can vary based on your needs, they generally include:

- *Nighttime Feedings:*
  If you're bottle-feeding, the night nurse can handle all feedings, allowing you to sleep through the night. For breastfeeding mothers, the night nurse can bring the baby to you for feeding and then take care of burping, diaper changes, and settling the baby back to sleep.

- *Diaper Changes and Soothing:*
  The night nurse takes care of all diaper changes and soothes the baby back to sleep, whether it's through rocking, swaddling, or other comforting techniques.

- *Monitoring the Baby:*
  The night nurse monitors the baby throughout the night, ensuring they are safe, comfortable, and well-cared for. This can be especially reassuring for first-time parents who may feel anxious about their newborn's well-being.

- *Sleep Training:*
  Many night nurses are experienced in gentle sleep training methods and can help establish healthy sleep patterns for your baby, which can lead to better sleep for everyone in the long run.

The Benefits of Hiring a Night Nurse

- *Rest and Recovery for Parents:*
  One of the most significant benefits of hiring a night nurse is the opportunity for parents to get uninterrupted sleep. This rest is crucial for physical recovery, especially for new mothers who are healing from childbirth, and for mental well-being.

- *Expert Newborn Care:*
  Night nurses bring a wealth of experience and knowledge in newborn care. Their expertise can be invaluable, especially for first-time parents unsure about handling certain aspects of baby care.

- *Reduced Stress and Anxiety:*
  Knowing that your baby is in the hands of a trained professional can significantly reduce stress and anxiety, allowing you to relax and enjoy your time with your newborn during the day.

- *Support for Breastfeeding:*
  A night nurse can support breastfeeding mothers by helping with night feedings and offering advice on breastfeeding techniques and challenges.

- *Flexible Arrangements:*
  Night nurses can be hired on a flexible basis, whether you need help every night, a few nights a week, or just occasionally. This allows you to tailor their services to your specific needs and budget.

Is a Night Nurse Right for Your Family?

Deciding whether to hire a night nurse is a personal choice that depends on several factors:

- *Budget Considerations:*
  Hiring a night nurse is an additional expense, and it's important to consider whether it fits within your family's budget. However, many of my clients find the investment worthwhile for the peace of mind and rest it provides.

- *Support Network:*
  Consider the level of support you already have. You may not need a night nurse if you have family or friends who can help with night care. However, if you lack support or your partner needs to return to work soon after the baby's arrival, a night nurse can be a great option.

- *Your Comfort Level:*
  Some parents may feel uncomfortable with the idea of having someone else care for their baby during the night. It's important to assess your comfort level with this arrangement and communicate your expectations clearly with the night nurse.

- *Specific Needs:*
  If you have a premature baby, twins, or a baby with special needs, a night nurse's specialized care can be particularly beneficial. Their experience can provide the extra care and attention your baby may require.

Finding the Right Night Nurse

If you decide that a night nurse is right for your family, finding the right person for the job is important. Here are some steps to help you in the process:

- *Research and Referrals:*
  Start by asking for referrals from friends, family, or your pediatrician. You can also look for agencies specializing in newborn care and night nurses. Online reviews and testimonials can also be helpful.

- *Interview Candidates:*
  Conduct interviews to ensure that the night nurse is a good fit for your family. Ask about their experience, qualifications, and approach to newborn care. It's important to find someone whose philosophy aligns with yours.

- *Check Credentials and References:*
  Verify the night nurse's credentials, certifications, and references. Ensuring they have the proper training and experience to care for your baby is essential.

- *Trial Period:*
  Consider starting with a trial period to see how comfortable you are with the arrangement. This allows you and the night nurse to adjust to the new routine and make necessary changes.

A night nurse can be a valuable asset during the early weeks and months of parenthood, offering much-needed rest, expert care, and peace of mind. Whether you're struggling with sleep deprivation or simply want an extra pair of hands during the night, a night nurse can help you navigate this challenging but rewarding time with greater ease. As with any parenting decision, it's important to choose what works best for your family and to communicate your needs and expectations clearly. With the right night nurse, you can ensure that you and your baby are well-rested, healthy, and happy.

D. GETTING A JUMP-START ON HIRING A NANNY OR APPLYING FOR DAYCARE

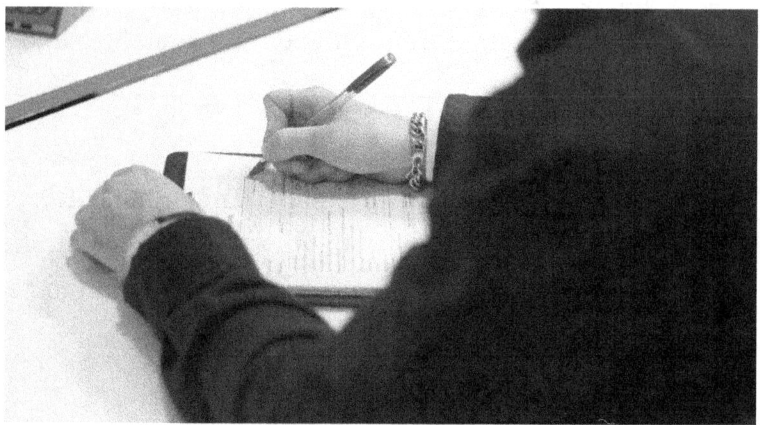

Photo credit: Mina Rad, Unsplash.com

One of the most significant decisions new parents face is arranging childcare, whether through hiring a nanny or securing a spot at a daycare. In many areas, particularly in large cities, the demand for quality childcare is high, and waitlists can be long. To ensure you have the care you need when you're ready to return to work, it's crucial to start the process early—often even before your baby is born. This chapter will guide you through the steps to take, what to consider, and how to navigate the often-overwhelming task of finding the right childcare for your family.

Why Start Early?

In many places, waiting until after your baby is born to start thinking about childcare can leave you scrambling for options. High-quality daycare centers often have long waitlists, and the best nannies can be booked months in advance. Starting early gives you the best chance of finding a situation that meets your needs and fits your family's values.

Understanding Your Options

Before diving into the search, it's important to understand the different types of childcare available:

- *Daycare Centers:*

  » *Pros:* Daycare centers often offer structured environments with socialization opportunities for your child. They are usually licensed and have multiple caregivers, which can provide peace of mind regarding reliability and safety.

  » *Cons:* High demand can lead to long waitlists, and the structured environment may not suit every child's needs. Additionally, centers often have fixed hours, which may not align with your work schedule.

- *In-Home Daycare:*

  » *Pros:* In-home daycares can offer a more personalized, home-like setting with smaller groups of children. They may also be more flexible with hours and care arrangements.

  » *Cons:* These settings may be less regulated than larger centers and finding one with the right fit can be challenging. Availability is often limited.

- *Nannies:*

  » *Pros:* A nanny provides one-on-one care in your home, allowing for personalized attention and flexibility in your child's routine. Nannies can also help with household tasks and may be more adaptable to your schedule.

  » *Cons:* Nannies are typically more expensive than other childcare options and finding the right person can be time-consuming. There's also the need to manage payroll and employment responsibilities.

Steps to Take Before Baby Arrives

Starting your childcare search early doesn't mean you need to have everything finalized before the baby is born, but getting a jump-start can save you a lot of stress later on. Here are some steps to consider:

1. *Research and Identify Your Priorities:*

    » Start by considering what's most important to you as a childcare provider. Do you value a structured learning environment, or is a more flexible, nurturing atmosphere better? Think about your work schedule, budget, and any specific needs your child may have.

2. *Explore Your Options:*

    » Research daycare centers, in-home daycare providers, and nanny agencies in your area. Look at reviews, ask for recommendations from friends or family, and check online parenting forums. If possible, visit some daycare centers to get a feel for their environment and ask about their waitlist policies.

3. *Get on Waitlists Early:*

    » For daycare centers, it's not uncommon to get on waitlists as soon as you know you're expecting. Some high-demand centers allow you to join waitlists before the baby is born, so don't hesitate to secure your spot early.

4. *Start the Nanny Search:*

    » If you're considering hiring a nanny, begin the process by drafting a detailed job description that outlines your expectations, schedule, and any specific qualifications you're looking for. Contact reputable nanny agencies or start networking within your community to find potential candidates. Even if you don't hire someone before the baby arrives, having a list of vetted candidates can make the process smoother when you're ready. Remember that "you get what you pay for," and consider the costs of having a trusted nanny suddenly leave for a higher-paying family.

» Please see "Chapter 30: The Caregivers Manual of You" for further thoughts on defining guidelines and directions for your caregiver beyond a basic contract.

» Also, here's an added "nanny" tip: there's a site whose target audience is nannies—https://www.reddit.com/r/Nanny/. It's worth taking a scroll through as a parent to see what nannies say about employer situations, and it has suggestions about how to stand out above and beyond (for example, "welcome baskets"—great idea!) and what "not" to do. Check it out as you think about hiring and onboarding.

5. *Conduct Interviews:*

» Whether you're looking at daycare centers or interviewing nannies, take the time to conduct thorough interviews. Ask about their experience, approach to childcare, and how they handle various situations. For daycare centers, ask to observe during childcare hours. You may also want to arrange a trial period for nannies to see how they interact with your family.

6. *Check References and Credentials:*

» Always check references and verify the credentials of any potential childcare provider. For nannies, this includes background checks and verifying any certifications, such as CPR and first aid. For daycare centers, confirm their licensing status and any accreditations.

7. *Plan for Contingencies:*

    » It's wise to have a backup plan in place. This could be a secondary daycare option, a list of temporary nannies, or arranging with family members to step in if needed. Flexibility is key, as your first choice might not always work out.

Finalizing Your Decision

Once you've researched and identified a few top choices, it's time to decide. Here are a few tips to help you finalize your childcare arrangements:

1. *Trust Your Instincts:*

    » Your gut feeling about a caregiver or center is important. If something doesn't feel right, don't ignore it. Keep looking until you find a situation that feels comfortable and trustworthy.

2. *Review Contracts and Policies:*

    » Carefully review any contracts or policies, whether you're hiring a nanny or enrolling in a daycare center. Understand the terms regarding payment, vacation, sick days, and what happens in case of emergencies or if the arrangement isn't working out.

3. *Stay Flexible:*

    » Even with careful planning, your needs or preferences might change after the baby arrives. Be open to reassessing your childcare arrangements if necessary, and don't be afraid to make changes if something isn't working.

Arranging childcare is one of the most significant steps you'll take as a new parent, and starting the process early can give you peace of mind and more options to choose from. Whether you decide on a daycare center, an in-home provider, or a nanny, the key is planning, researching, and trusting your instincts. By getting a jump-start on this important decision, you can ensure that you have the support you need when it's time to return to work, allowing you to focus on enjoying those precious early months with your new baby.

PART FOUR

TAKING YOUR LEAVE(S)

As you prepare to embark on your parental leave, it's important to recognize that this time is not just about stepping away from work—it's about stepping into a new chapter of life with intention and purpose. Part Four, "Taking Your Leave(s)," is designed to guide you through this transition, helping you to face the realities of your new role, adjust your mindset, manage responsibilities, and navigate the interpersonal dynamics that come with being a new parent.

We begin with **Facing Reality and Letting Go**, where you'll explore the importance of acknowledging the changes that come with parenthood and accepting that not everything is within your control. This section will help you ground yourself in the present moment, letting go of the need to micromanage every aspect of life and learning to embrace the unexpected.

Next, we delve into **Mindset and Presence**, focusing on the inner work that can help you stay centered and mindful during your leave. Through practices like being, not doing; engaging in magical dreaming; savoring the small things (like eating raisins); and rethinking the art of multi-tasking, you'll discover how to cultivate a presence that nourishes both you and your family.

In **Roles and Responsibilities**, we address the practical aspects of parental leave, such as how to effectively delegate responsibilities through Total Responsibility Transfer (TRT), how to be the best support partner for your child's mom, and how to engage others in your support network. This section is about creating a balanced and supportive environment for you and your partner.

Interpersonal Dynamics explores the complexities of interacting with others as new parents. In this section, you'll learn how to handle unsolicited advice gracefully, navigate the challenges posed by the "I Would Never" crowd, and understand the ten golden rules of what to say (and not say) to new parents. These insights will help you manage the often-tricky social terrain of parenthood, allowing you to maintain your confidence and peace of mind in the face of external pressures and opinions.

Enneagram and Parenting Style is dedicated to understanding how your Enneagram type influences your parenting style from the very start. This chapter delves into the strengths and challenges each type brings to the parenting journey, offering strategies for growth that can help you become the best parent you can be. By recognizing these tendencies early on, you can be more intentional in your interactions with your child, fostering a nurturing environment that supports both your child's development and your own personal growth.

Finally, **Staying Connected** will offer strategies for maintaining and nurturing your relationships—with your partner, support network, work colleagues, and yourself—during this transformative time. This part of your journey is about more than just surviving; it's about thriving in your new role and staying connected to what matters most.

As you read through this section, remember that taking your leave is not just about time away from work—it's about stepping into your life as a parent with grace, resilience, and intentionality. Whether you're facing challenges or celebrating victories, these chapters will provide you with the tools and insights you need to make the most of this unique and precious time.

In this Part, we will explore chapters:

18. Facing Reality and Letting Go

19. Mindset and Presence

20. Roles and Responsibilities

21. Interpersonal Dynamics

22. Enneagram and Parenting Style

23. Rewriting the Stories We Tell Ourselves as Parents

24. Staying Connected

Facing Reality and Letting Go

As you embark on the journey of parenthood, it's essential to face the realities of this new chapter with open eyes and an open heart. The transition into parenthood is one of the most profound changes you'll experience, and with it comes the need to adjust your expectations and embrace the unpredictability of life with a newborn. This chapter, "Facing Reality and Letting Go," invites you to confront the challenges and adjustments that naturally arise during this time and to recognize the importance of flexibility and adaptability.

The first step in facing reality is acknowledging that things may not go according to plan—and that's okay. Parenthood is full of surprises, and even the best-laid plans can be disrupted by sleepless nights, unexpected milestones, or simply your child's unique needs. Letting go of rigid expectations allows you to be more present, responsive, and compassionate with yourself and your partner. It's about understanding that perfection is neither attainable nor necessary; what matters most is your ability to adapt and respond to the ever-changing demands of your new role.

This chapter will guide you through letting go—of preconceived notions, unrealistic standards, and the need to control every aspect of your new life. By embracing the reality of parenthood, you can find peace in the chaos, joy in the unexpected, and strength in your ability to navigate this incredible journey with grace and resilience.

A. FACE REALITY

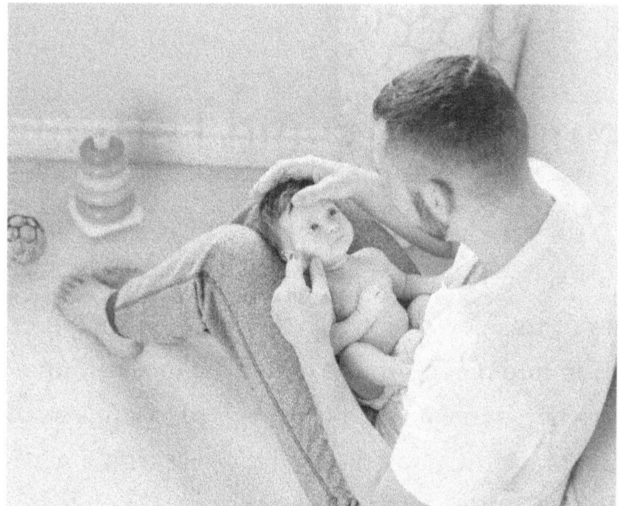

Photo credit: Getty Images, Unsplash.com

We are strong, thriving leaders with a certain mojo—a passion, focus, drive, direction, love of plans, and adherence to schedules. Whether you're a mom or a dad, you likely have a need to achieve, a plan to get there, and the determination to keep everything on track. No one can stop us, and if they try, we (sometimes gently, sometimes not so gently) steer them back on course.

Let's talk about that infamous "home to-do list" you've probably crafted. One list for everything that *must* be done *before* the baby arrives—right on that precise due date you've mentally circled in red. (Just so you know, babies don't care about your schedules. They're notoriously bad at sticking to them.) Then there's the second list for all the tasks you'll tackle *during* your leave: birth announcements, baby books, family bonding time, and maybe even finishing that home project that's been mocking you for months.

Now, reality doesn't care much about your to-do lists either. Babies, despite their adorable, cherubic selves, come with a few less-than-angelic traits, such as:

- Unpredictability (think plot twists, but less entertaining).

- Unreliability (ever tried to schedule a nap time? Good luck).

- Poor timing (because of course the baby will need you right when you sit down to relax).

- Sleep-sucking (like a tiny vampire, but of your energy and sanity).

- Demanding (as in, *"I need attention right now, and no, I don't care that you haven't slept in days"*).

- And Loud! (Yes, with a capital L).

I can say these things because you're in that wonderful stage of anticipating the joys of a new baby—so much so that you hopefully won't be offended when I pop the bubble just a tad. The truth is you might want to consider revising your to-do list to a "suggestions" list. Now and permanently. The only "do" you're responsible for is adjusting to your new life as a parent and giving your baby the best care possible. So, please, don't stress yourself trying to accomplish every task.

And let's put things in perspective—at the end of your leave, the world as we know it won't fall apart if your suggestions list is still hanging around, half-finished, like that gym membership you swore you'd use more often.

Here's one small exception: this book. In those rare (and I do mean rare) quiet moments of the day—or at 3 a.m. when you're wide awake for reasons that defy logic—consider picking this book up again to start thinking about your return to work. But remember, it doesn't have to be now. It can wait a month or two while you adjust to the beautiful chaos of new parenthood.

So, take a deep breath, embrace the unpredictability, and let go of the need to check off every box on that list. The most important task you have is already in your arms.

B. YOU CAN'T CONTROL THE WORLD

As I mentioned earlier, we cannot change the past, nor can we predict the future. And as much as we might want to, we can't control the world and everything around us. Yet so many of us, especially those used to thriving in fast-paced, high-stakes environments, allow our egos to convince us that we can. This relentless pursuit of control is exhausting. Sometimes, the most empowering thing we can do is to let go and allow things to evolve on their own.

The graphic below illustrates some things that fall within and outside our control. Understanding this can be a game-changer when adjusting to life with a new baby.

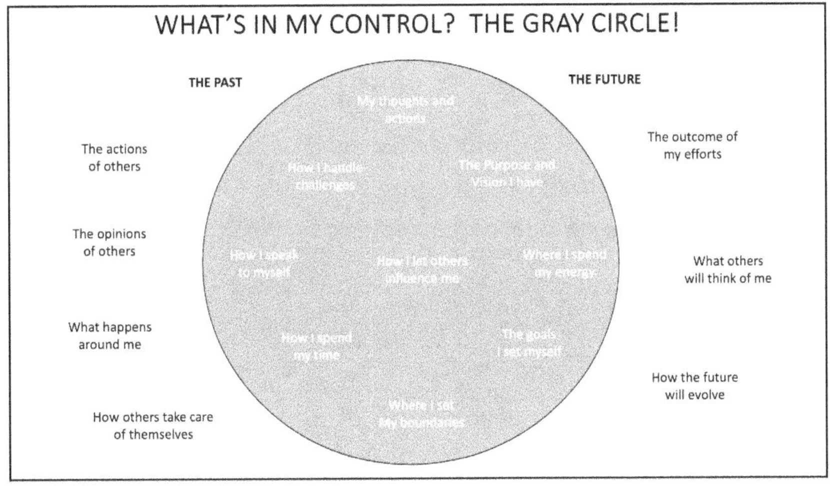

So, what does this have to do with the arrival of a baby? A lot! We leaders, who thrive on being:

- Perfectionists
- Planners
- Control freaks
- Doers
- Driven
- Confident
- Secure
- Reliable

... are suddenly faced with a tiny human who embodies none of these traits. Babies don't care about your plans, schedules, or desire to be in control. They can throw you off-kilter, thrusting you into a whirlwind of unpredictability, chaos, and even a little madness. They can stir up emotions and insecurities you never knew you had.

Here's the thing: It's okay. In fact, it's more than okay—it's a lesson in the art of surrender. My advice to you is to recognize and accept that you will no longer be "in control"—and that's perfectly fine. Embrace it. Let go and enjoy the ride. You'll still reach the destination, but one path offers a far more enjoyable journey. So why not take the scenic route?

Mindset and Presence

In the midst of new parenthood, it's easy to get lost in the endless tasks and to-do lists. But there's something even more important than crossing off items—your mindset and presence. How you engage with each moment can transform your experience during this intense period.

In this chapter, we'll focus on four key areas:

A. **The Art of Being, Not Doing**

Learn to step back from constant activity and embrace moments of stillness. This section encourages you to prioritize simply *being* over relentless doing.

B. **Eating Raisins**

Through a simple exercise involving a raisin, we'll explore the power of mindfulness and how paying attention to small, everyday activities can bring greater awareness and presence.

C. **Multi-Tasking Note to Self**

We'll challenge the notion that multi-tasking is beneficial, showing you the downsides of juggling too many tasks at once and encouraging a more focused approach.

By embracing these practices, you can cultivate a more mindful, present approach to parenting and life.

A. THE ART OF BEING, NOT DOING

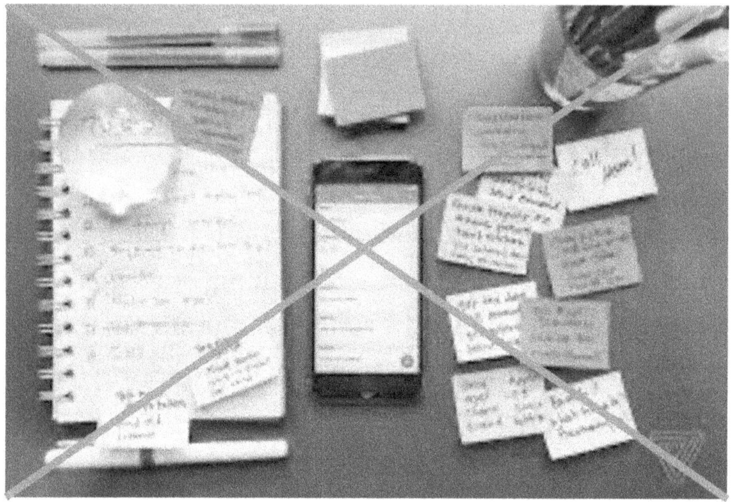

"To-do" lists—oh, they never stop, do they? They serve a purpose, sure, but if we're not careful, they can turn us into hamsters on a wheel, perpetually running but never arriving. We're not wired to be in constant motion, ticking off one task after another without pause. That's why it's crucial to discover the *Art of Being, Not Doing*. Trust me, it's a luxury worth indulging in.

Start by putting that to-do list aside or renaming it a "Suggestions" list. Remember, tomorrow is just another chance to get done what was on today's list. And guess what? Most of it isn't life-threatening.

Start small. Block off even 15 minutes a day to simply *be*. You might even find yourself venturing into a whole morning or day of it. If you need to, put this "being" on your to-do list, but make sure it's right at the top. Use this time to just *exist*—not to think about what's next, what to add to the list, or what needs fixing, changing, or perfecting.

This time is crucial for self-care (and sanity) and can be practiced in many ways. For example:

- Sit quietly and meditate on how awesome you are and what you're most grateful for today.

- Go for a walk and truly *see* your surroundings with an open mind and all your senses. Notice the beauty around you—you might be surprised by what you discover.

- Do something you love that has no immediate "value" attached to it—just for the joy of it.

- Bubble bath, anyone? Or maybe a massage? Fishing? Golf? How about a good book (and not a business one)?

- Do something silly in secret. When was the last time you jumped in a rain puddle? Or belted out a song in the shower?

- Try something new. How about some super-beginner, non-judgmental yoga in the privacy of your own home?

The possibilities are endless. Try this once a day and watch your "do nothing" tolerance grow.

B. EATING RAISINS

Well, this may be one of the odder practices to try. But it's enlightening about our senses (all of them) and how we ignore most of them most of the time.

Go grab a box of raisins (or another nonfrozen treat).

I invite you to start by Grounding yourself (see Chapter 42 if you are not familiar with the practice of grounding) to become more present and aware.

We will start with the raisins still in the box or your chosen treat. I'm quite certain not many of you selected carrot and celery sticks, but that's just my guess.

And we will SLOWLY notice the *box* of raisins with ALL five of our senses.

- What does the box *look* like?

- How does it *smell?*

- How does it *sound* when you shake it?

- How does it *feel* to the touch?

- How does it *taste?* (Go ahead, lick the box. I won't judge)

Next, take a raisin out of the box and put it in your hand. Repeat the same questions and observations.

Then place it in your mouth—but do not chew it yet—and engage your senses again.

Finally, chew the raisin very, very slowly. Savor each moment. This exercise might take you 10 minutes to eat just one raisin, but you'll be amazed at what you notice when you focus your attention on such a simple, everyday task. I'll let you draw your own conclusions from that.

C. MULTI-TASKING NOTE TO SELF

Photo credit: That-s-her-Business, Unsplash.com

We've all heard that multi-tasking is a must in our busy lives, right? Wrong. Research by the Center for Brain Health (yes, a real place with real experts) shows that chronic multi-tasking doesn't make us more productive—instead, it makes us:

- Constantly distracted

- Shallow thinkers

- Error-prone

- Suckers for irrelevancy

- Rude and dismissive to those who need our attention

- And it also leads to the following:

- Decline in fluid intelligence

- Greater brain atrophy

- Chronic stress

Scary stuff, huh? Yet, not too long ago, over half of all résumés boasted about "excellent multi-tasking skills." Thankfully, we've moved past that, but it doesn't mean we've stopped multi-tasking altogether.

There's a difference between "multi-tasking" (like chewing gum and walking at the same time—safe enough) and "multi-focusing" (like checking email while having a conversation with your partner).

Clearly, the latter is more problematic.

If you're still skeptical, try this simple exercise:

1. *Trial 1:* Remember the game "rock, paper, scissors"? With your left hand, roll through the sequence as many times as possible in 30 seconds without making a mistake. Start over with "count one" if you slip up and note how many perfect sequences you can string together.

2. *Trial 2:* With your right hand, execute the following sequence: pat your tummy once, snap your fingers once, pat your tummy twice, snap your fingers twice, and so on. As in Trial 1, start at over "count one" if you mess up, and note how high you can go in the sequence in 30 seconds.

3. *Trial 3:* Now, try doing Trial 1 and Trial 2 at the same time. Together. All at once.

I'll let you discover just how bad we all are at multi-tasking, even with simple tasks. If you took 90 seconds to try this, I hope it serves as a vivid reminder to keep those "multi-focus" moments to a minimum!

Roles and Responsibilities

Parenting is often described as a team effort, but it can quickly become a chaotic juggling act without clear roles and responsibilities. This chapter delves into the importance of defining who does what and how to ensure that nothing falls through the cracks. By clearly delineating roles, you can create a harmonious household where everyone knows their part and contributes effectively.

A. TRT: TOTAL RESPONSIBILITY TRANSFER

Parenting is a team effort, but as with any team, clear roles and responsibilities are crucial to ensuring everything runs smoothly. This is where the concept of Total Responsibility Transfer (TRT) comes into play. TRT is the idea that for any given task, there should be one person who is fully responsible for managing that task from start to finish. Think of it like having one head chef in the kitchen for each specific dish—only one person can oversee the entire process to ensure nothing falls through the cracks.

In the context of parenting, TRT means that when one parent takes on a task, they are not just responsible for a single action within that task but for the entire process. This approach helps to eliminate confusion, prevent overlap, and ensure that all aspects of the task are handled efficiently by one "boss in charge of."

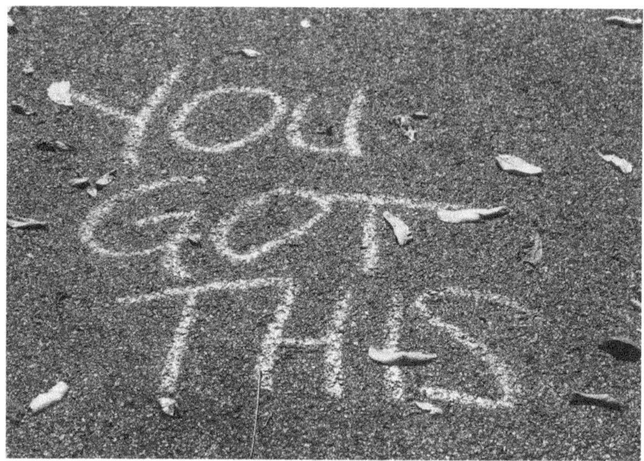

Photo credit: Sydney Rae, Unsplash.com

Why TRT Works in Parenting

TRT is especially valuable in parenting because the responsibilities are numerous and often complex. By clearly defining who is responsible for what, parents can avoid misunderstandings, reduce stress, and ensure that nothing is overlooked. When one parent fully owns a task, they can manage it more effectively, and the other parent can trust that it's being handled without having to micromanage or step in unnecessarily.

Examples of TRT in Parenting

Let's explore how TRT can be applied to various parenting tasks, ensuring that each one is managed from start to finish by a designated "head chef." It doesn't mean that the TRT parent necessarily has to *do* each step, but rather, like a boss at work, if they don't do it themselves, they are responsible for making sure it happens and for *overseeing* the person who does.

- *Pediatrician Well Checks:*
  - » *Total Responsibility Transfer*: One parent is responsible for all aspects of the baby's well checks. This includes knowing when the next appointment is due, scheduling it, taking the baby to the appointment, asking the right questions, and debriefing the other parent afterward.
  - » *Why It Works:* This ensures that nothing is missed, such as vaccination schedules or growth milestones, and keeps both parents informed without duplicating efforts. It doesn't just mean you show up at the appointment!

- *Introduction to Solid Foods:*
  - » *Total Responsibility Transfer:* If one parent is in charge of introducing solid foods, they are responsible for researching the best foods to start with, planning the baby's meals, purchasing the necessary ingredients, preparing the food, feeding the baby, and cleaning up.
  - » *Why It Works:* This comprehensive approach ensures that the process is consistent and that all aspects of the baby's diet are considered, including nutrition, safety, and hygiene. It doesn't just mean you feed the baby!

- *Nighttime Routine:*
  - » *Total Responsibility Transfer*: One parent may take full responsibility for the baby's nighttime routine. This includes setting the bedtime, preparing the baby for bed (bathing, dressing, etc.), reading a bedtime story, and soothing the baby to sleep.
  - » *Why It Works:* Having one parent manage the nighttime routine creates consistency, which can help the baby feel

secure and establish a healthy sleep pattern. It doesn't just mean you physically put the baby to bed!

- *Daycare or Babysitter Coordination:*
  - » *Total Responsibility Transfer:* One parent is responsible for all aspects of daycare or babysitter coordination. This includes researching options, scheduling interviews, choosing the right provider, managing payments, and communicating with the daycare or babysitter.
  - » *Why It Works:* With one parent overseeing this process, there's no confusion about who is responsible for drop-offs, pick-ups, or payments, and all communication is streamlined through a single point of contact. It doesn't just mean you show up to interview the caregivers!

- *Clothing and Diaper Inventory:*
  - » *Total Responsibility Transfer:* One parent is in charge of maintaining the baby's clothing and diaper inventory. This includes tracking what's needed, purchasing items as they run low, organizing the baby's wardrobe, and rotating outgrown clothes.
  - » *Why It Works:* Ensures that the baby always has the necessary supplies, and that clothing is organized and up to date without scrambling at the last minute. It doesn't just mean you picked up a cute outfit on the way home!

- *Health and Safety Management:*
  - » *Total Responsibility Transfer:* One parent might take on the role of managing the baby's health and safety. This could include baby-proofing the home, managing first aid

supplies, keeping track of the baby's medical history, and ensuring the baby's environment is safe and clean.

> » *Why It Works:* It ensures that the home is consistently safe and that the baby's health needs are always up to date without gaps in responsibility. It doesn't just mean you put the safety plugs in the outlet, which your spouse researched and remembered to order!

- *Social and Developmental Activities:*

  > » *Total Responsibility Transfer:* One parent could organize and manage the baby's social and developmental activities. This includes scheduling playdates, researching and enrolling in classes or activities, and ensuring the baby is engaged in age-appropriate developmental play.

  > » *Why It Works:* This approach ensures that the baby's socialization and developmental needs are met consistently and that both parents know the baby's progress. It doesn't just mean showing up for mommies-and-me or daddies-and-me class!

- *Financial Planning for Baby:*

  > » *Total Responsibility Transfer:* One parent might take charge of financial planning related to the baby. This could include setting up a college savings plan, managing the budget for baby-related expenses, and ensuring the baby has adequate health insurance coverage.

  > » *Why It Works:* Keeps the family's financial goals on track and ensures that the baby's future needs are planned for and funded without financial strain. It doesn't just mean remembering to pay the bill!

- *Emergency Preparedness:*

  » *Total Responsibility Transfer:* One parent might be responsible for all emergency preparedness related to the baby. This includes creating a family emergency plan, assembling a go-bag, knowing emergency contacts, and ensuring the baby's medical and safety information is readily accessible.

  » *Why It Works:* Provides peace of mind that the family is prepared for any emergency situation and that the baby's needs will be met in a crisis. It doesn't just mean grabbing the baby on the way out of a burning building!

- *Family Communication and Updates:*

  » *Total Responsibility Transfer:* One parent might handle communication and updates with extended family members about the baby's milestones, health, and progress. This includes sending photos, updating grandparents, and managing family visits.

  » *Why It Works:* Ensures that family members feel connected and informed, and that communication is consistent without overwhelming the other parent with additional tasks. It doesn't just mean showing up for Sunday family dinner at the grandparents'!

Benefits of Implementing TRT in Parenting

- *Clarity and Accountability:* With one parent fully responsible for a task, there's no confusion about who should be doing what. This clarity helps avoid miscommunications and ensures that each task is completed efficiently.

- *Consistency*: When one person manages a task from start to finish, there's greater consistency in how that task is handled. This is especially important for routines like feeding, sleeping, or health management.

- *Reduced Stress*: TRT can reduce the mental load on both parents by clearly defining responsibilities. Each parent knows exactly what they are responsible for, which reduces the chances of tasks being forgotten or overlooked.

- *Empowerment*: By fully owning a task, each parent can take pride in their role and feel more empowered in their parenting journey. This division of labor allows both parents to contribute in meaningful ways.

As a reminder, being responsible for (and potentially outsourcing parts of) a task does not mean the responsible parent necessarily needs to "do" all the pieces. Instead, they are responsible for making sure the holistic process happens in the way that both partners want it to be done, however that is executed.

Total Responsibility Transfer (TRT) is a powerful tool for managing the many parenting tasks. You create a clear, consistent, and effective approach to managing your baby's needs by assigning full responsibility for each task to one parent. TRT ensures that tasks are handled thoroughly and fosters a strong sense of partnership, where both parents can trust that the other is fully managing their responsibilities. By implementing TRT in your parenting routine, you can reduce stress, improve communication, and ensure your baby's needs are met with care and attention.

B. PARENTING MODELS

Understanding your parenting style from the very beginning is crucial in shaping how you interact with and guide your child. The choices you make in these early stages can have a lasting impact on your child's development, behavior, and the overall dynamic of your family. This chapter introduces you to the foundational parenting styles outlined in the well-known Diana Baumrind Matrix and expands on it by discussing the additional "Helicopter" parenting style that has emerged over time.

The Diana Baumrind Matrix

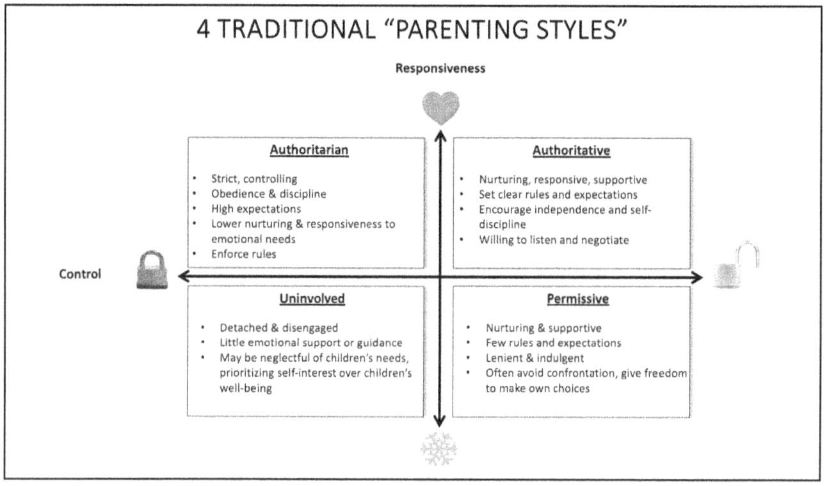

The Diana Baumrind Matrix presents four traditional parenting styles: Authoritative, Authoritarian, Permissive, and Uninvolved. Each style is characterized by varying levels of responsiveness and control, which significantly influence the parent-child relationship.

- *Authoritative* parents are nurturing, responsive, and supportive, yet they also set clear rules and expectations. They encourage independence while maintaining a willingness to listen and negotiate, fostering a balanced and positive environment for the child.

- *Authoritarian* parents are strict and controlling, with a strong focus on obedience and discipline. They have high expectations but tend to be less responsive to their child›s emotional needs, enforcing rules without much flexibility.

- *Permissive* parents are nurturing and supportive but often set few rules and expectations. They tend to be lenient and avoid confrontation, giving their children significant freedom to make their own choices, sometimes at the expense of structure.

- *Uninvolved* parents are detached and disengaged, offering little emotional support or guidance. This style may neglect the child's needs, prioritizing the parent's self-interest over the child's well-being.

Understanding these styles helps you recognize your natural tendencies and the potential impacts on your child's growth. From the beginning, being mindful of these dynamics can help you adjust your approach to better support your child's development.

The Emergence of the Helicopter Model

In addition to the four traditional styles, a new model has emerged: the Helicopter parent. This style is characterized by constant supervision, overprotection, and overinvolvement in a child's decision-making process. Helicopter parents often struggle with letting go, which can lead to high levels of pressure on the child and difficulties with independence.

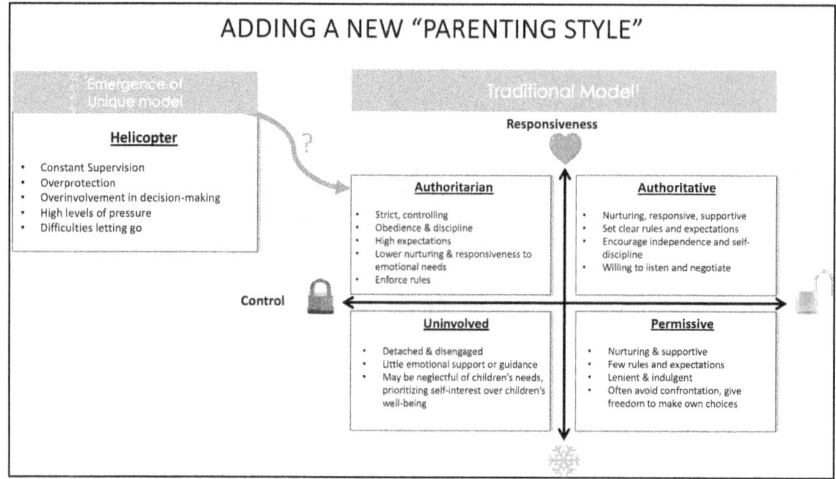

This second slide (above) builds on the Diana Baumrind Matrix by illustrating how the Helicopter parenting style adds to the traditional models, particularly those high in control and responsiveness. The addition of this model is important to consider, especially in today's fast-paced, competitive world, where parents might feel compelled to micromanage every aspect of their child's life to ensure success.

However, it's crucial to recognize that while the intentions behind Helicopter parenting are often good, this approach can sometimes stifle a child's ability to develop autonomy and problem-solving skills. Reflecting on your parenting style from the outset allows you to make conscious choices that balance guidance with the freedom your child needs to grow into a confident and independent individual.

C. HOW TO BE THE BEST SUPPORT PARTNER

Photo credit: Getty Images, Unsplash.com

Becoming a new parent is one of the most transformative experiences in life, and as the support partner, your role is crucial in ensuring that both the new mom and the baby are cared for during this time. For this chapter, "support partner" refers to the non-birth-giving parent. While the mother is physically recovering and bonding with the baby, your support can make all the difference in creating a positive, nurturing environment for your growing family. But being the best support partner involves more than being present—it's about actively engaging in various roles, communicating effectively, and taking care of yourself. In this chapter, we'll explore the roles and approaches that parenting partners can consider to best support the new mom, the baby, and themselves.

The Role of Emotional Support

One of the most important roles you can play as a support partner is providing emotional support. Pregnancy, childbirth, and the early days of parenthood are emotionally intense experiences, and your partner will likely experience a wide range of feelings, from joy and excitement to exhaustion and anxiety.

- *Be a Good Listener:*
  - » Sometimes, the best support you can offer is simply being there to listen. Whether your partner needs to vent about a challenging day, express concerns, or share a special moment with the baby, your willingness to listen without judgment is invaluable.
  - » Practice active listening by giving your full attention, acknowledging her feelings, and offering words of reassurance. Remember, you don't always need to "fix" things—often, just being present is enough.

- *Offer Reassurance and Encouragement:*
  - » The postpartum period can be overwhelming, and new moms often doubt their abilities. Offer encouragement and remind her that she's doing an amazing job, even on the tough days.
  - » Recognize her efforts, big and small, and celebrate the milestones together, whether it's successfully breastfeeding, soothing the baby to sleep, or simply making it through a challenging day.

The Role of Physical Support

While the new mom is recovering from childbirth and adapting to the demands of caring for a newborn, your physical support is essential in helping her navigate this period.

- *Take on Household Tasks:*
  - » One of the most practical ways to support your partner is by taking on household chores. Whether it's cooking, cleaning, doing laundry, or running errands, your help can relieve some of the daily pressures and allow her to focus on recovery and bonding with the baby.
  - » Don't wait to be asked—take the initiative to identify what needs to be done and handle it. This shows your partner that you're fully engaged in supporting the household.

- *Share in Baby Care Duties:*
  - » While the new mom might handle breastfeeding, there are plenty of other baby care tasks that you can take on, such as diaper changes, burping, soothing, and bedtime routines. The more involved you are, the more you can alleviate some physical demands on your partner.
  - » Taking on night shifts or bottle feeding (if your baby is bottle-fed or the baby's mom is pumping) allows your partner to get some much-needed rest, which is crucial for her recovery and overall well-being.

The Role of Communicator and Advocate

As a support partner, you're also a key communicator and advocate within your family and with external parties like healthcare providers or extended family members.

- *Facilitate Open Communication:*
  - » Keep the lines of communication open with your partner, discussing how she's feeling, what she needs, and how you can best support her. Check in regularly to ensure that

you're both on the same page and address any concerns or challenges as they arise.

>> Encourage her to express her needs and preferences and be willing to adjust your approach based on what she communicates.

- *Be an Advocate:*

  >> Whether during doctor's appointments or dealing with well-meaning but overbearing relatives, your role as an advocate is to ensure that your partner's wishes and boundaries are respected.

  >> Speak up on her behalf when necessary and work together to create a plan for how to handle external pressures or unwanted advice. This might include setting boundaries with visitors or making decisions about the baby's care.

The Role of Support Partner in Parenting

Parenting is a team effort; as a support partner, you play a critical role in co-parenting and creating a balanced partnership.

- *Share Parenting Responsibilities:*

  >> Parenting is a shared responsibility; the more involved you are from the beginning, the stronger your partnership will be. Discuss how you'll divide responsibilities, from baby care to household management, and adjust as needed.

  >> Consider attending parenting classes or reading books together to learn about different approaches to parenting. This can help you feel more confident in your role and ensure that you're both aligned in your parenting philosophy.

- *Be Present and Engaged:*

  » Make an effort to be fully present and engaged when you're with your partner and baby. Put away distractions like your phone or work and focus on spending quality time with your family.

  » Engage in activities that allow you to bond with your baby, such as tummy time, reading, or taking walks together. These moments are not only important for your baby's development but also for building a strong connection as a family.

The Role of Self-Care for the Support Partner

Taking care of yourself is as important as caring for your partner and baby. Parenthood is demanding, and you'll be better equipped to support your family if you also care for your physical and emotional well-being.

- *Prioritize Your Own Health:*

  » Make time for regular exercise, healthy eating, and adequate sleep (as much as possible). Taking care of your physical health will give you the energy and stamina you need to support your family.

  » Don't hesitate to seek help if you're feeling overwhelmed or stressed. Talking to a therapist, joining a new dads' group, or simply confiding in a friend can help you manage the challenges of parenthood.

- *Set Realistic Expectations:*
  - » Understand that you won't be perfect, and that's okay. Parenthood is a learning experience, and setting realistic expectations for yourself and your partner is important.
  - » Give yourself grace when things don't go as planned and focus on being present rather than striving for perfection.

Being the best support partner involves more than just being there—it's about actively engaging in various roles that help nurture and support your growing family. Whether it's providing emotional and physical support, being an effective communicator and advocate, sharing parenting responsibilities, or taking care of your own well-being, your role is vital in creating a positive and supportive environment for both the new mom and your baby. By embracing these roles and approaches, you'll strengthen your partnership and lay the foundation for a happy and healthy family life.

D. HOW ALL THE OTHERS WHO LOVE YOU CAN SUPPORT YOU

Photo credit: Getty Images, Unsplash.com

This segment is written for the non-parents! Yes, you, all the excited friends and family who want to jump in and help the new family (and cuddle the teensy baby). If you are the parents reading this, you might consider sharing it with your loved ones, especially the ideas and tips you would find most helpful.

Becoming new parents is a life-changing experience filled with joy, exhaustion, and everything in between. During this time, the support of friends and family can be invaluable—but not everyone knows how to help, especially those who haven't experienced parenthood themselves. While those of you who are already baby-familiar will likely have a good sense of what to do (or not do), others of you might be at a loss.

Often, loved ones ask a well-meaning *"Is there anything I can do to help?"* which gets met with a polite *"No, we're fine"* from the new parents because they may not know exactly what they need in the moment. Here are some tips for you non-parents:

Get Specific:

Instead of offering vague assistance, friends can make specific offers that are easy to accept. Here are some ideas:

- *Send Dinner:* Instead of asking, "Do you need anything?" a friend might say, *"I'd like to send you dinner tonight—what are you in the mood for?"* This takes the decision-making burden off the new parents and provides a much-needed meal without any effort on their part.

- *Offer Babysitting:* Friends can volunteer for specific tasks like babysitting to allow the new parents some much-needed alone time. For example, *"I'm free this Saturday and would love to babysit for you. How about you two have a date night?"*

- *Tackle the Laundry:* Laundry piles up quickly with a newborn, and it's one of those tasks that can feel overwhelming. A friend might offer, *"How much laundry do you have? I'm on my way over to take care of it."*

- *Provide Errand Support:* Offering to run errands or pick up groceries can be incredibly helpful. Friends can send a text like, *"I'm heading to the grocery store—text me your list, and I'll drop everything off."*

Creative Ideas for Local Friends:
Local friends can get creative in their support, making it easy for new parents to accept help:

- *Pre-Packaged Help:* Send a text with options like, *"I'm doing something for you today. Text 1 for groceries, 2 for laundry, 3 for a house tidy-up, 4 for a walk with the baby,"* and let the parents choose what they need most.

- *Surprise Drop-Offs:* Drop off a care package with snacks, diapers, or self-care items. Just leave it at the door with a note, so the parents don't feel pressured to entertain.

- *Household Chores:* Offer to take care of specific household tasks, like mowing the lawn, taking out the trash, or walking the dog. Text *"Hey, can I walk the dog this afternoon?"* These small acts can make a big difference.

- *Watching the Newborn:* For parents with an older child, offering to watch the newborn (even in another room) can give second- or third-time parents alone time with their older child(ren) who just might feel a bit neglected or jealous. Text *"Can I come over and play with (A or B), or take them to the park this morning?"*

- *De-Cluttering and Organizing*: We all know about those lurking cupboards. Like the Tupperware storage area, or the things we no longer wear section of the closet, or the "unknown but possibly important" box in the garage, or the "I can never find things in the pantry" dilemma. And now we add the "where am I going to put this pile of baby stuff?" corner. Close friends can help sort, while the parents supervise. Simply ask, *"Want me to come over and help sort all the baby clothes?"*

Creative Ideas for Distant Friends:

For friends who live far away, there are still plenty of ways to offer support:

- *Send Uber Eats or Grubhub*: Distant friends can order a meal delivery for the new parents. A simple message like, *"Dinner's on me tonight—expect a delivery around 6 pm,"* can be a huge relief.

- *Gift Cards for Essentials:* Sending a gift card for a service like Amazon, Target, or a local grocery store can help parents get what they need without leaving the house.

- *Virtual Check-Ins*: Offer to be a listening ear via video call. Sometimes, new parents just need to vent or chat with someone outside the baby bubble. Schedule a regular call to catch up and offer emotional support.

- *Odd Hour Calls:* Being a late night / early morning person to call can be invaluable for those in different time zones. Sometimes, it's lonely (or even boring!) in the middle of the night.

- *Subscription Services:* Consider gifting a subscription service like Netflix, Audible, or a meal kit delivery. These can provide entertainment, relaxation, or convenience at a time when the parents need it most.

- *Personalized Help:* If you know the new parents well, think of something personalized—like setting up a weekly grocery delivery service or arranging for a cleaning service to stop by. These thoughtful gestures can ease the burden in ways that truly make a difference.

- *Personalized Indulgence:* Again, if you know the parents well, you might know just what they need to relax. Basket of bath bubbles and scents? Candles and a bottle of wine? Golf game tee time reservation and payment? In-home massage (Soothe.com is a great on-demand / pre-booked option)?

The key to supporting new parents is to offer help in ways that are easy to accept and genuinely useful. By being specific, creative, and thoughtful, friends and family can provide the kind of support that makes this challenging time a little bit easier and a lot more enjoyable. Remember, it's not just about offering help—it's about showing love and understanding during one of life's most rewarding yet exhausting times.

Interpersonal Dynamics

Navigating interpersonal dynamics as new parents can be both challenging and rewarding. This chapter delves into the often-tricky waters of unsolicited advice, judgmental opinions, and how to handle well-meaning but potentially intrusive comments from others. It's essential to recognize that while advice can be well-intentioned, it can also feel like a criticism of your parenting choices. The chapter breaks down how to process these moments and respond in ways that protect your peace of mind.

A. UNSOLICITED ADVICE IS BY DEFINITION A CRITICISM

One of the most challenging aspects of becoming a new parent is the constant stream of unsolicited advice. It seems like everyone—from family members to complete strangers—has something to say about how you should raise your child. While some of this advice is well-intentioned, it can often feel like a thinly veiled criticism of your parenting choices. The truth is unsolicited advice, no matter how kindly it's delivered, is inherently a form of criticism.

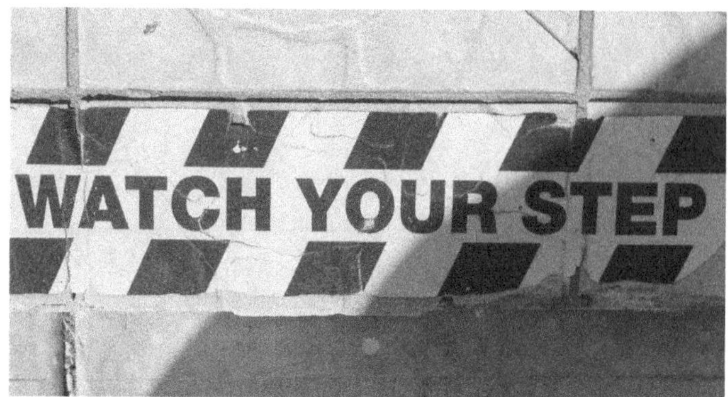

Photo credit: K Adams, Unsplash.com

Why Unsolicited Advice Feels Like Criticism

When someone offers advice without being asked, they are implicitly suggesting that you don't know what you're doing or that their way is better. Even when it's phrased as a helpful suggestion, the underlying message is that your approach is somehow lacking. This can be especially frustrating and hurtful when you're already doing your best to navigate the challenges of parenthood.

Parenting is a deeply personal journey, and every parent-child relationship is unique. What works for one family might not work for another, and what feels right for one parent might be completely wrong for someone else. Unsolicited advice often ignores this individuality, instead pushing a one-size-fits-all solution that doesn't consider your specific circumstances.

Recognizing the Criticism

Understanding that unsolicited advice is a form of criticism can help you process it more effectively. When you recognize it for what it is, you can choose how to respond—or whether to respond at all. Here are some key things to keep in mind when faced with unsolicited advice:

- *It's Not About You:* Often, the advice-giver is projecting their own fears, insecurities, or beliefs onto you. Their advice says more about them and their experiences than it does about your situation.

- *You Know What's Best:* Trust that you know your child and your family's needs better than anyone else. You're the one in the trenches, and you're the one who ultimately has to live with the consequences of your parenting decisions.

- *The Power of Silence:* You don't have to engage with unsolicited advice. Sometimes, the best response is no response. A polite nod or a simple *"Thanks for sharing"* can be enough to acknowledge the comment without giving it more weight than it deserves.

- *Setting Boundaries:* If someone repeatedly offers unsolicited advice that you find unhelpful or upsetting, it's okay to set boundaries. You might say, *"I appreciate that you care, but we've found what works best for our family."*

- *Reframe the Criticism:* If the advice feels particularly harsh, try reframing it in your mind. Instead of viewing it as a personal attack, see it as someone's attempt (however misguided) to connect with you or share their experience.

Choosing Your Response

When you recognize that unsolicited advice is a form of criticism, you can choose how to respond in a way that protects your peace of mind. Here are a few strategies:

- *Thank and Redirect:* *"Thank you for the suggestion! We're doing what feels right for us right now."*

- *Deflect with Humor:* "*I'll add that to the ever-growing list of advice we're getting—maybe I should write a book!*"

- *Acknowledge and Move On:* "*I hadn't thought of it that way. Anyway, how about those weather reports?*"

- *Express Gratitude:* If the advice comes from someone you care about and respect, even if it's unsolicited, you can acknowledge their good intentions while maintaining your boundaries. "*I appreciate that you're looking out for us. We're figuring things out as we go.*"

Unsolicited advice is an inevitable part of parenting, but it doesn't have to derail your confidence or your peace of mind. By recognizing it as a form of criticism and choosing your response carefully, you can navigate these interactions gracefully and focus on what truly matters—your relationship with your child. Remember, you are the expert on your own life and your own family, and you have the right to choose the decisions that feel best for you.

B. THE "I WOULD NEVER" CROWD

As a new parent, you'll quickly discover that everyone seems to have an opinion about how you should raise your child, particularly what not to do. From friends and family to strangers, unsolicited advice is inevitable. Perhaps the most challenging group to navigate are those who proudly declare, "*I would NEVER do that!*" or "*You should NEVER do this.*" Often, these statements come from people who don't have children or hold rigid views about parenting, and it's easy to feel judged or even offended by their comments.

Photo credit: Josiah Nicklas, Unsplash.com

First and foremost, it's important to recognize that these opinions are often more about the speaker than about you or your parenting choices. People who use absolutes like "never" or "should" often do so from a place of insecurity, inexperience, or a need to assert control. They may be grappling with their own fears or ideals, projecting their expectations onto you. Their statements are not a reflection of your capabilities as a parent but rather of their limited perspective.

Why "Never" and "Should" Are Problematic

The problem with absolutes like "never" and "should" is that they leave little room for the complexities of real life. Parenting is not a one-size-fits-all endeavor. What works for one child might not work for another, and what seems like a great idea in theory can quickly fall apart in practice. When someone tells you, *"I would NEVER let my child do that,"* they're ignoring the reality that every child is different, every family situation is unique, and parenting is often about choosing the best option in the moment, not adhering to rigid rules.

It's also worth noting that people without children often don't understand the nuances of parenting. They might have idealistic views about handling certain situations, but until they've walked in your shoes, their opinions are just that—opinions, not informed advice. Parenting is full of unexpected challenges, and what seems straightforward to an outsider can be incredibly complex when you're in the thick of it.

Choosing Your Response

When you encounter the "I Am Never Going To" crowd, protecting your peace of mind is important. Here are a few strategies to help you navigate these interactions:

1. *Smile and Nod:* Sometimes, the best response is no response. A simple smile and nod can acknowledge the speaker without engaging in a debate. You don't owe anyone an explanation for your parenting choices.

2. *Deflect with Humor:* If you feel the need to respond, consider using humor. *"Well, that's one way to do it! I'm just trying to keep the baby fed and happy today."*

3. *Set Boundaries:* If someone's comments are particularly intrusive or upsetting, it's okay to set boundaries. *"I appreciate your concern, but we've found what works best for our family."*

4. *Choose Your Counsel Wisely:* Seek advice from those who have experience and whose parenting styles align with your values. Surround yourself with people who support and uplift you rather than those who criticize or judge.

5. *Remember Your Confidence:* You know your child better than anyone else. Trust your instincts and the decisions you make for your family. Parenting is a journey of learning, and it's okay to make mistakes and change your approach as you go.

The "I Am Never Going To" crowd will always be around, but their opinions do not define your parenting. The best thing you can do is focus on what works for you and your child. Parenting is about love, patience, and flexibility, not adhering to someone else's rules. Embrace the journey, trust yourself, and let go of the need to please others. After all, the only people who truly matter in this equation are you, your partner, and your child.

C. TEN GOLDEN RULES OF WHAT TO SAY (AND NOT SAY)

Photo credit: PikBest.com

This chapter is written for the non-parents! It was inspired by both my clients, who often mention "dumb things well-meaning friends say" and by my daughter Charlotte, whose friends are now becoming parents.

When interacting with new parents, words can be incredibly powerful—either as a source of comfort and support or a source of unintended stress and frustration. It's important to be mindful of what you say, as new parents are often exhausted, overwhelmed, and deeply invested in their new roles.

Here are ten golden rules for what to say (and not say) to new parents:

1. *Don't Say: "The baby looks just like Dad."*
   Do Say: "The baby has your XX, Mom!"

> » New moms have gone through the physical and emotional labor of bringing the baby into the world and acknowledging that the baby resembles her can feel incredibly validating. While it's common for people to say that newborns look like their dads (likely due to evolutionary factors), giving the mom some well-deserved recognition is a nice gesture. If the baby really doesn't look like mom, surely one can find some eyes, nose or toes that remind you of mom.

2. *Don't Say: "I know you wanted a girl/boy, but..."*
   Do Say: "I am so excited for you!"

> » Regardless of the baby's gender, the focus should be on celebrating the arrival of a healthy baby and supporting the parents. Comments about gender preferences can be hurtful and unnecessary, especially when parents are adjusting to their new reality.

3. *Don't Say: "Enjoy every minute; they grow up so fast."*
   Do Say: "It's okay if this is hard; you're doing great."

> » While well-meaning, telling new parents to "enjoy every minute" can add pressure, especially when they're in the midst of sleepless nights and endless diaper changes. Acknowledging that it's okay to find some moments difficult can be far more reassuring.

4. *Don't Say: "Are you sure you should be doing that?"*
   Do Say: "You know what's best for your baby."

> » Whether it's about how the baby is being fed, how they sleep, or any other parenting decision, avoid questioning the parents' choices. Reinforce their confidence by reminding them they are the best judge of their baby's needs.

5. *Don't Say: "I know exactly how you feel."*
   Do Say: "I'm here to listen if you want to talk."

   » Every parent's experience is unique, and claiming to know exactly how they feel can come off as dismissive. Offering to listen without judgment is a much more supportive approach.

6. *Don't Say: "When are you having another one?"*
   Do Say: "How are you feeling?"

   » Questions about future children can add unnecessary pressure and stress. Instead, focus on how the parents are coping with their new baby and how they're adjusting to their new roles.

7. *Don't Say: "Your life will never be the same!"*
   Do Say: "This is such an exciting new chapter for you."

   » While it's true that life changes dramatically after a baby, framing it as a positive new chapter helps reinforce the joy and excitement of parenthood rather than dwelling on the sacrifices.

8. *Don't Say: "You look tired."*
   Do Say: "You're doing an amazing job."

   » New parents are often exhausted and pointing it out doesn't help. Instead, offer encouragement and acknowledge their hard work.

9. *Don't Say: "Should you be doing that while breastfeeding?"*
   Do Say: "Whatever you decide, I support you."

   » Breastfeeding decisions are highly personal and often fraught with anxiety. Avoid offering unsolicited advice on what a breastfeeding mom should or shouldn't do. Instead, support her choices without judgment.

10. *Don't Say: "Sleep when the baby sleeps."*
    Do Say: "Is there anything I can do to help you get some rest?"

    » While "sleep when the baby sleeps" is a common piece of advice, it's not always practical. Offering specific help, like watching the baby for a while so the parents can rest, is much more valuable.

Words matter, especially during the delicate period of new parenthood. By following these golden rules, you can offer support that is genuinely helpful, comforting, and respectful of the unique challenges that new parents face. Remember, your goal is to uplift and empower them as they navigate this new chapter.

I'll close with one last piece of advice – the hello greeting! Friends and family are accustomed to saying hello and giving/receiving hugs first. In the enthusiasm to see the newborn, the new parent is often overlooked and left standing there, like a second-class citizen. And that's hurtful because the new parent can feel rejected or slighted. So, say hi to the person you love first, and then fuss over that gorgeous bundle of joy!

Enneagram and Parenting Style

Parenting begins the moment your child is born, setting the foundation for years to come. Understanding your Enneagram type from the start can provide valuable insights into your natural parenting style, allowing you to be more intentional in your interactions with your child, whether a newborn, toddler, or older. If you haven't already identified your Enneagram type in Chapter 1, now is the time to do so, as it will deepen your understanding of this chapter.

From the first moment you hold your newborn, your Enneagram type influences your approach to parenting. Each type brings its own strengths and challenges to the table. For example, a Helper's warmth, a Reformer's structure, or an Enthusiast's energy shapes how you respond to your child's needs, manage parenting stresses and foster your child's development.

In addition to understanding your own type, knowing your parenting partner's Enneagram type is equally valuable. This awareness helps the parenting unit play to each other's strengths, fostering a more harmonious family dynamic. By recognizing how your partner's natural tendencies complement your own, you can better support each other and create a balanced approach to raising your child.

Starting early with an awareness of your and your partner's Enneagram types helps establish habits and patterns that positively impact your child's growth. For instance, a naturally protective parent might need to consciously encourage their child's independence, while a structured parent might work on fostering creativity and flexibility. Understanding your partner's approach can also help you adjust and adapt as you navigate parenting together.

This chapter isn't about labeling your parenting style but using the Enneagram as a lens to view your interactions and approach to family life. Whether you're a Helper, Achiever, Individualist, Investigator, Thinker, Enthusiast, Challenger, Peacemaker, or Reformer, your type offers insights into the gifts you bring to parenting and areas where you might need to grow. Understanding your partner's type further enriches this process, allowing you to collaborate more effectively as a parenting team.

To support your growth, the following pages provide common parenting characteristics and growth strategies tailored to each Enneagram type, helping you balance your natural tendencies with your child's needs. These strategies are about managing future challenges and setting a positive tone from the beginning—fostering emotional connections, encouraging independence, or finding balance in discipline.

Starting your parenting journey with self-awareness and mutual understanding as a parenting unit is a gift to you and your child. It enables you to be more present, patient, and supportive, creating a nurturing environment that honors both your needs and those of your child from day one through every stage of development.

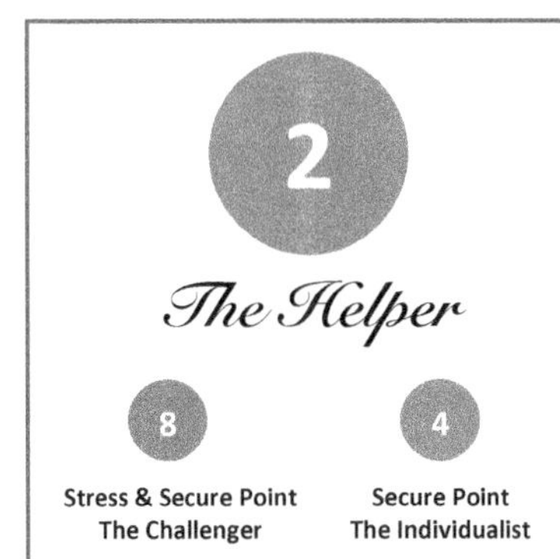

Common Parenting Characteristics	→	**Strategies For Growth**

Common Parenting Characteristics

- Good listeners
- Have fun together
- Warm & encouraging
- Pride in extension of self
- Can disempower by doing what others can learn to do
- Can be overly concerned about others' needs
- Can minimize child's sense of responsibility and problem-solving

Strategies For Growth

- Consider your own needs
- Encourage child's independence
- Think "Caring" vs "Carrying"
- Learn to support instead of rescue
- Avoid bailing a child out

Common Parenting Characteristics	Strategies For Growth
• Makes things happen • Consistent, dependable, loyal • Can be over-controlling, impatient • Too focused on achievement and results • Focus on getting things done over feelings • Paradox own achievement with time parenting	• Share your feelings • Respect qualities other than achievements • Be careful with expectations and pace

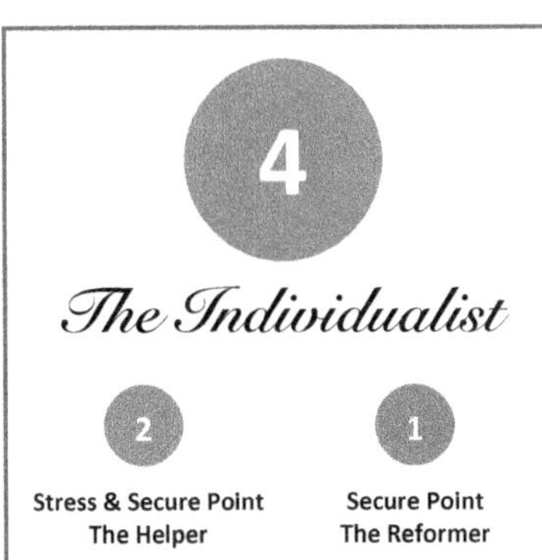

Common Parenting Characteristics		**Strategies For Growth**

Common Parenting Characteristics

- Want to make a unique connection
- Warm & compassionate
- Encourages to be in touch with feelings
- Can emphasize what's missing and become sad
- Can be overly critical and protective
- Can overwhelm with big feelings

Strategies For Growth

- Focus on facts over feelings
- Look for natural talents
- Practice gratitude
- Be aware of avoiding the ordinary
- Beware of creating drama

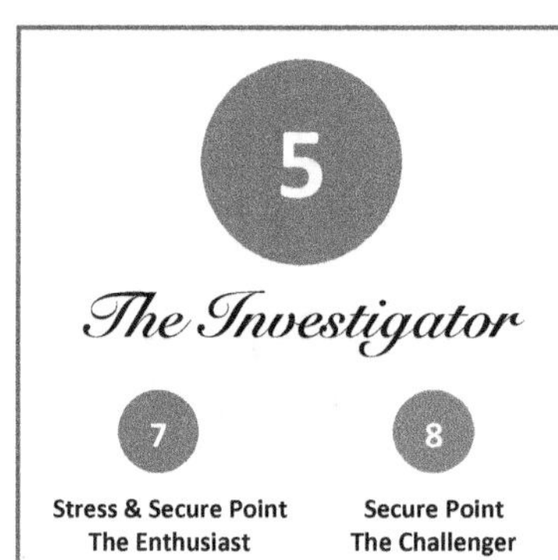

Common Parenting Characteristics	Strategies For Growth

Common Parenting Characteristics

- Enjoy sharing knowledge & big picture
- Kind, devoted
- Perceptive & objective
- Can be authoritarian & demanding
- Intolerant of others expressing strong emotions
- May withdraw detach, leaving perception of disinterest

Strategies For Growth

- Express your emotions
- Step out of your comfort zone and engage when uncomfortable
- Practice small talk and letting go of needing to know
- Find 1-on-1 time (for all)
- Say "I need time by myself" if retreating

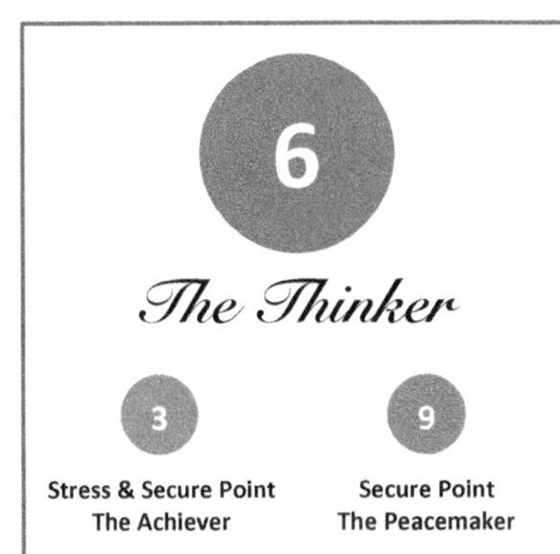

Common Parenting Characteristics		Strategies For Growth

Common Parenting Characteristics

- Loyal, loving
- Devoted, nurturing
- Strong sense of duty
- Scans for danger and tends to catastrophize
- Overprotects, worries a lot that children will get hurt
- Reluctant to give children independence

Strategies For Growth

- Manage your own stress and anxiety levels
- Learn to trust your children, and that they will be OK
- Become less rigid
- Learn to say "yes"

BLUE: HEAD • THINKING • SEPARATENESS • SECURITY • FEAR • Future

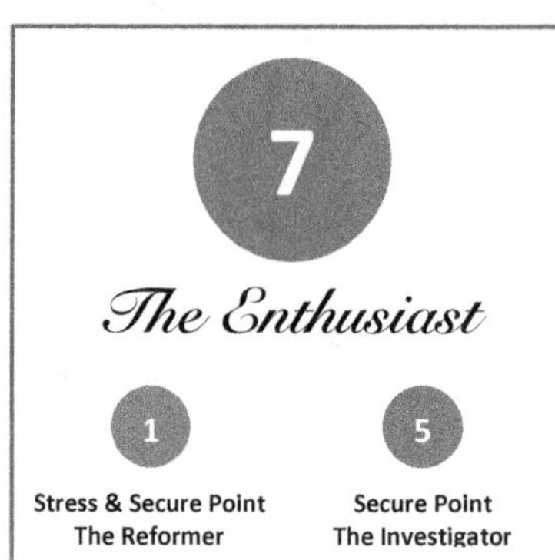

Common Parenting Characteristics

- Enthusiastic, generous and fun to be with (sometimes too much so)

- Loving & nurturing sense of duty

- Expose to many of life's adventures (but wants to lead the fun)

- Can be unfocused, not taken seriously

- Fragmented, busy mind can mean less attentive to and present for children

- Can feel trapped by obligations

- Not a good example of self-discipline

Strategies For Growth

- Remember children need your Presence not your Presents

- Check your upbeat energy

- Be aware of your positive spin

- Practice being more persistent and focused

RED: GUT • INSTINCT • REALITY • IMPACT • ANGER • Present

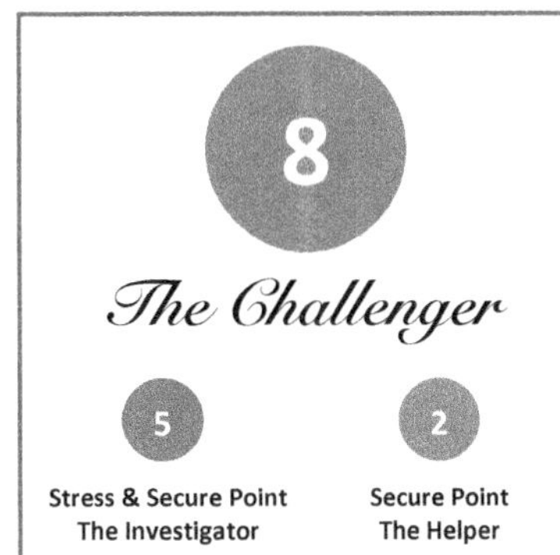

Common Parenting Characteristics	Strategies For Growth

Common Parenting Characteristics

- Loyal, caring, involved, devoted
- Can teach assertiveness
- Fix & solve; give answer & go
- Energy & intensity can be overwhelming, controlling, intimidating and too big for others
- Anger can scare
- Quickly moves on from an emotional event (and others do not)
- Hard to let go with need for control
- Dives into rescue to get control
- Once rules set, must be followed

Strategies For Growth

- Contain your energy
- Take responsibility for your anger
- Consider giving yourself a time-out!
- Work to be a "safe" person
- Shift from solver to coach – listen and negotiate

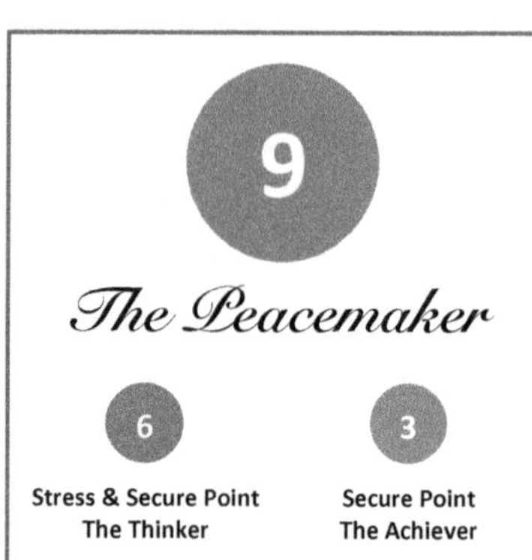

Common Parenting Characteristics		Strategies For Growth

Common Parenting Characteristics

- A patient diplomat
- Very supportive, kind, warm
- Good listeners, mediators – sees all sides of the issue
- Compassionate & flexible
- Gets along well with others
- Can be conflict avoidant, stubborn, overly permissive
- Can withdraw – "sort it out yourselves"

Strategies For Growth

- Learn to say "no" – it can be a complete sentence!
- Speak your own truth
- Resolve conflict in a positive way

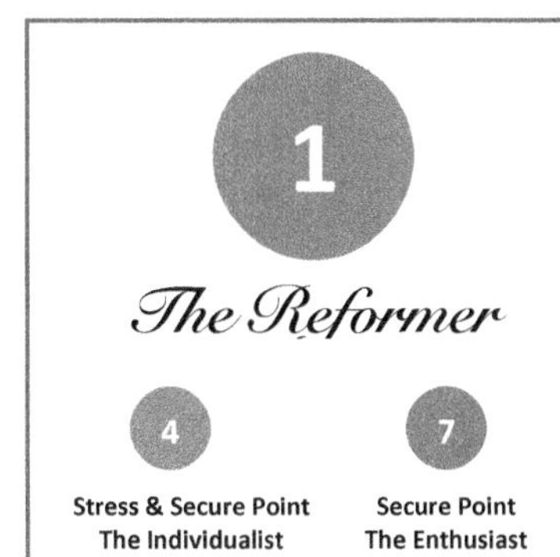

Common Parenting Characteristics	Strategies For Growth
• Discipline firmly	• Lower expectations
• Try hard to teach responsibility and strong moral values	• Suspend your judgment
• Try to find fault to make things better	• Be more flexible and accepting
• Can become highly critical and judgmental	• Find things being done correctly
• Child striving to meet expectations	• Ask *"do I want to be right … or kind?"*

Rewriting the Stories We Tell Ourselves as Parents

Image credit: Getty Images iStockphoto

We all have stories that shape how we perceive ourselves and respond to life's challenges. As parents, the narratives we create can either empower us or hold us back. When transitioning into parenthood, stories often emerge—whether about our abilities, our time, or how we "should" be doing things. It's important to recognize these narratives and understand when they serve us and when they don't.

Just like you might tell yourself, "I'm not patient enough," or "I'm failing at balancing work and home," these stories can become limiting beliefs. Let's approach them with curiosity and intention, using a four-question framework to help shift the narrative. The four-question framework is based on Acceptance and Commitment Therapy

(ACT) concepts, a psychological approach that promotes mindfulness and cognitive diffusion.

1. *Is It True?*

    Start by asking yourself if the story you are telling yourself is based on facts. For instance, when you think, "I'm not good at balancing everything," pause and examine the truth of that statement. What evidence do you have? Often, we're holding ourselves to impossible standards. Perhaps you've navigated work and home life many times with success, but one tough day triggers a critical narrative. Check in with reality before letting the story take hold.

2. *Is It Helpful?*

    Even if there's some truth to your story, is it really helping you? Let's say you've just put your baby to bed after a long day, and you're telling yourself, "I barely spent any time playing with them." Yes, you may wish you had more playtime, but beating yourself up over it isn't productive. Is the guilt useful, or would it be better to make a small change tomorrow to prioritize that time? By asking, "Is this story helpful?" you can create space for a kinder, more constructive response.

3. *Is It Kind?*

    Parents often engage in harsh self-criticism. "I should be doing more," or "I'm not good at this." But is this narrative kind? Imagine saying the same things to a close friend— would you? Instead of focusing on perceived shortcomings, try acknowledging your efforts. The shift toward kindness allows you to see the whole picture better and feel more compassionate toward yourself. Parenting is hard enough; treating yourself with kindness can make all the difference.

4. *Is It the Right Time?*

    Finally, ask yourself if it's the right time to deal with this narrative. Parenting, by nature, is chaotic and often overwhelming. When self-doubt or anxiety arise, it's usually in the middle of a busy moment or when your energy is depleted. For instance, 2 AM might not be the best time to evaluate your career path or rethink your parenting approach. Can you set aside time to address these stories when you're clearer and more grounded?

By applying these four questions, you can take control of the stories you tell yourself as you navigate parenthood. It's not about perfecting your responses; it's about giving yourself the grace and space to rewrite the narrative to serve you and your family better.

Staying Connected

As you transition into parenthood, the dynamics of your relationship and your connection to work undergo significant changes. This chapter is divided into two essential parts: "You, Me, We, and Us," and "Me and Work," each addressing different aspects of these evolving roles.

A. **You, Me, We, and Us:** In this first part, we explore the shift from focusing on the individual "you" and "me" to the shared "we" in your partnership and how the arrival of a child introduces the all-consuming "us"—the family unit. This new dynamic can challenge the balance of individuality and togetherness, making it crucial to consciously navigate these changes to maintain a healthy relationship while embracing your new roles as parents.

B. **Me and Work:** This second part addresses the importance of staying connected to your professional life during parental leave. We'll explore strategies for maintaining key relationships at work, making small contributions that keep you in the loop, and balancing these efforts with your primary focus on your new family. This section emphasizes the value of thoughtful engagement with your career, even as you prioritize your new responsibilities at home.

By understanding and adjusting to these shifts, you can maintain a fulfilling partnership and a balanced connection to your professional life, all while embracing the joys and challenges of parenthood.

A. YOU, ME, WE AND US

Credit goes to my Dad, Clive Minto, for sharing this wisdom with me many years ago. It's a concept I hold dear to my heart today. In any relationship, understanding the dynamics between "You," "Me," and "We" is crucial for maintaining a healthy balance between individual needs and the partnership. Initially, the focus is on two circles: "Me," representing your wants and needs, and "You," representing those of your partner. Where these circles intersect is the "We"—the essence of the couple. This intersection is where shared goals, values, and mutual support reside. It's the space where you navigate life together, finding common ground while respecting each other's individuality.

As you grow in your relationship, the "We" becomes a strong and vital part of your life, symbolizing the union of two people who support each other's dreams, meet each other's needs and work together to create a shared life. The balance of "You," "Me," and "We" is delicate and requires ongoing communication, compromise, and understanding. The first slide visually captures this balance, highlighting the importance of maintaining individuality and togetherness within a partnership.

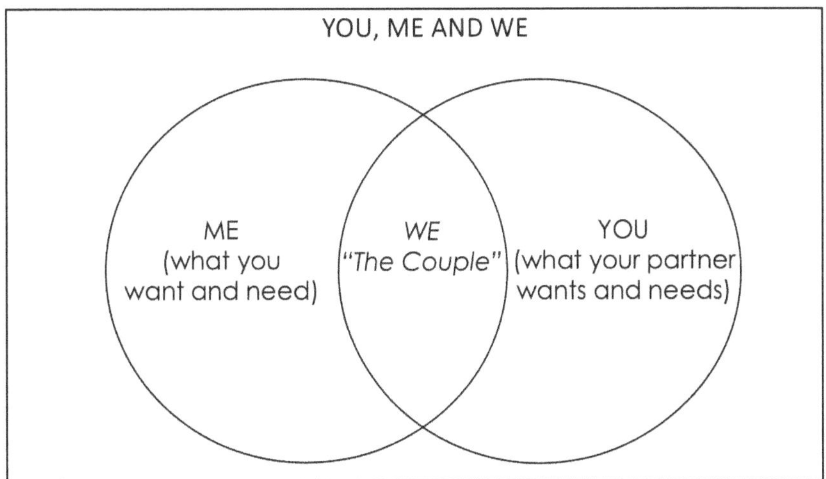

However, a new circle enters the picture when you become parents— "Us." This represents the family unit, which now includes the overwhelming demands of caring for your child and managing a household. The "Us" is powerful and all-consuming, often requiring immense time, energy, and attention. It can easily overshadow the "You," "Me," and "We," leaving little room for the individual needs of each partner or the couple's relationship.

The second slide illustrates this added complexity. The introduction of "Us" can stretch the balance, making it challenging to maintain the original circles of "You," "Me," and "We." The demands of the family unit can eclipse your desires and the connection you share as a couple.

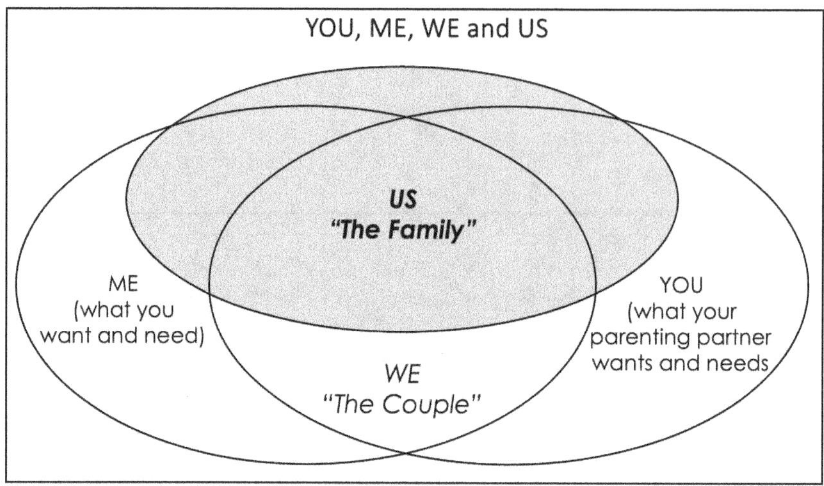

Recognizing this shift and consciously making space for each part of the equation is essential. By doing so, you ensure that while "Us" is a most significant part of your life, it doesn't completely overwhelm the "You," "Me," and "We" that are equally important for a healthy, fulfilling relationship.

To maintain this delicate balance, it's crucial to consciously and regularly nurture each of these circles—"You," "Me," "We," and "Us." Here are a few practical steps you can take to ensure that all aspects of your relationship and family life receive the attention they deserve:

1. *Schedule Regular Check-Ins:* Set aside time each week or month for individual and couple check-ins. For the «Me» circle, reflect on your goals, needs, and well-being. For the «We» circle, have open conversations with your partner about how you're both feeling, what's working well, and areas that might need attention. This ensures that both individual and shared needs are addressed.

2. *Prioritize Date Nights:* Amidst the demands of family life, it's easy to let the «We» slip away. Make a commitment to regular date nights or quality time together that's just for the two of you. This could be a simple dinner at home after the kids are asleep, a walk in the park, or a weekend getaway. The key is to reconnect as a couple and keep the «We» strong.

3. *Delegate and Share Responsibilities:* The "Us" circle can be overwhelming but doesn't have to eclipse everything else. Work together to share parenting and household responsibilities, ensuring both partners have time for themselves and each other. This might mean delegating tasks to each other or seeking help from family, friends, or hired services.

4. *Practice Self-Care:* Don't let the demands of «Us» consume your «Me» time. Prioritize self-care by carving out time for activities that recharge you—whether it's exercise, reading, hobbies, or simply taking a quiet moment for yourself. A well-nurtured «Me» leads to a stronger «We.»

5. *Communicate Openly About Changes:* As life evolves, so will the dynamics between «You,» «Me,» «We,» and «Us.» Keep the lines of communication open about how these shifts affect each of you. Acknowledge when the balance feels off and work together to adjust as needed.

By taking these steps, you can ensure that while the "Us" of family life is a central and joyful part of your relationship, it doesn't completely overshadow the individual and couple identities vital to your long-term happiness and connection. Balancing "You," "Me," "We," and "Us" is an ongoing process, but with intentional effort, it's entirely possible to create a harmonious and fulfilling family life

B. ME AND WORK

Taking parental leave is a vital time for bonding with your new child and adjusting to your expanded family, but it doesn't have to mean completely disconnecting from your professional life. In fact, staying connected to work during your leave can benefit you and your employer. This section explores why it's important to maintain those connections and offers practical strategies for doing so effectively.

Why Staying Connected Matters

Shutting down your laptop and fully stepping away might seem like the best way to focus on your new role as a parent, but maintaining some connection to your work can ease your eventual return. For your own sake, staying engaged with your professional world can help you feel less isolated and more in touch with the part of your identity tied to your career. This ongoing connection can significantly lessen the shock of "cold reentry" into the workforce, making the transition smoother and more comfortable when you do return.

For your employer, your continued involvement, even at a minimal level, ensures that you remain a visible and valued part of the team. This can prevent any disconnects that might occur during your absence and can also help you stay up to date with ongoing projects, changes in the organization, or new developments in your field.

Who to Stay Connected With

Being strategic about who you stay connected with during your leave is essential. Consider the key people in your career—mentors, sponsors, bosses, and close colleagues or friends. These individuals can offer you support, keep you informed, and advocate for you while you're on leave. Establishing a prioritized connection schedule with these people can help you manage your time and maintain those critical relationships without overwhelming yourself.

For example, you might schedule a monthly check-in with your boss or mentor, ensuring you stay informed about significant developments. A quick, friendly email or text exchange with close colleagues can also help you maintain your sense of belonging within the team.

Making Small Contributions

Another way to stay connected is by taking on small tasks or "asks" that can be done on your own time and terms. This might include reviewing documents, providing input on ongoing projects, or participating in a short call. These small contributions can keep you in the loop and demonstrate your continued commitment to your role, which benefits you and your employer.

However, tracking the time you spend on these activities is crucial. Documenting your hours can help you determine if you've accumulated enough time to warrant a couple of extra days of paid time off (PTO) or a delayed official restart date. This ensures that you're fairly compensated and helps you manage your workload and avoid burnout.

Balancing Connection and Rest

While staying connected is important, it's equally crucial to maintain balance and not overextend yourself. Your primary focus during this time is on your new family, and any work-related activities should not come at the expense of your well-being or your bonding time with your child. Be selective about what you take on, and always prioritize your own needs and those of your family.

By staying connected to work in a mindful and strategic way, you can ease your transition back into your professional life, maintain important relationships, and contribute to your employer's ongoing success—all while fully embracing your time as a new parent.

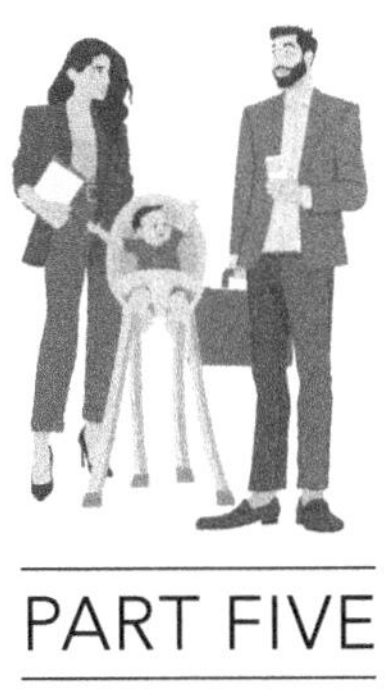

PART FIVE

PLANNING YOUR RETURN TO WORK

As your parental leave draws to a close, the next phase of your journey begins—planning your return to work. This transition is significant, not just in terms of logistics, but also emotionally and mentally. Part Five, "Planning Your Return to Work," is designed to help you navigate this complex process with clarity and confidence.

The first step in this journey, explored in **"To Return to Work or Not,"** is a deeply personal decision that requires careful consideration of your desires, needs, and circumstances. It's about assessing where you stand and what you truly want for yourself and your family.

Next, **"Opportunities Work Brings You"** invites you to reflect on the positive aspects of your career—what motivates you, what brings you fulfillment, and how work aligns with your broader life goals. Understanding these opportunities can help you approach your return with a renewed sense of purpose.

In **"Priorities and Important Matters,"** you'll delve into defining what truly matters to you personally and professionally. This chapter guides you in aligning your life with these priorities, ensuring that your return to work is not just a default decision but one that supports your long-term well-being.

"What You Left at Work" is an honest reflection on where you stood in your career before your leave. This chapter helps you assess your role, your trajectory, and the feedback you've received, setting the stage for a successful reentry.

As you prepare to return, **"Where You Want to Go"** encourages you to think strategically about your future. This chapter is about setting clear goals and aligning your career path with your personal growth and aspirations.

Engaging in the necessary conversations with your employer is crucial, and **"The Ask: Engaging in Conversation"** provides you with strategies to communicate your needs effectively and assertively. Whether it's negotiating flexible hours, discussing a new role, or addressing concerns, this chapter empowers you to find your voice and advocate for yourself with confidence.

"What Will Really Help You Thrive" focuses on the practical and emotional support you'll need to flourish in your return to work. From creating a supportive network to establishing routines that work for your family, this chapter offers insights into building a sustainable and fulfilling work-life balance.

Finally, **"The Caregiver's Manual of You"** goes beyond the basic construct of a caregiver contract to articulate your expectations, priorities, and values in care. It's essential to planning your return to work so that you are confident all is in alignment at home.

Part Five is about more than just returning to work—it's about doing so in a way that honors your needs, supports your family, and sets you up for success. With careful planning and intentionality, your return to work can be a positive and empowering step forward in your journey as a parent and professional.

To Return to Work or Not

Photo credit: Wesley Tingey, Unsplash.com

As I began writing this book, I asked myself, "*Who am I really speaking to?*" and "*Who is my target audience?*"—questions ingrained in me through my years of business training, particularly at Procter & Gamble as a Brand Manager. I realized that my goal is to reach women and men considering returning to work with their current employer after taking parental leave.

But let's face it, this decision is often filled with gray areas. Whether it's deciding if you want to return to work at all or whether you want to go back to the specific job you left behind, there's no crystal ball to predict the future, and there's certainly no one-size-fits-all answer.

If you're already certain that you want to focus solely on life at home, then this part of the book may not be for you—at least for now. Take that relaxing bubble bath and focus on the challenging and rewarding work of being at home. Come back to it if you change your mind.

But if you're planning or even just considering returning to the workplace, read on.

The question of whether or not to work outside the home is deeply personal, and there's no "right" answer—only the one that's right for you at this moment. And the reality is, that answer can change over time. My personal journey into motherhood unfolded as:

- From (on delivery day minus one): "*Absolutely, of course I'm a career-oriented woman who could never be a stay-at-home mom*" ("*Skipped 3 grades of school! Harvard MBA with Distinction! Fast-track BCGer!*")

- To (actual day of delivery): "*Hell no, I could never leave this precious baby girl to the care of anyone else. Are you crazy?!*"

- Then To (3 months later): "*OMG, I am going insane singing 'itsy bitsy spider,' and I need to get back to finding me—and something where my mind is more challenged.*"

Each maternity leave I took brought its own set of decisions, adjustments, and compromises. Here's a glimpse into my journey:

- *First Maternity Leave:* Charlotte was born weeks early, and I was just a month shy of my much-anticipated promotion from Consultant to Project Leader. Initially, I planned on taking three months off, with an office transfer from London to Boston, followed by a full-time return to work. But once Charlotte arrived, I could not imagine leaving her in someone else's care. I decided to quit. However, after a conversation with Sandy Moose, one of BCG's first hires and head of the New York office, I was persuaded to come back at 25%—one day in the office, plus a little extra—working on internal knowledge development. Sandy brilliantly enticed me with interesting client work, which gradually pulled me back to 50% and eventually to 60%, where I found a balance that worked for me and my family.

- *Second Maternity Leave*: Two years later, in the cold New York/ Connecticut winter, my son Matthew was born. With a February delivery and a planned three-month leave, my return to work was set for May. But summer was approaching, and my parents had a wonderful cottage in Canada where I wanted to spend time with family. So, I extended my leave by four months (unpaid) and returned in the fall. I initially went back at 60%, but as interesting work opportunities arose, I moved to 80%. However, 80% turned out to be too much, so I scaled back to 70%, working three days in the office plus some additional responsibilities. Eventually, another exciting opportunity pulled me back to full-time work, and I was also motivated by the prospect of a promotion. Fortunately, I had a great nanny situation, which provided stability during this period.

- *Third Maternity Leave:* Leading up to my third maternity leave, I was balancing work demands with an intense home life. My husband was involved in the early 2000s internet start-up scene and spent much of his time in Austin, Texas, while I was juggling a five-year-old, a two-and-a-half-year-old, and a third-trimester pregnancy. This was all while living in Stamford, Connecticut, commuting an hour to Manhattan, and managing a client in Los Angeles. It was a stressful time.

Sarah was born in May, and we joined my husband in Austin just before her due date. After the intensity of the previous months, I decided to quit—for good this time. However, BCG suggested I keep the laptop "just in case," which I did. After the internet bubble burst, we spent months traveling with our three children under five, enjoying a much-needed break from reality. But reality eventually called, and when it came time to decide who would return to work, we flipped a coin, and I lost. Since BCG didn't have an Austin office, we moved to Dallas, where I transitioned back to full-time work while my husband became the more at-home parent for a while.

My point in sharing my journey is that everyone's experience unfolds differently and unexpectedly. It's a bit like surfing a wave—you have to go with the flow and be agile, doing what's best for you and your family in the moment. You don't have to decide now how you will spend your entire parenting career.

Since you're reading this book, you are likely a high-achieving leader, and work options will always be available to you. Focus on what works for you now and be open to changing course as your situation evolves.

Let's get back to the root of the question. The question of "*Shall I work or not work?*" can seem daunting and permanent. But it doesn't have to be. Let's reframe it:

- *It's not "all or none" or "yes or no"*—there are varieties and nuances that best suit you.

- *It's what works for you now*—it's not a long-term forever decision.

- *You can always change your mind!*

Here is some space for you to jot down whatever comes to mind about the "*do I want to go back to work?*" question. Of course, think logically and analytically, but also pay attention to your feelings, gut, and instinct—they often have great wisdom.

Why?

____

____

____

____

____

____

Why Not?

____

____

____

____

____

____

Opportunities Work Brings You

Let's start with the fundamentals: What does your current employment provide YOU? Why are you choosing to work there? These questions might seem basic, but they are essential for understanding what truly drives you professionally. Too often, we get caught up in the day-to-day grind, moving along our career, development, and compensation paths without pausing to reflect on why we're on this journey in the first place.

Most of my clients are among the elusive 10% who work not just because they have to but because they genuinely love what they do and want to. For these individuals, their jobs are a source of joy and fulfillment—they find meaning and satisfaction in their work, and it becomes more than just a way to pay the bills. For them, work is not "work" in the traditional sense; it's a passion, a calling, and a major part of their identity.

So, why do you get up in the morning and go to (or Zoom to) work? What is it that motivates you beyond the paycheck? What aspects of your job do you genuinely enjoy, and what parts of your role get you excited? Is it the challenge of solving complex problems, the satisfaction of helping others, or the thrill of leading a team to success? What's your inspiration, and what keeps you going even on the tough days?

These are not just rhetorical questions but prompts to help you dig deeper into your relationship with your work. Take a moment to pause and jot down your reflections. Consider the specific ways your job contributes to your sense of purpose and fulfillment. Perhaps it's the intellectual stimulation, the opportunity to make a difference, or the sense of community you feel with your colleagues. Whatever it is, identifying these factors can help you understand why your work matters to you and why it might be worth returning to after your parental leave.

Understanding what work brings you can also guide your decisions moving forward. Whether you're contemplating a return to the same job, considering a new role, or thinking about a career shift, knowing what you value in your work can help you make choices that align with your true self. As you navigate the transition back to work, keep these reflections in mind—they are your compass, helping you stay true to what brings you joy and fulfillment in your professional life.

Here is some space for your reflections:

Why do you work?

____

____

____

____

____

____

What do you most like about work?

What would be the key elements that would excite you about a new job or role?

Priorities and Important Matters

In the hustle and bustle of everyday life, it's easy to lose sight of what truly matters. This chapter, "Priorities and Important Matters," is designed to help you regain clarity and focus by guiding you through two critical aspects of personal and professional management.

The first part, "**Defining Your Priorities**," encourages you to take a step back and identify the big-picture elements that are most important to you. By understanding what drives you, you can make more informed decisions aligning with your core values and long-term goals.

The second part introduces the "**Urgent/Important Matrix**," a powerful tool that helps you distinguish between tasks that require immediate attention and those that contribute to your long-term success. Together, these concepts will equip you with the tools to prioritize effectively, ensuring you invest your time and energy in what truly matters most.

In this chapter we'll explore:

A. Defining Your Priorities

B. Urgent/Important Matrix

A. DEFINING YOUR PRIORITIES

Figuring out your priorities is often more challenging than it might initially seem. At first glance, listing what's most important to you might appear simple, but once you start, you quickly realize that it's a more complex and introspective process. This is because your priorities are not just a list of things you care about; they're a reflection of your values, aspirations, and the life you want to create for yourself and your family.

Let's start at the conceptual level. What are the big-picture items that matter most to you? Your list might include a handful or two of major themes that resonate deeply with you. For example:

- *Personal Fulfillment:* What activities or pursuits make you feel content and whole? This could be creative endeavors, intellectual challenges, or personal growth experiences that bring you a sense of accomplishment and joy.

- *Family Security:* Ensuring the well-being and stability of your family might be at the top of your list. This could involve financial stability, emotional support, and creating a safe and nurturing environment for your loved ones.

- *Depth of Friendships:* Relationships are a cornerstone of life, and the quality of your friendships might be a significant priority. You might value deep, meaningful connections with a few close friends over a large social circle.

- *Exploring the World:* For some, travel and experiencing new cultures are vital to their sense of purpose. The desire to see the world, learn from different perspectives, and broaden one's horizons might drive many life decisions.

- *Contributing to Community:* Giving back to the community can be incredibly fulfilling. Whether through volunteer work, activism, or simply being a good neighbor, the desire to positively impact locally can be a powerful motivator.

- *Improving the World:* On a larger scale, some people feel called to contribute to global causes, such as fighting climate change, advocating for social justice, or supporting international development. This priority reflects a commitment to making the world a better place.

- *Serving the Underprivileged:* A dedication to helping those in need, whether through charity, service, or advocacy, can be a central priority. This might involve working directly with underprivileged communities or supporting organizations that do.

- *Growing a Strong Partnership:* Maintaining and nurturing a healthy, loving relationship with your partner may be a top priority. This could involve dedicating time and energy to communication, shared goals, and mutual support.

- *Adventuring in Life:* Some prioritize a life of adventure, whether through outdoor activities, trying new things, or taking risks. This reflects a desire to live life to the fullest and embrace new experiences.

- *Becoming an Expert on Something Unique:* Whether mastering a specific skill, becoming a thought leader in your field, or delving into a niche hobby, this priority is about achieving a deep level of knowledge and expertise.

- *Teaching Others How to Learn:* For some, sharing knowledge and helping others grow is incredibly rewarding. This could be through formal education, mentoring, or simply being a resource for others in your community.

- *Conquering Mountains:* This could be literal—climbing physical mountains—or metaphorical, such as overcoming significant personal challenges or achieving difficult goals. It reflects a drive for achievement and resilience.

- *Bettering the Environment:* Environmental stewardship might be a critical priority, whether through personal lifestyle choices, advocacy, or professional work aimed at preserving the planet.

- *Being the Best Possible Parent:* Raising children in a loving, supportive, and nurturing environment could be your most important goal. This priority involves dedicating yourself to the well-being and development of your children.

- *Achieving Career Greatness:* Professional success might be a significant priority, whether climbing the corporate ladder, building your own business, or becoming a leader in your field.

The list of possibilities goes on and on, and it's highly personal. For most people, this process of defining priorities is not easy. It requires honest introspection and sometimes confronting difficult truths about what truly matters to you.

Take a few minutes to think about these big-picture items and jot down your top 10 priorities as they come to you in a stream of consciousness. Don't overthink it—just let your thoughts flow naturally. Once you've done this, put the list away for a couple of days. Mark this page in your book to revisit later.

Your Incoming Priorities List:

1. ____

2. ____

3. ____

4. ____

5. ____

6. ____

7. ____

8. ____

9. ____

10. ____

Come back to it and reflect, modify, add, and delete. Iterate on this in the coming weeks until you have something that feels right. Not perfect, just close.

When you come back to your list, take time to reflect on it. Look at each priority and ask yourself why it made the list. Is it truly important to you, or was it something that you felt should be important? Modify, add, or delete items as needed. Iterate on this process over the coming weeks until you have a list that feels right.

More Space for Your Updated Priorities List:

1. ____

2. ____

3. ____

4. ____

5. ____

6. ____

7. ____

8. ____

9. ____

10 ____

Remember, this list isn't set in stone. Your priorities will evolve as your life circumstances change, and that's okay. The key is to stay attuned to what matters most to you at any given time and to let those priorities guide your decisions and actions. This exercise is about aligning your life with your values, ensuring that you're living in a way that's true to yourself.

By defining your priorities, you create a roadmap for your life that helps you focus on what's truly important and guides you through the complex decisions that lie ahead. Whether you're planning your career, balancing family responsibilities, or seeking personal fulfillment, knowing your priorities will help you navigate life's challenges with clarity and purpose.

B. URGENT/IMPORTANT MATRIX

So, now that you are clear on your priorities, take a look back on "Protecting the Rocks" (Chapter 5D) to reflect on what's most "important" to you in your daily life today. Contemplate how they do (or don't) dovetail together.

Next, let's look at how you are spending your time. Here's an interesting framework: the "Urgent/Important" matrix.

- *Urgent*: Things that really do need to be done now. The pressing issues. Things that you may have put off until they became urgent. The time-sensitive stuff.

- *Important*: Things that align most tightly with your Legacy aspirations and Priorities. What actually matters in the scheme of things (for whatever reason).

The four-quadrant matrix that emerges can be pretty telling. Consider for a moment where you are spending most of your time. Think about where your activities lie on the matrix. In concept, the "rocks" (big important stuff) fall on the right-hand side, the "sand" tends to lie on the left, and the pebbles are scattered throughout.

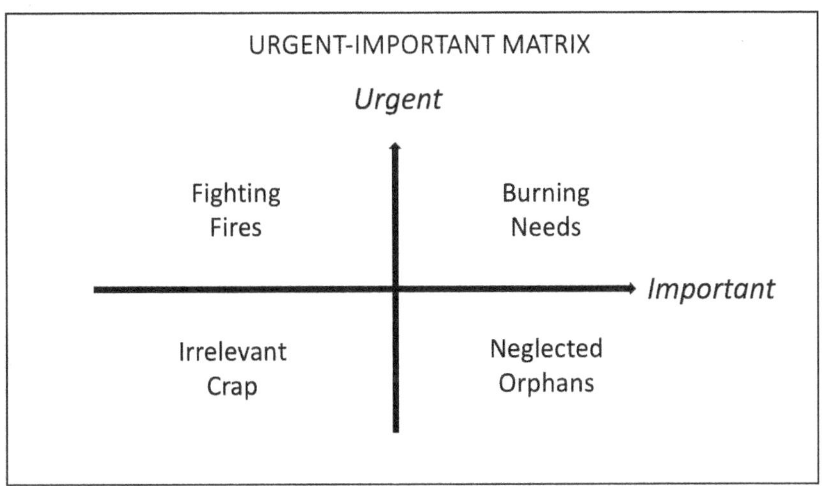

See if you can fill in the matrix where you have been spending your time. If you're stuck, take a look at your to-do list, explicit or implicit. Or look at your calendar for the last few months. Here's a blank matrix for you to contemplate.

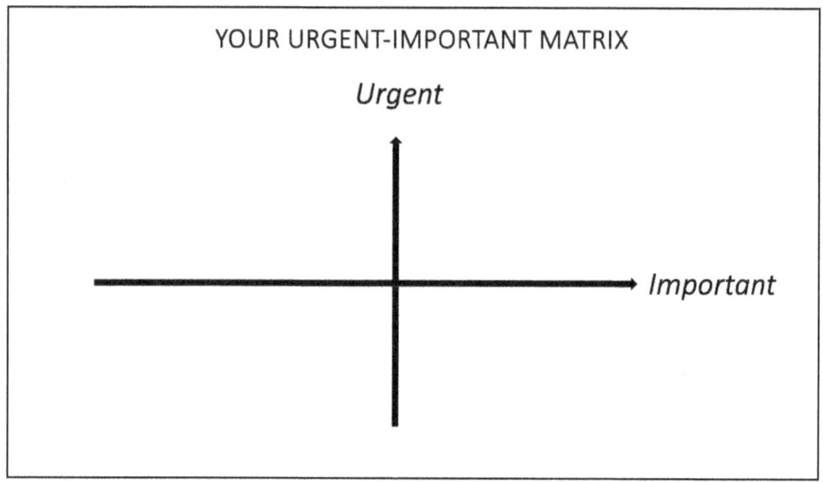

Some clients have chosen to keep a whiteboard of their urgent-important matrix rather than a linear list (e.g., the dreaded to-do list). A whiteboard keeps it fluid and helps put things in perspective. It also allows change on the fly—and wiping items off (as we have been accustomed to doing with that dreaded to-do list).

Finally, if you find this framework intriguing, here's how to kick it up a notch. Consider giving weight to how big some of these activities are. How much effort do they take? You can draw bigger circles for the items that take a lot of time and smaller circles for those that take less. It's conceptual. But it's rather enlightening. Many find that their:

- *Upper right (Burning Needs)*: Both Important and Urgent. It is often pretty big and heavily weighted.

- *Lower right (Neglected Orphans):* Important but not that Urgent. It is typically pretty sparse. (As a side note, reading this book likely falls into this quadrant. So, kudos to you for exploring this far and for making the time to focus on something that's important but never urgent).

- *Upper left (Fighting Fires):* Not that Important but Urgent. It often takes up the majority of time and causes a lot of anxiety and time pressure.

- *Lower left (Irrelevant Crap):* Neither Important nor Urgent. This matrix quadrant is where a bunch of the "sand" lies and takes up an inordinate amount of collective time.

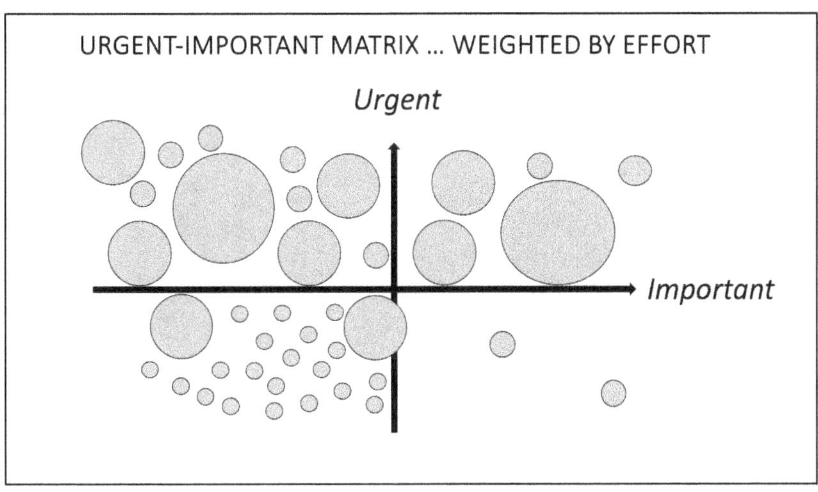

Here's some space for you to explore for yourself. Happy pondering and exploring!

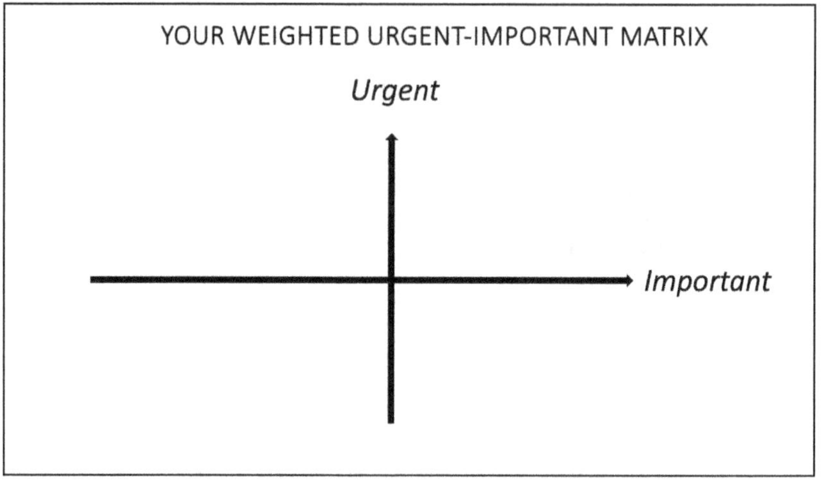

What You Left at Work

As you prepare to return to work, it's essential to reflect on where you truly stood concerning your career when you left. This chapter is designed to guide you through an honest evaluation of your professional standing before you took a break. This chapter is about more than just revisiting your role; it's an opportunity to reassess your career trajectory, your feedback, and how you're perceived within your organization.

The chapter begins with a **"Role Reality Check,"** where you'll take a closer look at your actual responsibilities and what you do and don't like about them. Next, **"Career Trajectory"** invites you to consider where your career was headed before your leave and whether that path still aligns with your goals. The **"Time-Warp Career Trajectory Game"** provides a fun yet insightful way to project your career's future based on different scenarios.

In **"An Honest Look at Feedback,"** you'll revisit the feedback you've received—both formal and informal—and consider how it shapes your professional identity. **"Your Brand Wordle"** helps you distill your personal brand into keywords and themes, giving you a clear picture of how others see you and how you want to be seen. Finally, the **"Johari Window"** exercise offers a framework for exploring your professional self's known and unknown aspects, helping you understand and manage how you present yourself at work.

By the end of this chapter, you'll have a comprehensive understanding of what you left behind at work, giving you the clarity needed to reenter the workforce with purpose and direction.

In this chapter we'll explore:

A. Role Reality Check

B. Career Trajectory

C. Time-Warp Career Trajectory Game

D. An Honest Look At Feedback

E. Your Brand Wordle

F. Johari Window

A. ROLE REALITY CHECK

Start by considering where you are at work *today*. Here are five prompting questions and some space to jot down your thoughts.

1. What role are you in?

---

2. What do you like about it?

____

____

____

____

____

3. What do you NOT like about it?

____

____

____

____

____

4. What would you KEEP doing, STOP doing, or CHANGE about it if you could?

____

____

____

____

____

5. Overall, are you HAPPY in it? What does it do for you? Why are you in it?

Seriously, write it down. If you just think about it in concept, you'll likely not really delve into the present. Take a moment to jot down the answers to the questions above here.

B. CAREER TRAJECTORY

Take a super-high level look at your career track to date. Draw a horizontal line (for a timeline) on the page, with "first big-girl job" at the left and the line extending out for, say, the following ten years. Note where you are today on the timeline and where key promotions and changes have happened. Then, look ahead a few years on what you aspire to. Do you see key promotions? Important career shifts? Key milestones?

Get a sense of where you've been, where you are, and where you are going. It doesn't have to be perfect. The aim is to be generally correct (though you know it will be specifically wrong!).

You might even overlay other key events in your nonwork life. For example, is another baby on the horizon sometime in the next few years? (Gasp, do I even suggest this to a third-trimester reader?!)

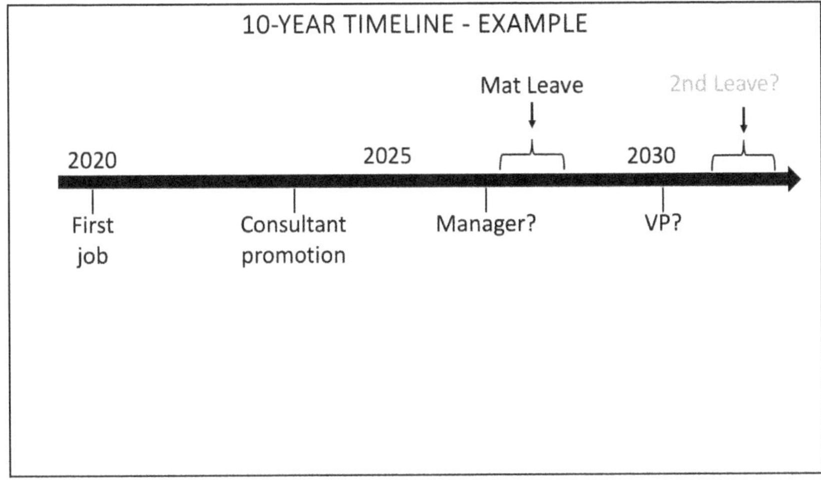

Now it's your turn to create one for yourself.

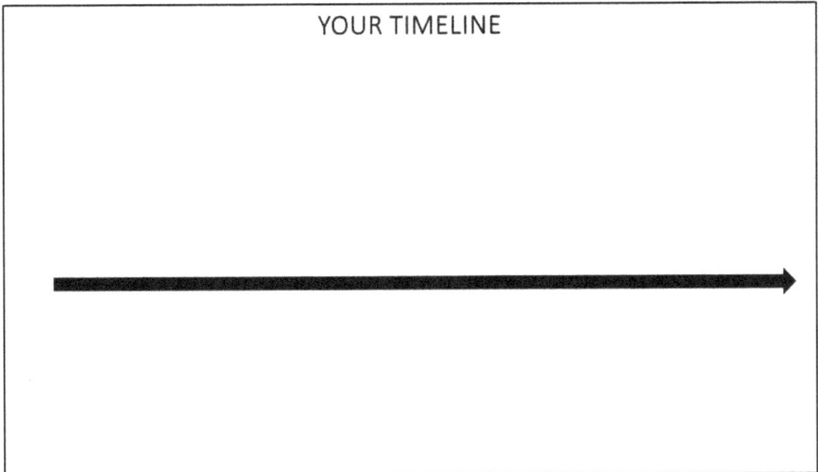

C. TIME-WARP SCENARIO GAME

You've probably written your timeline trajectory as though it was "business (or life) as usual" and working in your current capacity, which is likely "100%" right now.

Now it's time to play the career-planning (or time-warp) scenario game.

Consider the implications of what happens if you take extended leaves. What about if you go part-time for extended periods? What about another maternity leave somewhere on the horizon? At this point, it can get complicated, with timelines shifting and assumptions flying.

Some of my clients have used an Excel spreadsheet (admittedly, the highly analytical ones, and certain Enneagram types in particular). The basic concept is to create a spreadsheet that goes month-by-month or quarter-by-quarter—with the time block, the capacity in which you might work in that time frame, and the implications on career-path (and promotion) timing.

It simply puts in black and white the implications of decisions on path-forward. There's no right or wrong; it's simply an exercise in understanding your options. For example, if a promotion is 12 months out, and you decide to go 50% capacity at work, that promotion now becomes 24 months out. And if you are considering another maternity leave in a couple of years, that promotion becomes 30 months out with a 6-month parental leave. And so on.

Create one for yourself if you are perusing some key work-capacity options.

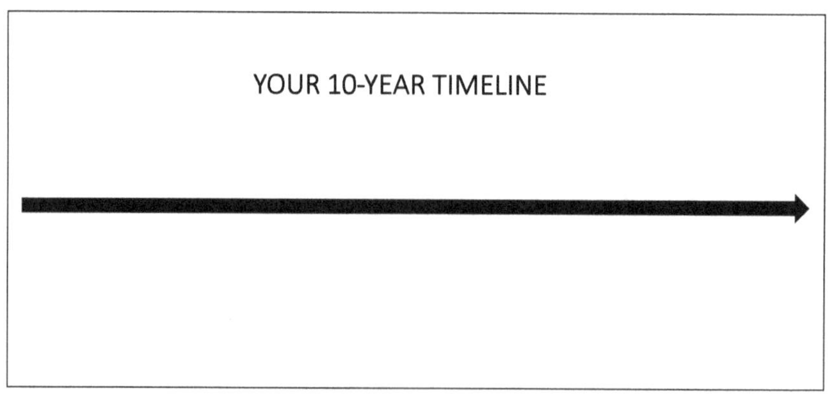

D. AN HONEST LOOK AT FEEDBACK

The dreaded F-word. No, not that one! Feedback.

Unless you are the most amazing, sky-rocketing superstar, those annual or semiannual performance reviews likely contain some stinging comments and piss-me-off suggestions. We high achievers are not generally pleased about hearing "opportunities for improvement." Yet there are some real nuggets in there. And if they are thoughtfully and authentically described, there's a lot to learn from it. Even if we don't like it.

So, pull out those reviews of the last few years. Reread them without getting judgmental about yourself or the author. Just take them for what they're worth and assume good intent. Highlight the insightful comments—the good and the bad.

Now, step back and write your own career performance review. Just for you. Consider answering the following three questions:

1. What am I really strong at? Great at? What helps me excel?

2. What truly are my "areas for development"? What could use some work? Where is my growth-edge?

____

____

____

____

____

3. What do I need to do to get from here to there? What will support my growth? Where are my resources?

____

____

____

____

____

E. YOUR BRAND WORDLE

Now that we've finished that (humbling) experience of looking ourselves in the mirror regarding career feedback, let's move on to something more fun!

Have you ever heard of a wordle? It's where you create a list of words, assign them weighted importance, and get a graphical output of how that looks—a word "cloud." They are often used in concept development, visioning, and branding.

Consider what your brand wordle might look like and create one now. Two free sites I appreciate are www.WordClouds.com and www.EdWordle.net. Set aside 30 minutes to start, create a list of the words you want your career brand to stand for, and get started in seeing what the output looks like. This is fun to noodle on.

Please note that as you revise your inputs, each graphic you create is unique and will be replaced when you push the return key again. So, if you find one that is pretty good and you might want to keep it, be sure to screenshot it. You might not like the updated graphic as much as the previous one.

I really hope you do this because it's a lot of creative fun. You might not get to the perfect wordle on the first go-round, but you can always come back and play with it. Some of my clients keep it in their top desk drawer as their own personal North Star that they aspire to. A couple of clients even framed it and hung it (discreetly) on their wall.

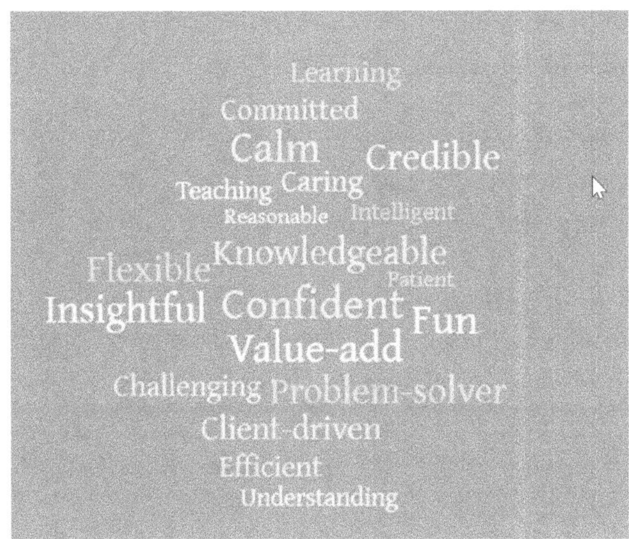

What words belong in yours? Start with a random string of thoughts—then start *wordling* it.

———————————————————————————

———————————————————————————

———————————————————————————

———————————————————————————

———————————————————————————

———————————————————————————

———————————————————————————

F. JOHARI WINDOW

The Johari Window may be a bit of a sidebar here, but I think it's worth mentioning. Now that you've clearly identified what your "Brand You" is, the Johari Window framework looks at how visible your brand is to you and others.

- *Open:* In the upper left is what you know about you and what others know about you. It is the "you" that comes to the top of your mind.

- *Blind:* In the upper right is what others know of or see in you but that you might not be naturally aware of. On the encouraging side, these can be the kinds of things about which you say, *"Oh wow, that's great to hear—I didn't realize that!"*

- *Facade:* In the lower left is what you truly know about your-self, but others simply don't see. They are the hidden gems, the things you wish people knew about the real you: the opportunities you have to make your authentic self more visible.

- *Unknown:* In the lower right is what no one sees—you or others—that might be hidden beneath the tip of the iceberg. It's uncharted, undiscovered territory that might reveal itself as your journey unfolds. It can often be driven by the Clifton Strengths (discussed in the Appendix) that lurk beneath the surface.

<table>
<tr><td colspan="3" align="center">JOHARI WINDOW FRAMEWORK
To Self</td></tr>
<tr><td></td><td align="center">Known</td><td align="center">Unknown</td></tr>
<tr><td>To Others

Known</td><td align="center">OPEN</td><td align="center">BLIND</td></tr>
<tr><td>Unknown</td><td align="center">FACADE</td><td align="center">UNKNOWN</td></tr>
</table>

After you have thought about "Brand You," pausing to consider your Johari Window can often reveal some interesting insights. You might even consider asking trusted others what they see. Their input may well surprise you!

YOUR JOHARI WINDOW

<u>*To Self*</u>

	Known	Unknown
<u>*To Others*</u>		
Known		
Unknown		

Where You Want to Go

Preparing to return to work is not just about picking up where you left off; it's about envisioning where you want to go next. This chapter is dedicated to helping you map out your professional future with intention and clarity, guiding you through key considerations that will shape your career path moving forward.

We begin with the "**Intersection (of You and Work)**," where you'll examine the alignment between your personal goals and your employer's needs. Understanding this intersection is crucial to ensuring your aspirations and contributions are valued and fulfilled. Next, we'll explore "**Work's Ebb and Flow**," delving into the natural rhythms of your work and how you can adapt to them while staying true to your career goals.

The chapter then moves into "**Work/Life 'Balance,'**" a realistic discussion on creating a sustainable balance that supports your career ambitions and your personal life. We'll encourage you to consider various career possibilities in "**Laying Out Options**," helping you visualize different scenarios and outcomes.

Following this, "**Negotiables and Non-Negotiables**" will help you identify the aspects of your work that you're willing to compromise on and those you are not. This clarity will be essential as you move forward in discussions with your employer or consider new opportunities.

Finally, "**Warning: Inference Ladders**" introduces this critical concept for navigating workplace communication and decision-making, helping you avoid the pitfalls that can lead to misunderstandings.

By the end of this chapter, you'll have a well-rounded understanding of where you want to go in your career, equipped with the tools to make informed decisions and navigate the complexities of returning to work with confidence and purpose.

In this chapter we'll explore:

A. Intersection (of You and Work)

B. Work's Ebb and Flow

C. Work/Life "Balance"

D. Laying Out Options

E. Negotiables and Non-Negotiables

F. Warning: Inference Ladders

A. INTERSECTION (OF YOU AND WORK)

At the highest level here, we're searching for and creating the overlap space between *you* (what you want and need) and *them* (what your employer is willing to provide). This is the elusive overlap in the Venn diagram—"The Opportunity" sweet spot. For some, the circles do not meet, yet alone have a significant size for exploration. It's more likely that there is an overlap space—often a large one. We simply need to be honest and creative to find it and brave enough to ask for it. Now is the time to find your Voice.

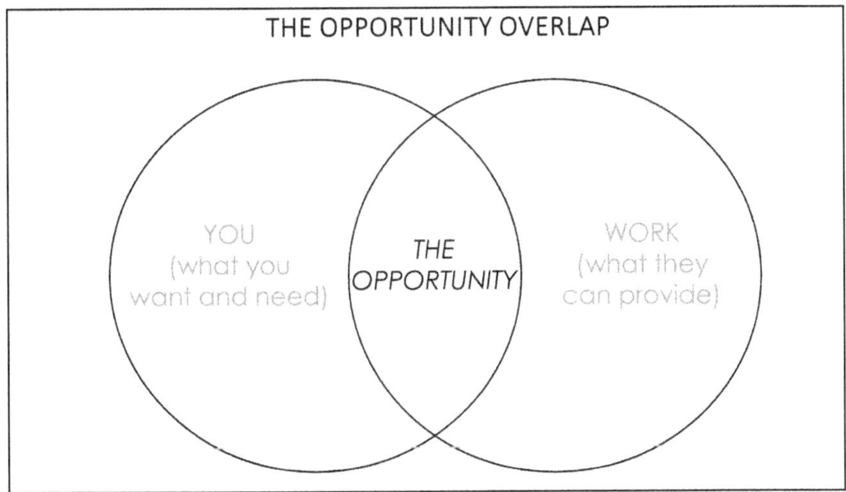

Here's a blank template for you to jot down your notes:

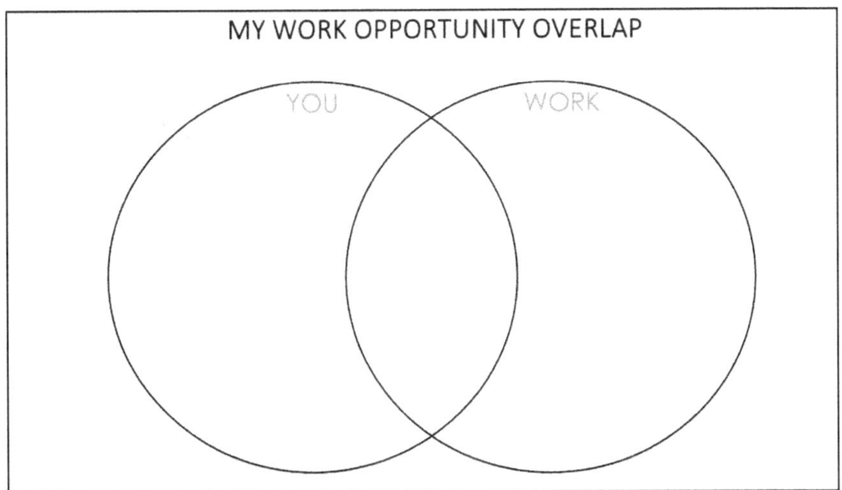

B. WORK'S EBB AND FLOW

The term "work/life balance" is heard all over the place and is traditionally used to describe some kind of magical weighting on each side of a scale that gives us a stable, centered, fixed way of steadying ourselves. Delightful and aspirational, right?

Some liken it to a balanced scale.

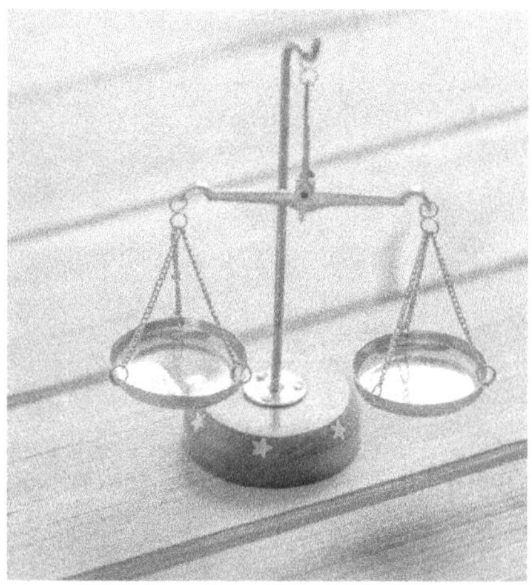

Photo credit: Elena Mozhvilo

I call BS on this static concept of "balance." It's more like surfing a shape-shifting wave than creating static balance on an unchanging scale.

My observation is that life's journey is not a straight line. It's more like a meandering river, taking twists and turns. Sometimes heading straight through the shoot and sometimes bumping the banks. Sometimes seeking shelter in a quiet tributary.

Likewise for work demands. Sometimes, they are intense; other times, they are eerily calm. It ebbs and flows. It simply does.

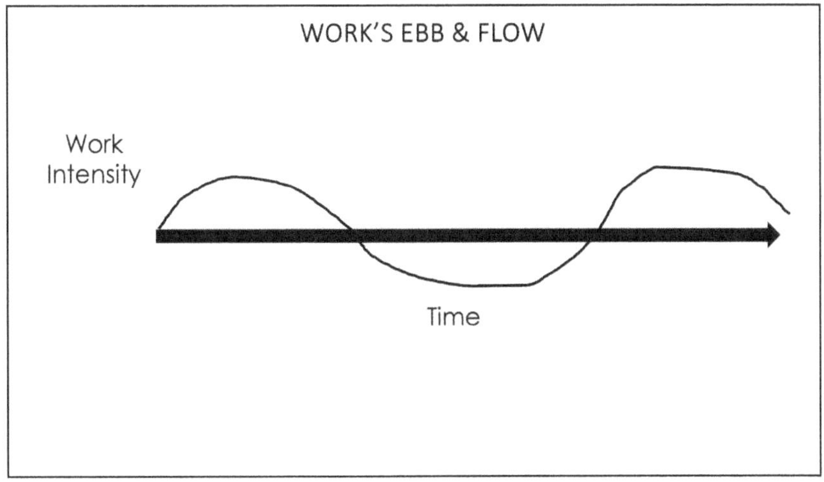

Now, the maddening thing about us high-achieving leaders is that we are incredibly able to create anxiety about *both* phases. Both the ups and the downs. The too-busy and the not-so-busy ebbs and flows. How clever of our Saboteur brains!

- Busy: "*I am so overwhelmed. Work is crazy. I have no time for my family. Everyone is clawing at my time. I have no time for myself. I am exhausted. How am I going to get everything done? No one understands or appreciates me. This sucks!*"

- Not so busy: "*I feel guilty that I'm not doing as much as I should at work. Maybe they don't really need me? What if I get fired? What if someone finds out I snuck out of the office for the afternoon and didn't take a personal day? Maybe I should offer to do that extra project? I'd better look busy, or I might get fired!*"

Pretty incredible when you think about it! So, what to consider about the oscillations:

1. *Accept the phase.* Be aware of what part of the cycle you are in. Know that it will change with time. Decide how long you are willing to stay in it. And decide what (if anything) you are going to do about it.

2. *Reduce the amplitude.* Yes, we all get "busy at work." But how busy is *busy*? Is working all weekend, four weekends in a row acceptable to you? What about one weekend? Or one late night? Know how much you are willing to do. What are you, personally, capable of, and what is acceptable to YOU right now?

3. *Manage the length.* Recognize how long it's been going on and set yourself boundaries. You are the boss of you, and at some point (which you decide), you choose to manage yourself out of the phase. Remember, also, that you are likely the culprit in not adhering to the boundaries you set for yourself in the first place. We usually cross our own boundaries before others do (see Chapter 28).

4. *Accept yourself.* Returning to the stories we tell ourselves in each phase, keep those Saboteurs (upcoming in Chapter 43B) in check. If we're working too hard, we are actually making that choice for ourselves. If we're not working too hard, that lazy sneak-out afternoon is highly unlikely to exceed the many extended evenings and weekends we've put in time in the past. And I've never heard of high-achieving leaders accused of being slackers.

C. WORK/LIFE "BALANCE"

Before considering the kind of support you need and the kind of work situation you will put yourself in, it helps to get crystal clear on the key stress factors that work contributes to your life. Simply put, there are three primary drivers:

- *Sustainability.* How many hours you will work, and over what period of time. The volume of work over the year (and the remaining hours in a week you will have to do other things).

- *Flexibility.* The extent to which family needs and desires can be dovetailed into traditional work hours. The seamlessness of integrating life activities into the workday (and vice versa).

- *Predictability.* How often work emergencies crop up and plans change at the last minute. The ability to anticipate work demands and plan the week's schedule well in advance.

How important is each of these to you today? Prioritize the list by understanding why each matters to you. Consider the circumstances of any partner in the equation and how that might shift what you need for yourself and for both your careers at this point in time.

Thoughts to self:

____

____

____

____

____

In addition to flexibility, sustainability, and predictability, other intangibles might be critical to your satisfaction with your career role. For example, inspiration (excitement, engagement, challenge) or affiliation (friends, inspirational leaders, social outlets). Pause for a moment and think about what those might be for you. Why is it that you want to continue your career in the first place? And yes, you can add "money" if that's one of the motivators (or even the primary one!) driving you.

Notes to yourself about what matters most to you in your desire to return to work:

____

____

____

____

____

All these underlying needs and desires (sustainability, flexibility, predictability, and others) are typically translated into policies and expectations along five dimensions. Understand what these are for your employer and think about their implications for the underlying "what will really help me thrive" factors you just explored. Here are the five (sometimes unwritten) expectations to look for and consider:

1. *Workload:* The standard workload is typically about 2,000 hours per year (40 hours a week, 50 weeks a year). But what is the "typical" week? Is the expectation in reality more like 60 hours/week? Is it six days/week? Understand the workload expectations (usually unwritten but commonly held beliefs/ experiences of your cohort). Also, consider that, a 50% part-time role in a job that typically requires 80 hours a week may be a reasonable 40-hour-per-week job (and the premium pay for the premium job that is usually associated with long hours, but super-high all-in compensation may well be great compensation for "part-time"!).

2. *Work hours:* Some companies publish typical work hours (e.g., *"9–5 with a 30-minute lunch break"*). Most also have culturally typical work hours (e.g., *"we're usually in the office by 8, but done by 6, with a couple of hours on the weekend"*). Know whether there are certain expectations, particularly with global companies across multiple time zones (for example, super-early mornings for West Coasters working with Europeans, super-late nights for East Coasters working with Australians). Be aware of any expectations about Saturdays (Middle Eastern affiliates) and Sunday evenings (Asia Pacific affiliates). They are what they are and be aware of what the cultural expectations actually are. You are highly unlikely to single-handedly shift the company's cultural norms.

3. *Regular PTO:* This can range from two meager weeks to more than six weeks (with tenure, especially in European countries). Know the policy and the (sometimes unwritten) caveats that come with it. Know whether you can "buy" extra vacation or take a sabbatical (paid or unpaid). Some companies encourage taking large time blocks (for example, insisting that at least one time block be a minimum of two weeks); others suggest taking only shorter time blocks (for example, with a midweek check-in or an expectation to sift email daily). Some expect you to shut down the laptop and be entirely gone; others expect at least some availability for those "critical calls" (are they really?). The point is to understand the culture behind the written PTO policies. And to think about how that expectation fits with what you know best rejuvenates you and gives you joy. And whether you will consider going counterculture (someone has to be the first).

4. *Physical location:* While many companies now have a WFA (work from anywhere) approach, even more have strange matrix policies like *"be in the office at least three days a week"* or *"everyone must be in the office on Wednesdays."* There are all kinds of (often not ideal) practices out there. And they seem to migrate and change with experimentation (and as justification for those long, large office leases). Know what your company expects and how that impacts your life and your choice of living location). It's likely not realistic (for you or for them) to be the only employee who *"doesn't do Wednesdays."*

5. *Travel:* This one is rarely written into job descriptions and even less commonly written into a corporate policy. However, the expectation is real and can vary widely by role and

client case assignment. So, it's a bit murkier but tends to be more situation-specific and, therefore, more negotiable in setting expectations. Please don't avoid having a conversation about travel, even if it feels awkward. Think about what you can tolerate (or might even look forward to!). For example:

- The annual retreat that takes you halfway around the globe for ten days (and do you really need to be there live)?

- The out-Sunday-back-Thursday on-the-ground-at-the-client commitment (and can you be assigned to another type of client, at least in the short term)?

- The two-days-every-other-week scenario? Is that two days, with one overnight in between? Or two very long day trips, but you're back at home in your bed?

The permutations (and possibilities) are endless. So, know what you want and ask for what you need at this point in your career.

D. LAYING OUT OPTIONS

Hopefully, by now, you've spent quite some time considering all the possibilities. And hopefully, your head is not spinning, and you haven't worked yourself into a state of extreme anxiety. Let me start by reminding you that nothing (nothing!) is fixed, irreversible, or unchangeable. You're just looking for the options that best suit you (and your partner) and your baby. It's a stake in the ground for now, not a lifetime commitment.

If you're sure you know what you want and it will work (for now), carry on and get cracking.

But if you're sure you know what you want and it's just not going to work with your current employer, then resign. Without guilt. And start polishing off that résumé in search of a place where you can be you and make the choices you want to make. It's your life to live, and we don't want to make choices that we already know are going to make us miserable.

If, however, you are now rather confused about what the heck to do, lay it all out—on paper. Think of the possibilities and distill them down to two or three options. Then, think about the pros and cons of each. It may sound rather simplistic, but simplification can often add clarity. Here's a template and some space for thinking it through. Use a pencil and an eraser—it will shift and evolve as you ponder it.

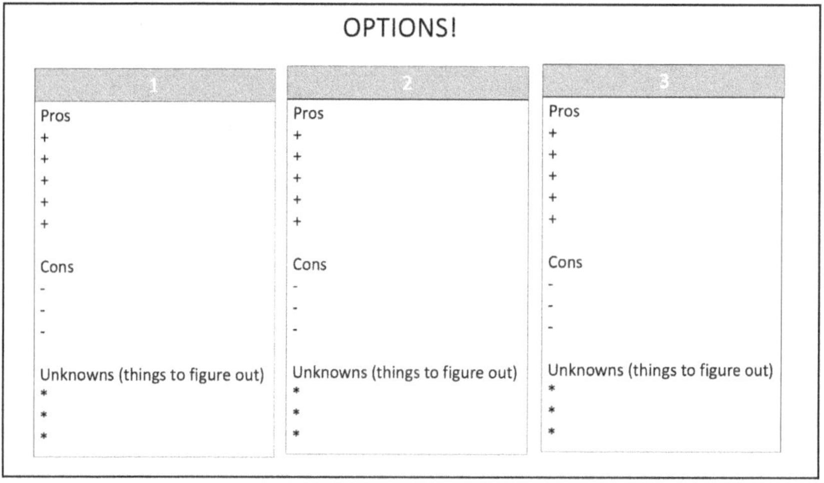

E. NEGOTIABLES & NON-NEGOTIABLES

Let's get a little more tactical about these priorities, needs, and wants. What does it mean for your discussions about returning to work?

A useful exercise is to consider what "I MUST have" (non-negotiables) and what "I'd LIKE to have" (negotiables). Get crystal clear on it. Write it down on the template below. Come back to it. Ponder it. Really establish in your own mind what these are.

Consider that these are not "forever and a lifetime" decisions. These are important to you in your reentry—say, for the next three to six months. Priorities change, and you can always revise the list. Note that this "time frame" context will be important in your planning for reentry discussions, covered later.

Here's a laundry list of the factors some of my clients have considered:

- NO travel

- Never working past 6 p.m.

- Not being available 5–7 p.m.

- Not working weekends

- Going to Mommy & Me on Thursday afternoons

- Not taking calls after 11 p.m.

- Working from home when my child is sick or the nanny no-shows

- Daddy Saturdays – no work, ever!

- Not attending weekend company retreats

- Accommodating planned childcare activities (e.g., doctor's appointments)

- Not attending evening recruiting and social events

- Working from home three days per week

KNOWING WHAT REALLY MATTERS TO YOU!	
NEGOTIABLE	**NON-NEGOTIABLE**
•	•
•	•
•	•
•	•
•	•
•	•

F. WARNING: INFERENCE LADDERS

At this point, I believe it's worth taking a brief, self-imposed time-out (It will be great practice for when you are dealing with "time-outs" for a toddler.)

While exploring options, we can sometimes get inside our own heads and make assumptions about our "others" (employers, partners, and other support resources).

You may have heard this before: We are experts at creating our own "inference ladders." This means that we make assumptions about how others think and feel and, therefore, about what they are or are not willing to do. We set the narrative in our own minds and then expertly look for confirming points of evidence, often connecting the dots in a somewhat pathological way. From this, we weave our warped view of reality and thus limit the art of the possible.

So, if you hear yourself thinking thoughts like *Oh, they will never consider that*, or *This would never work*, reconsider. Are you making assumptions about what is and is not possible, in a world where opportunity might abound with good exploration, consideration, and communication?

I suggest pausing and considering whether you are climbing any inference ladders. And if so, how to step back and consider how the narratives of others might differ from yours.

Photo credit: Tommy Bond, Unsplash

The Ask:
Engaging in Conversation

Negotiating your return to work or any significant career move requires more than just knowing what you want—it requires effective communication and a strategic approach to asking for it. This chapter is about equipping you with the tools and confidence to engage in these crucial conversations with power and poise.

We'll begin by exploring the **"Position of Power for Women,"** where you'll learn how women, in particular, can recognize a strong negotiating position. Understanding your value and the unique contributions you bring to the table is key to confidently advocating for your needs and desires.

Next, we'll introduce the concept of the **"Power Pose,"** a physical stance that can help boost your confidence and presence in any conversation. This simple one-minute technique can profoundly impact how you are perceived and feel during negotiations, setting the tone for a successful dialogue.

"Finding Your Voice" is about more than just speaking up—it's about articulating your needs clearly and assertively while staying true to your authentic self. We'll guide you through strategies to ensure your voice is heard and respected, even in challenging conversations.

In "'**No' is a Complete Sentence**," you'll learn how to set boundaries and stand firm in your decisions. Sometimes, saying no is the most powerful thing you can do to protect your time, energy, and priorities, and this section will help you do so with confidence and grace.

Finally, "**A Gentle Warning on Timing**" offers insight into starting conversations early. Timing can be everything and can greatly influence the outcome.

By the end of this chapter, you'll be ready to engage in conversations about your work and career with clarity, confidence, and power, ensuring that your voice is heard and your needs are met.

In this chapter we'll explore:

A. Position of Power for Women

B. Power Pose

C. Finding Your Voice

D. "No" is a Complete Sentence

E. A Gentle Warning on Timing

A. POSITION OF POWER FOR WOMEN

Source: Shutterstock.com

Surprisingly, many women seem unaware of their inherent position of power—or even worse, they fear that asking for modified roles during the parenting phase might seem like a plea for special treatment. Let me be clear: *nothing* could be further from the truth!

There are both upsides and downsides to being a working mother, and it's important to understand both:

- *The Downside: Maternal Bias*
  Ah, bias. We all have them—it's part of our human wiring. Our brains create shortcuts based on stereotypes to help us navigate life more efficiently (thanks, evolution!). But while biases might be helpful when identifying threats in the wild, they're not so great when applied to the workplace. One particularly pesky bias that working mothers face is *maternal bias*—the subtle but insidious idea that mothers (and even pregnant women) are somehow less competent or less committed to their jobs. It's often referred to as a *"micro-bias"* because it operates under the radar. But make no mistake—it's real and

can influence how you're perceived at work. The key is to be aware of it and challenge it. Don't let it define your worth or your capabilities.

- *The Upside: Over-Indexed Interest*
Now, here's the good news. Despite the biases, there's a powerful force working in your favor—companies *want* to retain high-performing women. This is especially true for women in senior positions or those with dual minority status (race, country of origin, sexual orientation, etc.). Why? Because:
  » Women, particularly senior women, are still underrepresented in the workforce.
  » Diversity, equity, and inclusion (DEI) initiatives are top priorities for many companies.
  » Companies have already invested heavily in your development, and losing that talent is costly.
  » Turnover, especially of key employees, is expensive and considered a "regrettable loss."
  » Flexibility in the workplace is growing, both formally and informally, and companies recognize its value in retaining talent.

Given all of this, you are in a position of strength. So, when it's time to negotiate or discuss your role, do not—*I repeat*, do not—go in apologetically, as if you're asking for a favor. You're not. You're simply ensuring that both you and the company can thrive. Walk into those conversations with your head held high, knowing that retaining you is just as much in the company's best interest as it is in yours to find a working arrangement that supports your needs. Confidence is key.

So, young lady, stand tall. You're not asking for a handout—you're securing your future and contributing to a company that values what you bring to the table.

B. POWER POSE

Photo credit: Ryan Moreno, Unsplash.com

Ah, the Power Pose. Think of it as the bold, confident sister to the calming and serene Grounding practice (you can find all the Zen details about that one in Chapter 44A). While grounding helps you center and settle, the Power Pose is all about standing tall and taking up space—literally. It's like a shot of espresso for your body and mind, minus the caffeine jitters.

Why does it work? Well, it's scientifically proven that how we hold our bodies directly affects our mental state. And vice versa. Want to feel powerful? Then, show up with power—starting with your posture. It makes sense to prime your body to feel strong, especially before an important meeting where you want to bring your A-game.

And the best part? This little exercise takes just one minute. Science says it needs at least 60 seconds to kick in (which is shorter than the time it takes to scroll through your social feed). Plus, you can do it *almost* anywhere. I've even snuck in a Power Pose in a bathroom stall before a big meeting. Yes, really. Had to share that!

So, what's the secret? It's all about taking up as much space as humanly possible for one glorious minute while treating yourself to some empowering, positive thoughts. This can be especially important for women, who often aren't conditioned to *take up space* in the same way men are—and let's face it, we're generally working with smaller frames compared to our male counterparts. But here's the deal: at this minute, *you own the room.*

Here's how you do it:

- *Step 1:* Stand with your feet wider than your hips. (Think Wonder Woman, but without the cape.)

- *Step 2:* Reach your arms up and out, spreading them as wide as humanly possible—like you're trying to hug the entire sky. Tip your head back and look up, whether at the ceiling or the sky.

- *Step 3:* Take the deepest breath you can muster, and as you do, expand your chest forward like you're about to belt out an epic power ballad.

- *Step 4:* While you're in this power-packed position, feed your brain some positive affirmations like *"I'm strong," "I rock," "I've got this,"* or the classic *"I am a superstar."*

- *Step 5:* Don't forget to enjoy the moment! Smile, laugh, and if you're in a place where it won't scare people, shout those affirmations out loud. Own it!

- *Step 6:* Hold it for at least 60 seconds. You can do anything for one minute, right?

When you finally return to earth, take a moment to notice how you feel. Energized? Strong? Ready to take on the world? That's the magic of the Power Pose. Pretty amazing what one minute can do!

C. FINDING YOUR VOICE

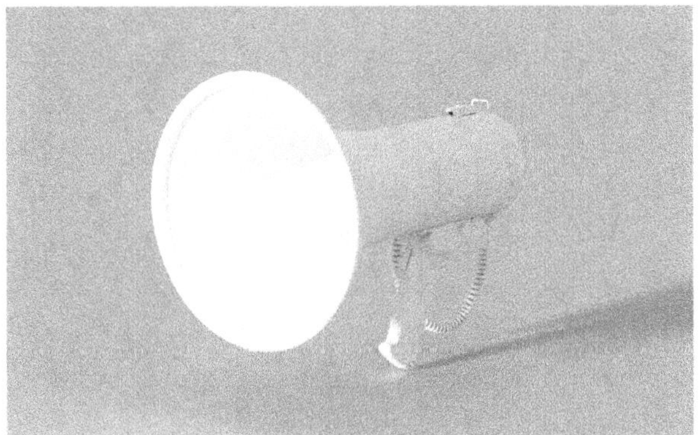

Photo credit: Alexander Mils, Unsplash.com

Some of us will stride into your reentry conversation like a boss—confident, clear, and ready to *own* the room. I'm talking Beyoncé-at-the-Grammys levels of poise. You know exactly what you want, and you're ready to ask for it with the kind of resolve that could make grown adults cry (in a good way).

But not everyone feels like Beyoncé on negotiation day. For some of you, it's more like that moment before your turn in a spelling bee—sweaty palms, slight nausea, and the faint hope that maybe no one will notice if you just quietly sneak out the back door. Sound familiar?

Let me give you a little pep talk if you fall into the latter category. You've *got* this. Why? Because you've been through the process of figuring out exactly what you need to thrive in that beautiful Venn diagram intersection of "You" and "Work" (Chapter 29A for those keeping track). That center of balance where your needs and career ambitions overlap like two circles in a strategic hug. You know what you want, what you're willing to negotiate, and what's a hard pass. So, take a deep breath—you're in control here.

Now, let's talk about how to walk into that meeting with confidence. So many good books give you 400-page treatises on how to have a stellar conversation. I don't know about you, but I don't have time for that, and I'm guessing you don't either. So, let's distill that wisdom into something we can all remember.

1. *Be honest:* Speak and act the truth. Unless the truth is you ate all the brownies and blame your kid—let's keep that between us.

2. *Be direct:* Say what you mean and mean what you say. No need for poetic riddles or overthinking.

3. *Be present:* Focus on the here and now. (Yes, that means no thinking about what's for dinner halfway through the meeting.)

4. *Be personal:* It's okay to be human. Share a little about yourself—it'll make the conversation warmer and less robotic.

5. *Be sincere:* Say things with heartfelt compassion. Like a bad perfume, people can sniff out insincerity from a mile away.

6. *Be a great listener:* You know the drill. Eyes on them, nod at appropriate times, and for the love of all that is good, don't interrupt.

7. *Be real:* If you don't know something, just admit it. You're not auditioning for "Jeopardy."

8. *Be candid:* It's okay to talk about the uncomfortable stuff. If they caution you about part-time roles or extended gaps in your resume, explain what "parenting" really means.

9. *Be consistent:* No flip-flopping. Stand by what you say. No one likes trying to follow a moving target.

10. *Create opportunities for dialogue:* This isn't a monologue. Leave space for them to contribute. It's a conversation, not a TED Talk.

11. *Don't be judgmental:* Especially when it comes to yourself. That's wasted energy you could spend on something useful— like thinking of what TV series to binge next.

You've done the hard work of figuring out your goals, so now it's time to go into that meeting and simply communicate them. Chances are that your employer will say "*yes*" (or at least work out some form of a modified "yes" solution that keeps everyone happy). But—brace yourself—what if they say *no*? What then? (Cue dramatic music).

First off, *don't panic.* That "*no*" isn't the end of the world—it's just a redirection. Sure, a "*no*" can sting initially, but it's actually doing you a favor. If this role, this setup, or this organization wasn't going to give you the support you need, why waste precious time trying to squeeze a square peg into a round hole? You've got bigger things to do, like finding a place that *does* fit.

And guess what? You're a strong leader with skills that other organizations will jump at. There are plenty of roles out there that align with your values, your needs, and your future vision. So, if you get hit with a "*no*," just smile, nod, and smoothly shift into *Plan B*— finding that perfect fit elsewhere. The right opportunity is out there waiting for you. And you've already got your voice—now go use it!

D. "NO" IS A COMPLETE SENTENCE

No.

There, see? Short, sweet, and deliciously to the point. Now, let's try it again, this time with a little flair. Go ahead and practice in front of a mirror if you need to.

No!

Maybe throw in a hand gesture or two for dramatic effect. We've all seen toddlers pull it off with conviction—now it's your turn.

This magical two-letter word seems elusive for many of us, like a unicorn or finding five minutes of quiet during nap time. And it's particularly tough for women. Why? Because somewhere along the way, some societies decided that women should always be polite and nurturing and say *"yes"* to everything. (Especially those of you lovely Enneagram Type 2 "Helpers"—your superpower is saying yes to every request within a five-mile radius. But it's okay, we'll fix that. See Chapter 1 for more about your lovely Type 2 tendencies.)

If saying "no" gives you the cold sweats, I've got a gentler solution for you: The Power of a Positive No. Think of it as the classy, diplomatic cousin to the blunt "no." It's also a sandwich. A "yes-no-yes" sandwich, to be exact, with the fluffiest artisan bread and just enough "no" in the middle to make your point without causing a scene.

Let me break it down:

1. *YES:* Start with a warm slice of agreement. Find common ground, even if it's something tiny. *"Yes, I see where you're coming from."* But don't stop there—give it a little meat! Show them you get it. Be specific, not vague, like *"Yes, and…"*

2. *NO:* Here's the spicy middle. State clearly what you won't be doing. No waffling, no meandering through excuses. Just a firm, polite *"No."* And don't feel pressured to provide a 10-minute explanation unless you really want to (or if they give you puppy eyes—watch out for that trick).

3. *YES:* Finish strong with a helpful suggestion (that, ideally, has nothing to do with you!). *"Yes, why don't you try this instead?"* It's like a parting gift they didn't expect, but it's really just a clever way to end the conversation on a positive note. You're helpful, but you're also free of that obligation.

Voilà! You've got yourself a "Positive No" sandwich. Now let's serve it up with some real-life examples:

- *Example 1:* Your boss asks you at 6:00 p.m. on a Friday to deliver a report by 8:00 a.m. Monday. (Cue internal groaning.) You say:
  "I understand how important the analysis is ('yes'). But I won't be able to work on it this weekend ('no'). How about I get it to you by 10 a.m. on Monday—does that work? ('yes')."

See? You acknowledged the need, said no to ruining your weekend, and then offered a compromise that doesn't involve pulling all-nighters. Genius!

- *Example 2:* Your preschooler wants to play in the street. (Cue internal gasp.)
  You say:
  "*Wow, what a fun idea to play outside* ('yes'). *But no, you may not play where the cars are whizzing by* ('no'). *How about playing in the backyard where your tricycle is the only thing speeding by?* ('yes')"

You acknowledged their desire for fun, said no to danger, and directed them to a safer option. Parenting win!

The beauty of the "*yes-no-yes*" framework is that it gets easier with practice. Start small—try it out when you're tempted to say yes, just to avoid conflict. You'll find that, over time, it saves you from agreeing to things you didn't want to do in the first place. And bonus: early testing ground includes your children, where you're the boss (well, for now). So go ahead, sharpen your "*no*" skills, and before you know it, you'll be handing out Positive No sandwiches like a pro!

E. A GENTLE WARNING ON TIMING

Maybe I should have put this warning right at the start of the book, but you know what they say: "*It's never too late to get started!*" or, as the proverb goes, "*The early bird catches the worm!*" (Though frankly, who decided worms were so desirable? Why not coffee or a cinnamon roll?)

Let me paint you two scenarios. Some of you may have picked up this book early—perhaps even before entering your third trimester. You've thoroughly read it, digested every bit of advice, and are well on your way to a smooth transition. If you're an Enneagram Type 3 Achiever (go back to Chapter 1 for a refresher), this is you. You've already color-coded your return-to-work plan, crafted your elevator pitch for flexible hours, and laminated a list of your daily affirmations. Bravo!

Then there's the rest of you. And listen, no shame here, we're all busy! Maybe you've decided to procrastinate the "what's next?" conversation, and you're pretending that maternity/paternity leave is an infinite abyss where time doesn't matter. You'll deal with all those questions "later," right? But there's no such thing as "later"—just an increasing pile of decisions waiting for you.

Photo credit: Maria Ivanova, Unsplash.com

Here's the thing. The reasons for procrastination usually boil down to two common culprits:

1. *"I don't want to think about it yet. I'm busy on my leave. I'll make a decision the week before I return."*

   Ah, the week before. If I had a dollar for every time I heard this, I could retire *myself* on maternity leave. The truth? The week before, reality smacks you in the face, and you're left scrambling for childcare, work arrangements, and a miracle.

2. *"Well, I'll just go along with whatever they expect when I get back and figure it out as I go."*
   Going with the flow sounds nice—until the flow feels more like a tidal wave of expectations. You've handed over control of your work life, and now you're surfing the dangerous waters of ambiguity with no life jacket in sight.

Both approaches are risky. If you don't think about what you truly want, if you don't find the confidence to ask for it, and if you let those boundaries blur into oblivion, things can turn ugly fast. Not just for you but also for your employer. Trust me, everyone will feel it.

So, here's the gentle nudge (or maybe more of a loving shove): don't bury your head in the sand. Lift it up, look ahead, and start having those conversations *now*. The sooner, the better. It's never too early to begin shaping your return to work. These conversations may evolve over time, but give yourself the gift of time to think, explore, and engage.

You may just be surprised by how many doors open when you show up with clarity and confidence. So go on, be that early bird (or at least a bird with a plan in hand). Your future self will thank you.

What Will Really Help You Thrive

In this chapter, we focus on the essential elements enabling you to flourish as you navigate the challenges of balancing work, family, and personal well-being. Thriving isn't just about surviving; it's about finding joy, fulfillment, and success in your professional and personal life.

This chapter delves into practical strategies and mindset shifts that can significantly impact your day-to-day life. We'll explore the importance of setting realistic expectations, creating supportive environments, and prioritizing self-care. In addition, we'll examine how to leverage your strengths, seek out resources, and build a network of support to help you overcome obstacles and achieve your goals.

Ultimately, this chapter is about empowering you to take control of your circumstances, make intentional choices, and cultivate the resilience and mindset needed to survive and truly thrive in all areas of your life. By applying these principles, you'll be better equipped to handle the inevitable challenges that come your way and to create a life that is both fulfilling and sustainable.

In this chapter we'll explore:

A. Outsource What Is Not a Priority

B. You Get What You Pay For

C. You Are Not Alone

D. Co-CEOs Divide, Conquer and Communicate

E. Experts: Avoid the Temptation to Take Over

F. Transition Week(S)

G. Plan for "Oh Crap"

H. Over Planning and Magical Thinking

I. I Don't Care what You Think of Me

J. Realize that Now Is Not Forever

A. OUTSOURCE WHAT IS NOT A PRIORITY

Ah, the great illusion of doing it all. For those of you who found your Enneagram selves to be the Achiever, Pleaser, Perfectionist, Thinker, or Stickler (see Chapter 1 for a reminder), you might still be clinging to the belief that you can juggle everything—work, parenting, self-care, home chores—with grace, a smile, and not a hair out of place. Let's go ahead and burst that bubble now: *You can't do it all.* Not without turning into a stressed-out octopus with a baby strapped to one of your many arms. (And even then, I bet your octopus-self would still struggle.)

The reality is, especially with a tiny human now demanding your attention, something's gotta give. So, the real question becomes: *What can you take off your plate?*

Remember those earlier chapters where you reflected on your Purpose, Values, and Priorities. Now, look at the *everyday grind*—the stuff you do every day, every week, every month, maybe even every year. How much of it is just sand and pebbles (see Chapter 5D "Protecting the Rocks" for a refresher)?

Remember the Urgent/Important matrix from your corporate days (or from Chapter 27B)? Chances are, your plate is full of "meh" tasks sitting on the lower-left side of that matrix, and you've got a huge baby-shaped boulder taking up prime real estate on the right.

It's time for some thoughtful jettisoning.

Let's be honest: you probably don't *need* to mow the lawn, scrub the house from top to bottom, do the grocery shopping, or whip up home-cooked meals every single day. If these tasks light up your soul and spark your joy, then great! They should stay on your plate. But it's time to outsource if they fall firmly into the "mundane" category. Yes, I said it. Outsource.

Most of us in senior executive positions have the flexibility (and the budget) to pay someone else to handle the things that drain us. And the Net Present Value (NPV) here is sky-high. Why? Because by outsourcing the mundane, you're freeing yourself up to focus on what truly matters—whether it's work, family, or simply activities that bring you joy.

Still not sure? Test it out for a month. Drop a task—say, cleaning the bathroom—and see how it feels. If you *truly* miss scrubbing toilets, you can always fire the cleaning service. But chances are, you won't.

And here's some space for you to jot down your own thoughts.

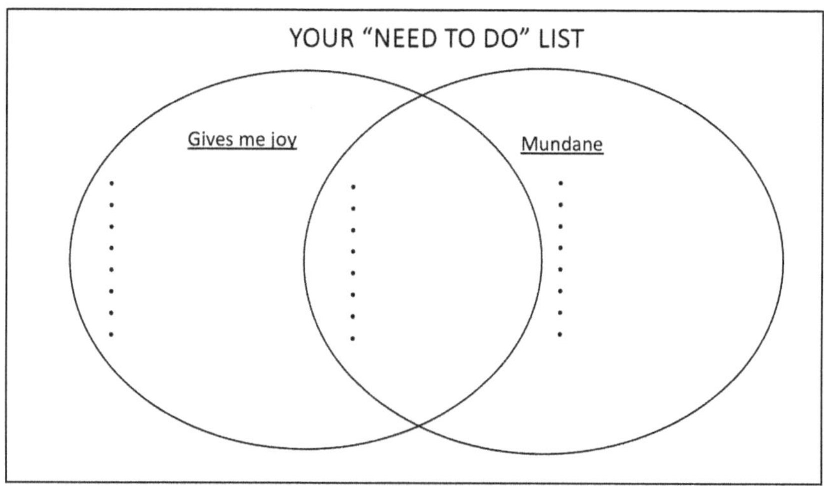

B. YOU GET WHAT YOU PAY FOR

Photo credit: Giorgio Trovato, Unsplash.com

Which brings me to the next point about outsourcing and support: the age-old wisdom, *"You get what you pay for."* And when it comes to something as crucial as childcare, this saying holds *especially* true.

Childcare costs can feel astronomical, and many of my clients find themselves balking at the price tag. But here's the thing: if you can afford to pay for premium support (and most of my clients can when they really sit down and crunch the numbers), then you can seriously consider doing it. I'm not going to tell you what type of childcare is best for you—that's a deeply personal decision, and the options are as varied as they are numerous: daycare, live-in nanny, live-out nanny, au pair, at-home spouse, and the list goes on.

Let me illustrate the point with a story about one of my clients, and you'll see exactly what I mean about getting what you pay for.

- *Plan A:* About a month before returning to work, "Jenny" and her partner decided that their best option was to hire a live-out nanny. They worked with a nanny agency to ensure a thorough screening process and cast a wide net. They offered a reasonable rate—$20 an hour—and created a thoughtful job description. Everything seemed to be going smoothly for the first month. Until it wasn't. One Friday evening, the nanny announced she was quitting, effective immediately. While she'd enjoyed working with them, she'd found a new position that offered better pay, fewer chores, and more predictable hours. Jenny and her husband were left dumbfounded—and scrambling. Panic mode had officially kicked in.

- *The Transition:* They frantically searched for a replacement over the weekend but found no suitable candidates. Jenny had a critical client workshop on Monday, and her husband, "Ben," had to use some last-minute vacation days to cover childcare. His boss wasn't thrilled, but it was their only option. By Wednesday, the agency found temporary help, but it was a revolving door of caregivers. Each new week brought someone new, and with that, the endless cycle of re-explaining routines, rules, and expectations. Jenny and Ben were stressed—*really* stressed. Their minds were constantly split between work and worrying about their daughter. Every hour, they were texting, checking in, and agonizing. Their daughter seemed perfectly fine, but the strain on Jenny and Ben was palpable.

- *Enter the backup cavalry: Mom.* Moms can be heroes and often swoop into the chaos (mine sure did, repeatedly, as did my aunts and best-friend-cousin). But let's be real—moms have lives, too, and not everyone is thrilled about the prospect of their mother-in-law moving in permanently (even the *best* of them). So, while Jenny and Ben appreciated the support, the stress was still simmering beneath the surface.

- *Plan B:* At their wits' end, Jenny and Ben decided to make a bold move: they upped the pay to $30 an hour. At first glance, that extra $10 might seem outrageous—an additional $400 a week, $20k a year! But when they really looked at their finances (and their combined $400k income), they realized it was less than five percent of their earnings. And guess what? Within 24 hours of posting the new pay rate, they had over a dozen qualified candidates. They interviewed six and could have happily hired three. They finally selected "Amanda," a standout who was incredibly qualified and aligned with their family's values and needs. Amanda has been with them for nearly two years, offering the stability they craved, the flexibility they needed, and peace of mind that allowed them to excel at work without worrying about sudden nanny resignations.

The best part? The bonuses they earned from excelling at work last year—work they could only focus on thanks to Amanda's stellar support—more than offset the higher cost of childcare. Not to mention the priceless value of their daughter's well-being and their sanity.

So, while I'm not here to tell you what to pay your nanny, I ask you to consider the true cost-benefit of quality support. Sometimes, we're quick to say, *"Oh, we can't afford that!"* But I challenge you to ask: *Can you afford not to?*

C. YOU ARE NOT ALONE

Navigating the journey of returning to work after becoming a parent can feel overwhelming, but it's important to remember that you don't have to do it alone. In fact, relying on the support systems around you—both at work and in life—can make all the difference. This section is designed to help you recognize and utilize the valuable resources available as you transition back into your professional role while managing the demands of a growing family. These include:

1. *Work Resources:* Learn how to effectively leverage your professional network, including sponsors, mentors, and peers, to support your career development and reentry into the workforce.

2. *Life Resources:* Discover the wealth of wisdom and support available from family, friends, and external resources to help you manage the challenges of balancing work and family life.

3. *Reading Recommendations:* Explore a curated list of books that other moms and dads have recommended for navigating pregnancy, early parenting, and the return-to-work journey.

4. *Double Safety Nets:* Prepare for the unexpected with strategies for creating contingency plans, ensuring that you have backup options in place for those inevitable surprises.

With these, you can build a strong foundation of support so you can confidently face the challenges of parenthood and career with the knowledge that help is always within reach.
Indeed, you are not alone!

1. Work Resources

There are many resources to help leaders lead within an organization.

All types provide valuable input; however, each role is explicitly different and should be clear in your mind. The four primary roles are highlighted below.

WORK SUPPORT RESOURCES

Sponsor	Advisor
A person who is <u>responsible</u> for, and <u>investing personal capital in</u> the actions, development, and career path of another.	*A person who helps another decide on or plan a course of <u>action</u> for a <u>particular topic</u> of their expertise.*
• Internal • Ongoing promotion • Vested support in success • Mutually beneficial to highlight the "good"	• Internal or external • Discrete soundbites • Incentives can be mutually intertwined • Personal opinion, "good or bad"

Mentor	Coach
A person who gives another advice on <u>actions</u> AND has the personal relevant expertise to tailor <u>career</u> advice.	*A person who dovetails their broad external perspective, with deep personal understanding, to guide another's <u>actions in life AND career path</u> choices.*
• Internal or external • Ongoing relationship • Incentives can be mutually intertwined • Full transparency (the "good" and the "bad")	• External • Holistic, integral "work" and "life" • Deeply personal relationship • Full transparency (the "good" and the "bad")

First, make a list of who provides each of your roles. Seriously, write them down.

Sponsors:____

Advisors: ____

Mentors: ____

Coaches: ____

Peers:____

Others: ____

Now think about what communications you have had with them recently. When did you last check in and say hello? Are you still top-of-mind with them?

- How can they help you?

- What can they share about anything that's shifted in your absence?

- Do they have any words of wisdom or advice for you?

- What might you be able to offer to support or help them?

- Have you set up a time to reconnect (live or virtually)? And what will your agenda be?

Think of it like a key stakeholder management plan. Communication is key. And people, at least nice people, are happy to help but won't unless they know how to be helpful, and you've set up time with them.

Key actions you will take, and by when:

____

____

____

____

____

____

2. Life Resources

There is so much wisdom, knowledge, and experience around us to support us working-outside-the-home parents. Not to mention the mistakes made and lessons learned from those who have journeyed the path before us. It's not like we're the first to navigate this.

Yet, we can sometimes get all caught up in our independence and a false belief that we can solve every problem ourselves. Why would anyone want to reinvent the wheel? Or spend time learning a skill that we are highly unlikely to ever want to use again, let alone enjoy (toilet cleaning, anyone?). There are experts out there for that.

Here are some examples of the types of *external resources* that are out there to support parents returning to work. It is not exhaustive, and I have no personal incentive to endorse any of the brands mentioned. It's simply that they are loved by more than one of my clients. What's on your list?

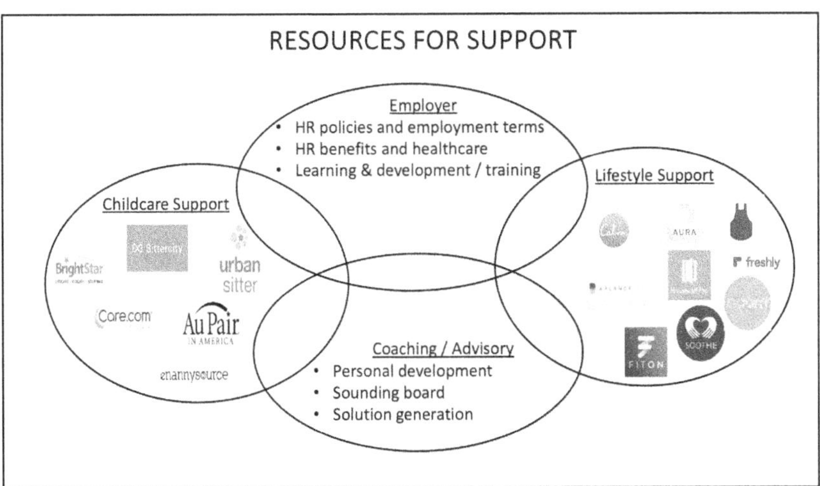

Take a moment to jot down what support resources you think might be helpful to you. Make a list; decide how/when/what to do to leverage them. Don't be shy. As the saying goes, "*It takes a village.*"

____

____

____

____

____

____

____

In addition, and often way more significantly and importantly, *friends and family* can provide support. Many of them have been through this return-to-work journey before us, and they can provide a wealth of support—both in terms of advice and experiences and in terms of just being there for you (and letting you grab a nap!). I was lucky enough to have both my mum and my cousin in residence for most of those early infant (sleep-depriving) days. In most cases, grandparents are highly enthusiastic volunteers who are more than willing to help out you, your partner, and your baby. Don't underestimate their helpfulness and value! Use them wisely, and clearly communicate what you need (and where your boundaries are). Review Chapter 17 A/B for more thoughts about scheduling and putting grandparents to work.

3. Reading Recommendations

Along the client-journey, I've heard (and checked out) many recommendations for favorite pregnancy and parenting books. I have no vested interest in any of them (and people look at me oddly when I read them in public since I am clearly not of an expecting age anymore).

Here's a list of pregnancy and early-parenting books my clients applaud as must-reads:

- *Expecting Better: Why the Conventional Pregnancy Wisdom Is Wrong—and What You Really Need to Know* by Emily Oster. Fantastic statistics, facts, and myth-busting!

- *Moms on Call* by Laura Hunter. Great book on schedules (and the logic behind them). A three-part series (0–6 months; 6–15 months; and 15 months to 4 years) of great wisdom on creating predictability (can anyone say "sleep schedules"?).

- *1000 Questions about Your Pregnancy: Everything Every Expecting Woman Needs to Know* by Dr. Jeffrey Thurston. Straightforward, humorous, and informative.

- *What to Expect When You're Expecting* by Heidi Murkoff. An oldie but updated classic. Even I read this during my first pregnancy (ahem…) 25+ years ago. At least it's not from the "Dr. Spock" era. (Ask your grandma about that if you haven't heard about him.)

- *What to Expect the First Year*—you guessed it, also by Heidi Murkoff!

4. Double Safety Nets

I'd like to highlight something here: Life is unpredictable, but babies are even more so. And the margin for error is a bit slimmer with newborns. The anxiety and guilt for "*getting it wrong*" can also be bigger and much more significant for you and for the baby.

I encourage you to think through the "what if?" scenarios, because if all kinds of things *can* happen, then the chances are pretty good that a few *will* happen. It's a fine line—I certainly don't want to encourage you to be a doomsday-imagining Chicken Little running around with your head cut off. But a little preparation and forethought can go a long way. Here are some examples:

- *If your nanny suddenly falls ill or quits, what will you do?* Is the first call to your friend or your mom? Is there a backup plan, or is the plan *you* (or your partner)?

- *If your little one were to get sick next week, who is going to stay home with them?* Consider sharing calendars and flex for who's on point for any contingency plan—well before it surprisingly happens.

- *If you'd like to have date night every Friday, do you have a permanent standing order for a sitter? How about a Sunday morning sitter, where you lounge in bed and the sitter takes the children out to an activity or to another room or floor?* You can always cancel with enough warning or pay for the option to have the unused availability

- *If one caretaker starts at noon, and the other ends at noon, does it make sense to build in a 15-minute overlap?* It may be better to have double coverage than no coverage.

You get the idea. Not to make anxious, scenario-planning worriers out of all of us. But what I have learned over the years is that if something *can* happen, it most likely *will* happen—you just don't know what and when. So, a little forethought goes a long way to preventing scrambling, disappointment, or disasters.

D. CO-CEOS DIVIDE, CONQUER AND COMMUNICATE

When you become parents, you and your partner are no longer just individuals or even just a couple—you are now the co-CEOs of "*Family, Inc.*" This concept reframes the responsibilities and challenges of family life as a shared leadership role, with both partners acting as equal leaders in the most important organization they will ever be part of. Just like in a corporation, Family, Inc. has its own Purpose, Mission, Values, and, of course, a new and very critical stakeholder—the latest addition to your family.

The Concept of Co-CEOs:

In any successful organization, the role of a CEO is to guide, lead, and make decisions that align with the company's mission and values. As co-CEOs of Family, Inc., you and your partner are responsible for jointly leading your family, ensuring that everything from daily logistics to long-term goals are managed with care and purpose. This partnership requires clear communication, mutual respect, and a shared vision for what you want your family to be and achieve.

The 70-70 Effort Principle:

One key to making this co-CEO model work is understanding that it's not about dividing tasks and responsibilities 50-50. Instead, think of it as a 70-70 effort. Each partner should feel like they are contributing more than their fair share, putting in 70% or more effort. If you strive to give more than 50%, you'll create a strong, supportive partnership where both feel fully invested. The reality is that one partner might need to shoulder more of the load some days, and on other days, it might be the opposite. However, the ongoing effort to go above and beyond fosters a sense of teamwork and shared responsibility that's essential for the health of your family dynamic. For more detail about key home, family, and financial role responsibilities, you can jump to Chapter 39— *"Is it Really 50-50?"*

Recognizing Invisible Work:

Much of the work that goes into running Family, Inc. is invisible, especially if one partner is at home full-time while the other is working outside the home. The partner at home may be handling countless tasks that go unnoticed—everything from managing the household schedule to caring for the child's needs, often without the breaks or social interactions a work environment might provide. Both partners must acknowledge and appreciate this invisible work.

Knowing Where 112 goes:

One way to maintain balance and ensure that the workload is distributed fairly is to regularly evaluate how you're both spending your time. The week has approximately 112 waking hours, assuming you sleep eight hours a night. How are those hours being used? Are both partners getting the time they need for personal activities, socializing, or simply relaxing? Here is some space to assess those hours:

<table>
<tr><td colspan="4" align="center">YOUR 112 HOURS</td></tr>
<tr><td><u>Activity</u></td><td><u>Current Hours</u></td><td><u>More or Less?</u></td><td><u>Quality</u>?</td></tr>
<tr><td>•</td><td></td><td></td><td></td></tr>
<tr><td>•</td><td></td><td></td><td></td></tr>
<tr><td>•</td><td></td><td></td><td></td></tr>
<tr><td>•</td><td></td><td></td><td></td></tr>
<tr><td>•</td><td></td><td></td><td></td></tr>
<tr><td>•</td><td></td><td></td><td></td></tr>
<tr><td>•</td><td></td><td></td><td></td></tr>
<tr><td>•</td><td></td><td></td><td></td></tr>
<tr><td>•</td><td></td><td></td><td></td></tr>
<tr><td>•</td><td></td><td></td><td></td></tr>
<tr><td>•</td><td></td><td></td><td></td></tr>
<tr><td>•</td><td></td><td></td><td></td></tr>
<tr><td>•</td><td></td><td></td><td></td></tr>
<tr><td>•</td><td></td><td></td><td></td></tr>
</table>

<table>
<tr><td colspan="4" align="center">YOUR PARTNER'S 112 HOURS</td></tr>
<tr><td><u>Activity</u></td><td><u>Current Hours</u></td><td><u>More or Less?</u></td><td><u>Quality</u>?</td></tr>
<tr><td>•</td><td></td><td></td><td></td></tr>
<tr><td>•</td><td></td><td></td><td></td></tr>
<tr><td>•</td><td></td><td></td><td></td></tr>
<tr><td>•</td><td></td><td></td><td></td></tr>
<tr><td>•</td><td></td><td></td><td></td></tr>
<tr><td>•</td><td></td><td></td><td></td></tr>
<tr><td>•</td><td></td><td></td><td></td></tr>
<tr><td>•</td><td></td><td></td><td></td></tr>
<tr><td>•</td><td></td><td></td><td></td></tr>
<tr><td>•</td><td></td><td></td><td></td></tr>
<tr><td>•</td><td></td><td></td><td></td></tr>
<tr><td>•</td><td></td><td></td><td></td></tr>
<tr><td>•</td><td></td><td></td><td></td></tr>
<tr><td>•</td><td></td><td></td><td></td></tr>
</table>

Practical Suggestions for Balance:

1. *Weekly Check-In*: Schedule a weekly "*What Do I Need and Want to Do?*" check-in, where both partners can express what they need in terms of time, help, or emotional support. This open communication can help prevent resentment and ensure both partners get what they need to thrive.

2. *Sanity Check on Sleep*: Keep an eye on who consistently gets to bed first. If one partner is winding down with social media while the other is still folding laundry or doing dishes late at night, it's a sign that something might be out of balance. Adjusting the distribution of tasks can help both partners get the rest they need.

3. *Equal Opportunity for Breaks:* Make sure that both partners can step out of the house, grab coffee with friends, or take a break. This might mean scheduling specific times when the at-home partner can have some time to themselves while the other takes over childcare or household duties.

By embracing the co-CEO model, committing to the 70-70 effort principle, and recognizing invisible work you and your partner can build a strong, balanced, and resilient family dynamic.

It's not always easy, and there will be times when things feel overwhelming, but you can lead Family, Inc. to thrive by continuously communicating, adjusting, and supporting each other.

E. EXPERTS: AVOID THE TEMPTATION TO TAKE OVER

Ah, the joys of new parenthood! It's a beautiful, messy, and sometimes downright confusing time for both parents. But what happens when one parent—let's call them the "Expert"—has significantly more experience with the newborn? Maybe they've spent more time at home during those first few weeks, or maybe they've just gotten the hang of things a little quicker. Either way, there's a tendency for the Expert to step in and "fix" every problem, leaving the less experienced parent feeling like they're just along for the ride.

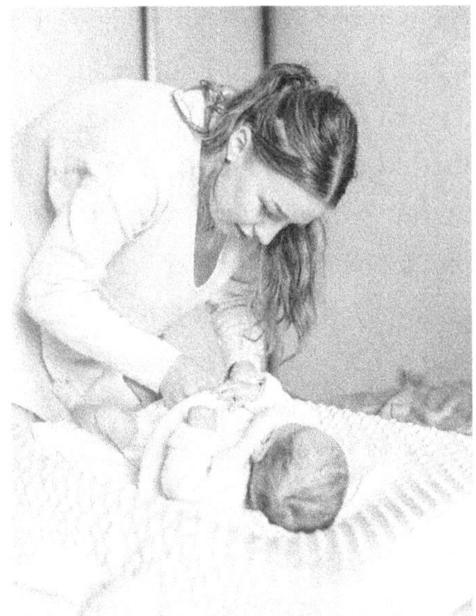

Photo credit: Daiga Ellaby, Unsplash.com

Let's be clear: we're not saying the Expert cannot make suggestions. By all means, share your wisdom! But when the Expert swoops in to take over every time the less experienced parent is fumbling through a diaper change or struggling to get the baby to sleep, it can have some unintended consequences. Suddenly, what started as a well-meaning attempt to help can turn into a situation where only one parent feels confident enough to handle certain tasks—and that's not good for anyone.

Take the classic case of diaper changing. Picture this: the newbie parent bravely attempts to wrangle a squirming, wailing baby into a clean diaper. Things are going okay-ish—sure, there's some mess, a little confusion about which end is up, and a lot of second guessing—but they're getting there. Enter the Expert, who can't bear to watch another second of this chaotic scene. They step in, take over, and change the diaper in record time, with barely a drop of baby goo out of place.

But what happens next? Now feeling like a bumbling fool, the newbie parent is likely to defer all future diaper changes to the Expert. "*You're so much better at it,*" they might say, "*I'll just let you handle it.*" And just like that, the division of labor becomes a little more lopsided, and one parent feels less capable.

Here's the thing: a few dirty messes aren't going to kill anyone. Sure, it might take the newbie parent a few tries to get it right, but that's how we all learn, isn't it? By stepping back and letting the less experienced parent find their own way, the Expert is actually doing their partner—and their relationship—a huge favor. They're giving them the space to build confidence, develop their own techniques, and even make a few mistakes along the way.

Plus, sometimes those "mistakes" are pretty hilarious. Like when the diaper ended on backward, or a simple burping session turned into a full-on milk fountain. As messy as they are, these moments are all part of the learning process. And who knows? The newbie parent might just discover a genius diapering hack that the Expert never even considered.

So, Experts, take a deep breath and step back. Let your partner get in there, get messy, and figure it out. It might not be perfect, but that's okay. Parenting is a team sport, and the best teams know how to let every player find their groove. Before you know it, the newbie parent will be an Expert, too—and you'll both be sharing the joys and challenges of parenthood equally. After all, the more hands on deck, the smoother the sailing will be, even if that deck occasionally gets covered in spit-up and baby powder.

F. TRANSITION WEEK(S)

Photo credit: Getty Images, Unsplash.com

The week one partner returns to work after parental leave is a significant adjustment period for the entire family. Here we will explore how the non-transitioning parent—whether they are already back at work or still on leave—can support their partner's return to the workforce. While some strategies apply universally, others are tailored to the specific situation of the non-transitioning parent.

Common Strategies for Both Scenarios:
Regardless of whether the non-transitioning parent is already back at work or still on leave, several approaches can help support the partner returning to work:

- *Increased Household Responsibilities:* Taking on more household tasks—such as cooking, cleaning, laundry, and errands—can significantly reduce stress for the transitioning parent, allowing them to focus on their work responsibilities without the added pressure of managing the home.

- *Emotional Support and Communication:* Create space each day to check in with your partner about how their day went. Focus on both the logistical aspects of their return and, importantly, their emotional well-being. Ask how they feel about the transition, what challenges they're encountering, and how you can support them more effectively.

- *Special Gestures:* Planning small surprises, such as a special dinner or a relaxing evening activity, can provide much-needed comfort and show your partner their efforts are appreciated. These gestures can remind them that they are not alone in navigating this transition.

- *Maintaining Routine and Stability:* Ensuring that routines at home remain as stable as possible can help the transitioning parent feel more secure as they navigate the changes at work. Consistency in the baby's schedule, household rhythms, and daily activities can provide a sense of normalcy and balance.

Unique Strategies for When the Non-Transitioning Parent is Still on Leave:

If the non-transitioning parent is still on leave, they have a unique opportunity to provide additional support:

- *Full-Time Management of Household and Childcare:* With more time available, the non-transitioning parent can take on full responsibility for household management and childcare during the workday. This allows the returning parent to focus entirely on their job without worrying about what's happening at home.

- *Facilitating the Transition:* The non-transitioning parent can prepare everything the returning parent might need for their workday, from packing lunches to ensuring their work clothes are ready to making sure the car's gas tank is full. This can help the returning parent start their day smoothly and minimize stress.

- *Creating a Calming Home Environment:* Ensuring the home remains peaceful and stress-free can help the transitioning parent unwind after a long day. The non-transitioning parent can create a welcoming atmosphere by keeping the house tidy, preparing a favorite meal, or setting up a relaxing evening routine.

Unique Strategies for When the Non-Transitioning Parent is Already Back at Work:

For the non-transitioning parent who has already returned to work, there are different challenges and opportunities:

- *Prioritizing Quality Time*: Since both parents are now balancing work and family responsibilities, it's important to prioritize quality time together. This could mean scheduling evenings or weekends to focus solely on family activities, ensuring both parents feel connected and supported.

- *Lightening the Workload at Home:* The non-transitioning parent can adjust their work schedule to help more at home. For example, scheduling fewer late meetings, minimizing travel, or even taking a half-day off can allow more time for family responsibilities, reducing the burden on the transitioning parent.

- *Supporting the Transition Back to Work*: The non-transitioning parent, already accustomed to balancing work and home, can share insights or strategies that worked for them. This can include tips on managing time effectively, setting boundaries at work, or maintaining energy throughout the day.

Whether the non-transitioning parent is still on leave or has already returned to work, their role during the transition week(s) is crucial in supporting their partner's return to the workforce. By stepping up with practical help, emotional support, and thoughtful gestures, both parents can navigate this adjustment period together, ensuring a smoother and more positive experience for the entire family.

G. PLAN FOR "OH CRAP"

Photo credit: Valeriia Miller, Unsplash.com

No matter how meticulously you plan, life has a way of throwing curveballs that can derail even the most carefully laid-out plans. Here, we will explore some big and small challenges that can pop up, leaving you feeling overwhelmed, scared, or simply wondering, *"What do I do now?"* While these moments can be daunting, having a plan in place for when things go sideways can make all the difference.

Big Challenges:

1. *The Nanny Quits Unexpectedly:* One of the most common "oh crap" moments for working parents is when their trusted nanny suddenly quits, leaving them scrambling to find childcare. The sudden loss of a nanny can create a major disruption, whether due to illness, family emergencies, or a career change. It's crucial to have a backup plan in place, whether that's a list of trusted babysitters, a temporary daycare option, or a network of friends and family who can step in during the interim.

2. *Both Partners Are Scheduled to Travel:* In dual-career households, it's not uncommon for both partners to face overlapping travel schedules. This can create significant stress as you try to figure out who will care for the children while both parents are away. To mitigate this, consider coordinating travel schedules well in advance, utilizing grandparents or other family members, or even enlisting the help of a live-in nanny or au pair for those particularly busy weeks. Some clients use a "first on the calendar" takes priority approach. Others use the every-other-week, or the assigned travel days of the week approach. When both partners have Executive Assistants, they can be particularly helpful in coordinating between themselves before meetings are set in stone.

3. *A Child Gets Sick:* Few things throw a wrench in your plans like a sick child. Whether it's a minor illness or something more serious, a sick child often requires one parent to stay home, cancel meetings, or rearrange their work schedule. Having a contingency plan, such as flexible work arrangements or a shared sick day plan between partners, can help manage these situations without too much disruption.

4. *Workplace Emergencies:* Sometimes, the "oh crap" moment comes from work itself—whether it's an urgent project that suddenly demands your full attention, a crisis that requires immediate travel, or an unexpected layoff. In these cases, having a support network at home is critical, as is open communication with your employer about your boundaries and needs during family emergencies.

5. *Family Emergencies:* Beyond the immediate household, extended family emergencies—such as a parent or in-law falling ill—can require immediate attention and disrupt your daily routine. It's essential to discuss with your partner how you'll handle such situations in advance, including who will take time off, how you'll manage your children's needs, and how you'll support each other through the emotional and logistical challenges.

Smaller Challenges:

- *Unforeseen School Closures:* Snow days, teacher strikes, or unexpected school closures can catch you off guard and leave you scrambling for childcare. Keep a list of backup options, like emergency childcare services or neighbors who can help in a pinch.

- *Last-Minute Work Demands:* Whether it's an unexpected deadline or a late-night request from your boss, these smaller yet still stressful, work demands can disrupt your carefully balanced schedule. Practice setting boundaries where possible and consider whether certain tasks can wait until after your child's bedtime or be delegated.

- *Minor Health Issues:* Things like a child's minor cold or a bout of teething can still throw off your routine, even if they don't require a full day off. Having some flexibility in your workday, such as the ability to work from home, can help you manage these smaller disruptions without too much stress.

- *Household Mishaps:* From a burst pipe to a broken appliance, household mishaps tend to happen at the worst possible times. Maintaining a list of reliable repair services and having a financial buffer for emergency repairs can ease the stress when these things occur.

Planning for the Unexpected:
While it's impossible to predict every "oh crap" moment, the key to managing them is flexibility and preparation. Start by acknowledging that these challenges are inevitable and build a network of support—whether it's a list of backup caregivers, flexible work arrangements, or a strong partnership with your spouse. Communication is also crucial; regularly discussing potential challenges with your partner can help you stay aligned and ready to tackle whatever comes your way.

Remember, these moments, while stressful, are a normal part of life. By planning and remaining adaptable, you can navigate these challenges with resilience and ensure that your family stays on track, even when things don't go as planned.

H. OVERPLANNING AND MAGICAL THINKING

Overplanning: The Best-Laid Plans

Photo credit: Patrycja Jadach, Unsplash.com

Parenthood is an adventure filled with unexpected twists and turns, and while it's natural to want to plan every detail, the reality is that even the best-laid plans are likely to be derailed. This book offers a wealth of advice on preparing for your new role as a parent, from coordinating schedules to navigating your return to work. However, it's crucial to recognize that sticking rigidly to "the plan" is neither realistic nor beneficial. Parenting requires flexibility, the ability to go with the flow, and a willingness to adapt to the ever-changing needs of your newborn and the environment around you.

As new parents, you may find yourself meticulously crafting a plan for every aspect of your baby's life—feeding schedules, sleep routines, childcare arrangements—but it's important to remember that babies are unpredictable. They have their own rhythms and needs, which don't always align with your carefully constructed plans. Instead of becoming frustrated when things don't go as expected, embrace the unpredictability of this journey. Allow yourself to adjust, change course, and find new solutions that work for you and your family. The key is to approach planning with a mindset that values adaptability over perfection, understanding that your ability to pivot and respond to the realities of parenthood is just as important as any plan you put in place.

Magical Thinking: Reclaiming Imagination

Photo credit: Chris Nagahama, Unsplash.com

When we start dating, conversations often flow with a sense of limitless possibility. One partner might dream aloud about having a "castle in the sky," and the other eagerly adds to the fantasy, imagining unicorns and luxurious furnishings filling this magical space. This type of "magical thinking" fosters creativity, connection, and a shared sense of wonder. However, as the responsibilities of life—and especially parenting—take center stage, these imaginative exchanges are often replaced by more pragmatic concerns.

With the transition to parenthood, it's easy to fall into a pattern where practicalities dominate your conversations. Once filled with dreams and playful imaginings, date nights may now revolve around two main topics: the baby and the household. Discussions become focused on the next pediatrician appointment, the latest baby milestone, or how to manage the household budget. While these conversations are necessary, they can also crowd out the joyful, imaginative exchanges that once brought so much lightness and fun into your relationship.

To counter this, consider reintroducing magical thinking into your relationship. Plan a date night with two simple rules: no talk about children and no talk about the home. Use this time to reconnect with the imaginative, dream-building conversations that once defined your relationship. Let yourselves dream wildly again, even if just for an evening. What fantastical ideas can you come up with together? What dreams can you reignite that have been pushed aside by the demands of daily life?

By allowing space for magical thinking, you're nurturing your relationship and reminding yourselves of the importance of keeping creativity and wonder alive, even amidst the responsibilities of parenthood. This balance between practical planning and imaginative dreaming can help sustain your relationship, making the parenting journey not just a series of tasks and plans but a shared adventure filled with possibility.

I. I DON'T CARE WHAT YOU THINK OF ME

This one was a touchy topic for me for quite a while (and it took me a while to realize it). As an Enneagram Type 3 Achiever, I always pushed myself to be the best, fastest, and most spectacular. I had way overachieved academically (skipping three grades of school, graduating from college as one of three female Genetic Engineering majors at age 20, earning a Harvard MBA with Distinction), and then in my career (coveted Procter & Gamble Brand Manager, then Boston Consulting Group consulting career, culminating in becoming Managing Director & Partner, fast-tracked, and transferred between four offices, Lead Officer for the global Organization and Consumer Practice areas). Not to brag but to share the track record and expectations I had set for myself.

And so it was that I found myself walking through the cafeteria of BCG's Chicago office, having recently been promoted to Manager in the New York office, and getting ready to kick off a major global acquisition piece of work for a top consumer packaged goods client. On a roll and feeling awesome! Having taken two maternity leaves (three months and seven months) and worked in various part-time and full-time capacities over the previous three years, I felt comfortable in my fast-track but different-track trajectory. Although "behind time" in elapsed years and months (and a full cycle behind my peer cohort), I was actually "fast-tracking" it from a full-time equivalent of months of tenure.

Then I heard them—huddled together at a table in the cafeteria: the team that was to become my new hot-shot A-team to tackle this challenging case. The scene went something like this: *"Well, I heard she may not be very good because she's really behind on the promotion track. She's been here for over five years, and she only just made Manager. I hope we're not in for incompetence here. Those people are a nightmare to work with."* I just about imploded. Well, I didn't, but I did go to the restroom and have a good cry. A really good one. The injustice! The unfairness! My ego was crushed with the knowledge that others thought I wasn't a superstar.

I got over that one (the case went well). But I still got that jealous sinking of the stomach as I watched my peer group get elevated to the next level up—and then even two levels up from where I appeared to be stagnated. It was irritating. Then, it was downright annoying when someone who had worked for me a couple of years back was suddenly my boss. Huh? Wow, reality check. Ego blow!

At some point, though, I had an epiphany and changed my perspective. I knew the truth. My career development and promotion advisors knew the truth. And in most ways, it didn't matter what other people thought about my career track. In fact, most people don't even think about my career track, except perhaps in passing.

When I really stopped and thought about it, I was on the amazingly fast track of life. My life. I had made choices that made the most sense for me, and I was loving my life. Others who had made different parent-path choices and continued flat-out in their careers may have looked like superstars. However, they were often saddened by the role they were able to play in raising their children and being a real part of their family.

So, if you plan to work anything less than full-time, be prepared to put your career progress in the context of your life context—what your Purpose, Values, and Priorities lead you to know what you want and choose to do.

Oh, and don't forget to put your ego in check!

J. REALIZE THAT NOW IS NOT FOREVER

Photo credit: Paul Campbell, Unsplash.com

Unlike diamonds, maternity leave and return-to-work plans are not forever. They are not hard, cold, set-in-stone plans that will last a lifetime. They are flexible, adaptable, and subject to change. Life has a funny way of throwing curveballs—unexpected opportunities, challenges, or even a change in perspective as you settle into your new role as a parent. If you try to plan out the next decade of your career and personal life with rigid precision, you'll quickly find yourself overwhelmed by the countless variables and unknowns.

So, give yourself a break. Instead of getting bogged down in long-term projections, focus on what works for you and your family today. What feels right for the next three, six, or twelve months? Yes, it's important to consider the impact of today's decisions on your future goals, but it's equally important to avoid getting paralyzed by the "what-ifs." Sometimes, thinking "just for now" is not only more manageable but also more realistic.

When discussing your return to work, it's helpful to frame the conversation in the context of the immediate future—the first few months back, for instance. The non-negotiables you have while your child is an infant, such as limiting travel or needing flexible hours, are often temporary. Your needs and priorities will evolve as your child grows and as you adjust to the new dynamics of balancing work and family life.

Employers are often more amenable to accommodating your needs when they know these requests aren't permanent. For example, it's easier for an employer to agree to a "no travel" policy for the first six months after your return than to commit indefinitely. By framing your needs as part of a phased approach, you allow room for future adjustments that reflect your changing circumstances and help maintain a positive dialogue with your employer.

Remember, the plan you set today is not forever. It's a flexible, living document that can and should be revised as needed. Your return to work, much like parenting itself, is a journey that will unfold in its own time and rhythm. So, take a deep breath, embrace the fluidity of the situation, and give yourself the grace to adjust. After all, flexibility is one of the most valuable skills in both parenting and career management.

The Caregiver's Operating Manual of You

Photo credit: Kelly Sikkema, Unsplash.com

This chapter is for parents who employ a caregiver in their home. When it comes to entrusting the care of your children to someone else, whether it's a nanny, daycare provider, or even a grandparent, having clear expectations is key.

As table stakes, the typical (basic) contracts I've seen can range from two to as many as ten pages. They usually contain most of these "basic" elements:

- *Employment Dates*

- *Hours and Schedule* (minimum, maximum, average; fixed vs variable)

- *Job Responsibilities/Duties/Expectations* (childcare, home care, meals, pet care)

- *Live-in / Overnight arrangements* (space, boundaries, cleanliness, use of property)

- *Compensation* (base; over-time; bonus)

- *Benefits* (e.g., health care, club memberships, food, sick pay)

- *Taxes/Deductions* (payment method, deductions, timing)

- *Automobile* (use of for work/personal; insurance coverage; mileage/gas reimbursement; cellphone & GPS use)

- *Expense Reimbursement and Credit Card Use* (limits, approvals)

- *Vacation/Personal/Bad Weather/Statutory Days/Holidays*

- *Training/Health* (CPR, First Aid, Flu/Covid Shot, Vision tests, smoking, alcohol, use of masks, dress codes, cleanliness)

- *Termination* (with and without cause; severance; notice terms; return of property)

- *Confidentiality*

- *Technology* (use and posting on social media, TV, texting/phone calls)

- *Monitoring* (electronic surveillance – disclosure (or not) of location and access)

- *Approvals* (outside-home activities, guest visitors, expenses)

- *Background, references, and qualification checks*

- *Performance Reviews & Salary Increases*

- *Trial periods* (at the beginning of the contract)

- *Signatures* (notarized)

But beyond providing this basic contract, families often overlook the importance of creating an even more comprehensive document—the "Caregiver's Operating Manual of You." It is a separate document that captures your family values, communication style, routines, and emergency plans. It also creates a team-oriented environment where caregivers are empowered to align with how your family operates, ensuring a consistent and nurturing experience for your children.

Let's dive into ten essential components that make up this guide and why each piece is crucial for harmonious caregiving:

1. *Family Values: The Heart of Your Home*

   » Every family operates with a set of values, whether they're explicitly stated or not. These values shape how you parent, how you communicate, and what you prioritize in daily life. Do you value creativity, education, respect for others, or a strong work ethic? Is kindness a core value in your household? Do you have cultural or religious considerations? These pillars guide how your children are raised, and your caregiver should understand them.

   » By sharing your family's core values, you empower your caregiver to align their actions and interactions with your children accordingly. This way, they can reinforce the same messages and lessons you want to instill in your kids, creating consistency even when you're not around.

2. *Daily Routines: A Blueprint for Success*

    » Children thrive on routine, and sharing your family's daily schedule ensures a smoother transition when someone else steps in to help. In this section of the manual, outline your typical daily routines, including wake-up times, mealtimes, nap schedules, playtime, and bedtime routines.

    » A predictable schedule offers structure for the caregiver and your children, fostering a sense of security. Be as detailed as you can, particularly with rituals that are meaningful to your family—whether it's reading a story at nap time or a specific way you wind down the day.

3. *Communication Expectations: Keeping Everyone in the Loop*

    » Effective communication between you and your caregiver is crucial for trust and transparency. Be clear about how and when you expect updates on your children. Would you prefer daily check-ins, a text message after meals, or only reports when there's an issue? Clarify if you expect these updates at certain times (e.g., after naps) or on specific platforms (e.g., text, email, or an app).

    » Consider setting up an "end-of-week wrap-up," where the caregiver can recap the week: what went well, any challenges, developmental milestones, or upcoming plans. This allows for a healthy exchange of feedback and allows both sides to adjust as needed.

4. *Food Guidelines: What's on the Menu?*

   » One of the most important parts of caregiving is ensuring that your children are eating well. In this section, provide clear guidelines about your family's approach to food. Are there any allergies or intolerances the caregiver should be aware of? Do you prefer organic food, minimal sugar, or balanced meals? Include a list of preferred snacks and meals and consider offering a sample weekly meal plan for added guidance.

   » For older children, you may want to provide insights on encouraging healthy eating habits—whether you use rewards, praise, or allow children to make their own choices within limits.

5. *Emergency Protocols, Health & Safety: Staying Secure and Prepared for the Unexpected*

   » No one wants to think about emergencies, but being prepared is essential. This section should clearly outline emergency contacts, medical information, and instructions for dealing with unexpected situations. Ensure your caregiver knows where to find critical items like first-aid kits, medications, allergy-related items, and emergency phone numbers. Also, provide the pediatrician's contact information and any relevant health insurance details in case of an emergency.

   » Include a clear action plan for different scenarios. What should they do if your child gets sick, has an allergic reaction, or needs to be picked up unexpectedly? What should they do in case of a minor injury? How should they respond in more serious emergencies? Provide clear action plans for each situation and ensure they know who to contact first (whether it's you, your partner, or another trusted family member) and where they should go for medical assistance.

6. *Fun Activities and Enrichment: Keeping Kids Engaged*

   » Beyond the practical side of caregiving, providing ideas for activities that align with your family's values and your children's interests is helpful. Whether it's a list of favorite games, outings to local parks, or art projects that stimulate creativity, offering suggestions shows that you care about your child's enrichment.

   » If you have guidelines for screen time or preferred outdoor activities, this is the place to share them. A caregiver who knows your child's favorite activities will be better equipped to create positive experiences that support their development.

7. *Defining Boundaries: Balancing Flexibility and Structure*

   » It's important to define where flexibility is allowed, and structure must remain firm. Are there non-negotiable rules in your home, like no TV after a certain time or a strict bedtime? Are there areas where you're willing to allow the caregiver some freedom, such as choosing an afternoon activity or managing behavior during a playdate?

   » Setting clear boundaries empowers your caregiver to make decisions confidently while still adhering to your core principles. This balance ensures that your children are well cared for and your values are upheld, even in your absence.

8. *Extended Family and Trusted Contacts: Your Support Network*

   » Your caregiver needs to know who else is in your family's circle. This section of the manual should include a brief description of the extended family, starting with you and your partner. Share where you work, your typical hours, and any regular commitments you have that might affect your availability. Then, provide details on key members of your extended family, such as grandparents or close family friends who may be involved in caregiving or emergency situations.

   » In addition, list trusted friends and neighbors who can serve as backup contacts in case you can't be reached. Be sure to include their names, phone numbers, and relationship to your family. This network can provide extra peace of mind for both you and your caregiver.

9. *Your Home and the Neighborhood: Navigating Daily Life*

   » Familiarity with your home and surrounding area is important for any caregiver. This section outlines key information about your home—where important items like the first-aid kit, fire extinguisher, and cleaning supplies are kept. You may also want to include instructions for operating household appliances, security systems, or anything unique to your home's setup.

   » Also, provide a guide to your neighborhood. Are there nearby parks or play areas you recommend? List places to go for fun activities with the kids, from museums and libraries to local playgrounds or nature trails. If your caregiver will be driving, include any car seat or driving guidelines that are important for your family

10. *How We Work as a Team: Communication and Collaboration*

» To foster a successful caregiving relationship, it's important to emphasize teamwork and ongoing communication. Set aside time for a regular "team check-in," ideally at the end of each week, where you and your caregiver can reflect on the past week, discuss what worked well, and address any challenges. This check-in can be an opportunity to set goals for the coming week, share feedback, and ensure everyone is on the same page.

» Encourage openness and honesty from both sides. The caregiver should feel comfortable expressing any concerns or questions, and you should offer feedback in a way that supports growth and understanding. This ongoing dialogue helps keep expectations clear and ensures your children receive the best care possible.

» In this section, outline the structure for these team check-ins. Do you want to focus on milestones and routines or emotional well-being and development? Are there specific goals you want to prioritize, such as introducing new activities or focusing on a particular developmental area? Planning these discussions creates a collaborative environment where both parties feel heard and supported.

Putting It All Together

The "Caregivers Operating Manual of You" is not just about making sure the chores get done. It's about aligning the caregiver's actions with the way you parent—your values, routines, and expectations. It's about making sure that, even in your absence, your children experience a consistent environment reflecting the essence of your family life.

Creating this document may feel like a lot of work, but it is an investment in peace of mind. It gives your caregiver the tools they need to confidently care for your children in a way that feels right to you. Most importantly, it creates a shared understanding, ensuring your children receive the same love, attention, and guidance you provide, no matter who is in charge for the day.

In the end, the more comprehensive you are in creating this manual, the more likely you are to feel at ease, knowing that your children are in good hands—ones that care not only for their physical well-being but for the spirit of your home.

THE TRUTHS ABOUT RETURNING TO WORK

As you prepare to re-enter the workforce after parental leave, you're entering a phase filled with excitement and challenges. This Part, "The Truths About Returning to Work," delves into the realities you'll encounter as you navigate the complexities of balancing your career with your new role as a parent. It's not just about getting back to your desk—it's about re-establishing your professional identity while managing the changes in your personal life.

In this part, we'll explore the importance of setting boundaries and how we often are our worst enemies in enforcing them. You'll learn why even successful people fear failure and how to overcome that fear by embracing the idea that excellence doesn't equate to perfection. We'll discuss the critical skill of emotional regulation and how maintaining your cool can make all the difference in high-stress situations.

Returning to work after an extended leave can feel like dusting off cobwebs, trying to regain momentum. We'll address this challenge, offering strategies to help you shake off the rust and re-engage with your professional life. The chapter on "The New Homecoming" will guide you through the emotional and logistical adjustments that come with reintegrating into your work environment.

But it doesn't stop there—sustaining your energy, focus, and work-life balance is key to long-term success. We'll explore how to keep the momentum going once you're back in the swing of things.

Finally, we'll leave you with some "Inspirational Quotes and Words of Wisdom"—nuggets of encouragement and insight to carry with you as you continue to navigate the dual worlds of career and parenthood.

This part of the journey is about facing the truths of returning to work with honesty, resilience, and a mindset ready to embrace the challenges and rewards ahead.

33. Boundaries: Your Own Worst Enemy

34. Successful People Fear Failure

35. Excellence Is Not Perfection

36. Emotional Regulation

37. Cobwebs

38. The New Homecoming

39. Is It Really 50-50?

40. Sustaining It

41. Ready for Round 2?

42. Inspirational Quotes and Words of Wisdom

Boundaries:
Your Own Worst Enemy

Photo credit: Robert Linder, Unsplash.com

Whose boundary is it, anyway? It's yours. Employers have far less incentive to hold the boundary than you do. After all, it's your life!

We all set boundaries (implicitly or explicitly) with work, children, partners, and many others.

Work boundaries often come down to the three underlying drivers of work/life balance highlighted in Chapter 29C. Recall:

- *Sustainability:* how many hours, on average, we will designate for "work."

- *Predictability:* how often work plans change, and with what kind of warning.

- *Flexibility:* how much traditional "work hours" can flex to accommodate non-work-related needs.

Most of us, either explicitly or intuitively, are weighing and drawing those lines with our employers. Employers have recently become much more receptive to accommodating requests if we have the courage to find our voice and ask for whatever it is that will work for us.

Setting boundaries with employers (both hard, like a concrete wall, and soft, like a strand of yellow warning tape) is often the easy part.

The tricky part is setting and maintaining boundaries with ourself. Yup, the person sitting right here with us. We define boundaries, get buy-in from our work teams. And then choose to run into or step over them ourself.

- Sometimes, it's *fear* of repercussions (like promotion-track timing).

- Sometimes it's just spontaneous *excitement* in the moment (like a super-engaging problem to finish analyzing at midnight).

- Sometimes it's just *neglect* (it creeps up, we ignore it, and somehow, some day, we lift our heads and realize we've drifted from our own intent).

So, the big question is: What are you doing to keep *yourself* in check?!

Successful People Fear Failure

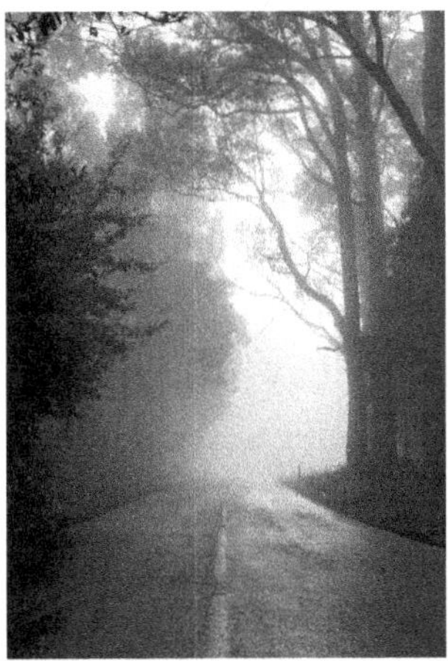

Photo credit: Michael Mouritz, Unsplash.com

We've all heard the term "fear of failure." But have you ever really thought about it for yourself?

What makes successful people successful is that, well, they've been successful. Top of Class, A-Performer, risen to the top, accelerated progression, a Superstar, a High Performance/High Potential Rising Star. All good stuff.

But what many hyper-successful people have not contemplated is that they are often not good at failure. They have pretty limited experience with it. They don't know how to handle the setbacks that other mere mortals may have experienced often (!) during their rise to midlevel management.

How many of our top leaders typically encounter career trials and tribulations—and *failure* (gasp)? How many of us failed and failed and failed again and then rose to the top? Not many. It's not that some amazing examples aren't out there, but, as a whole, our top leaders have limited experience with the big F-word: Failure.

High performers sometimes discover that they can be quite risk averse and actually fear failure. They don't put themselves in positions where failure is a real outcome. They would rather steer the ship slow and steady than place a big bet or take a chance. They would rather not try a new activity or hobby that they're not experienced with or good at because they might not look perfect in their attempts to learn. Someone might laugh at them. So they miss out on a lot of growth and a lot of fun.

You're about to enter into a whole new territory—parenting. And there will be failures, missteps, and bumps along the road. Both in your work and in your life. And that's OK! It's hard to imagine real growth without any failure. If you never fail, you're probably not really pushing your growth edge.

What's your fear-of-failure factor? What have you tried recently that you're not likely to succeed at and might even look silly doing? It's OK to fail. In fact, it can be liberating.

Hopefully, you will have some (not too traumatic) failures. Because if you don't, you're unlikely to truly be exploring life along your journey.

> *What would you do if you knew you could not fail?*
> —Robert H. Schuller

Excellence Is Not Perfection

Photo credit: Matthew Schwartz, Unsplash.com

"Excellence is the result of caring more than others think is wise, risking more than others think is safe, dreaming more than others think is practical, and expecting more than others think is possible."

A poster of a soaring eagle, with that inspirational inscription by Ronnie Oldham, has hung on my office wall for decades.

Striving for excellence is very aspirational and keeps us on our growth edge. However, the quest for excellence does not imply the quest for perfection. We hyper-achiever types often push ourselves to do it all. To make it perfect. To answer everything. We, of course, want to keep moving forward with agility and speed. However, the cost of getting the last 10% perfect, or even more the cost of getting the last 1% perfect, can be very high. It can sap our energy away from other activities and indulgences that delight us.

So, next time you are pushing yourself for Excellence, take a moment to pause and ask yourself whether you are actually pushing for unnecessary (and costly) perfection.

Emotional Regulation

Big transitions like becoming a new parent or returning to work after a leave are not for the faint of heart. It can be an emotional roller coaster of feelings. Expect it, roll with it, talk about it, and take time out for you.

The most common not-so-nice feelings my clients share at points during their reentry are anxious, overwhelmed, insecure, discouraged, and even angry. OK, so that makes it sound like returning to work will be awful overall. It won't be.

Clients share that they have a deep appreciation, for the most part, for the important role that outside-the-home work plays in their lives. Most delight in and love the contribution that their careers provide to their holistic selves. It's part of who they are and how they grow.

But there will be some not-so-good days and even more not-so-good moments. Just as there were before parenthood—but these times are driven by different events, they can be more of a surprise, and they can be amplified. As my parents often said, *This too shall pass.* Here are some suggestions for when those not-so-nice feelings arise:

SUGGESTIONS FOR REGULATING EMOTIONS

Anxious	Focus on the present moment and take deep breaths. Search for root causes and reality.
Overwhelmed	Write down what needs to get done, based on importance & urgency. Focus on one task at a time.
Insecure	Focus on appreciating and accepting yourself, flaws and all. Give yourself credit for who you really are and quell the Saboteurs.
Discouraged	Be kind to yourself. Remind yourself of the reason why you are trying.
Angry	Pause so you can give yourself space to think clearly. Respond rationally instead of reacting and going up inference ladders.

Stop, pause, ground
Question FEAR (Future Events Appearing Real)

Cobwebs

Photo credit: Simon Maage, Unsplash.com

Returning to work after a long parental leave can feel like stepping into a dusty, long-forgotten room—there are cobwebs everywhere, and it takes some time to clean up and settle back in. The longer your leave, the more those cobwebs can accumulate. It's common to experience imposter syndrome during this time, as you may worry that you've lost your edge or that you're not performing at the level you once did. But here's the truth: most of this is just adjustment, not a true reflection of your abilities.

The Reality of the Ramp-Up Period

After a long break, it's perfectly normal to experience a "ramp back up" period where you're not immediately operating at full capacity. This period is necessary and healthy as you readjust to your job's cognitive, emotional, and physical demands. Your brain needs time to shift back into work mode, re-engage with the complexities of your role, and rebuild the mental muscles that may have gone a bit soft during your time away. It's similar to how athletes gradually return to training after an off-season; they don't expect to perform at their peak immediately, and neither should you.

Adjustments to Anticipate:

- *Cognitive Adjustment*
  The cognitive ramp-up involves getting back into the rhythm of problem-solving, decision-making, and strategic thinking. It's common to feel a bit rusty at first—perhaps you find yourself taking longer to complete tasks that used to be second nature, or you feel overwhelmed by the sheer volume of information you need to process. This is all part of dusting off the cobwebs. With time, your brain will reacclimate, and those neural pathways will strengthen again, making those once-challenging tasks easier and more intuitive.

- *Emotional Adjustment*
  Emotionally, returning to work can be a rollercoaster. You might feel excited to be back yet simultaneously anxious about leaving your child, concerned about the expectations of your role, or worried that you've been out of the loop for too long. Imposter syndrome can rear its ugly head, convincing you you're not as capable as you used to be. Recognize these feelings for what they are—temporary. As you settle back into

your role and regain your footing, these emotional challenges will ease, and you'll start to feel like yourself again.

- *Physical Adjustment*
  There's also a physical component to the ramp-up. Whether it's getting used to the commute again, adjusting to long hours at a desk, or simply managing the energy required to juggle work and home life, your body needs time to adapt. Be kind to yourself during this period—take breaks, prioritize sleep, and listen to what your body needs as you rebuild your stamina.

Recognizing the Process

It's important to acknowledge that this ramp-up period does not reflect your abilities or potential. It's a natural part of returning to work after any significant break, especially one as life changing as parental leave. The key is giving yourself grace during this time and recognizing that you're not underperforming—you're simply readjusting. Over time, those cobwebs will clear, and you'll find yourself hitting your stride again.

So, when you return to work, and things feel a bit off at first, don't panic. Understand that it's a process, and with patience and self-compassion, you'll soon be back to your old self—or, even better, a new and improved version who has grown through the experience of parenthood. After all, just as cobwebs are easy to sweep away with a little effort, these initial challenges will also fade as you settle back into your professional life.

The New Homecoming

Photo credit: Hans Isaacson, Unsplash.com

Before your baby's arrival, transitioning from work to home was often a straightforward process.

After a long day at the office, you could look forward to stepping into your home, a sanctuary of peace and quiet. It was easy to kick back, pour a glass of wine, sink into the couch with bonbons, and binge-watch your favorite series.

But now, with a baby in the mix, coming home after a workday is a whole different experience. Instead of a haven of relaxation, home is now another intense environment, filled with the demands of parenting and your partner's needs.

Navigating this transition requires a new approach—one that balances the demands of your professional life with the realities of parenthood and partnership. How you make this transition can significantly impact your evening, your relationship, and your overall well-being. Some prefer a *"hard landing"* approach, moving directly from work mode into parenting mode, while others opt for a *"soft-landing,"* taking time to decompress and engage in self-care before diving into family responsibilities. In this chapter, we'll explore these different approaches and offer strategies for creating a transition routine that works for you and your family.

The Hard-Landing Approach: Jumping Straight In

For some, the best way to transition from work to home life is to dive right into parenting and partnership duties. This "hard landing" approach involves shifting gears immediately upon walking through the door, putting work behind you, and focusing entirely on your family.

- *Pros of the Hard-Landing Approach:*
  - » *Immediate Engagement:* Jumping straight into parenting duties allows you to be present with your family from the moment you get home. This can be especially important if your partner has been caring for the baby all day and needs immediate relief.

  - » *Maximizing Family Time:* By not delaying your involvement, you maximize your time with your partner and baby, ensuring that you're fully participating in the evening routine.

> » *Creating a Clear Work-Life Boundary:* For some, shifting directly from work to home life helps create a clear boundary between the two, reducing the temptation to bring work-related stress into your family time.

- *Strategies for a Successful Hard-Landing:*

  > » *Establish a Homecoming Routine*: Create a routine that signals the end of the workday and the start of family time. This could be as simple as changing into comfortable clothes, washing your hands, and greeting your partner and baby with full attention.

  > » *Prioritize Key Tasks:* Identify the most important tasks that need your immediate attention—whether it's taking over baby care, preparing dinner, or helping with bedtime routines—and focus on those first.

  > » *Communicate with Your Partner:* Make sure your partner knows your plan so they can be ready for the hand-off. Clear communication ensures that you are both on the same page and can transition smoothly into your evening roles.

The Soft-Landing Approach: Easing into the Evening

On the other hand, some parents prefer a "soft-landing" approach, where they take a brief period to decompress and practice self-care before fully transitioning into their parenting and partnership duties. This approach acknowledges that work can be draining, and taking a moment to recharge can help you be more present and effective in your home life.

- *Pros of the Soft-Landing Approach:*

  » *Decompression Time:* Taking a short break to unwind after work can help reduce stress and prevent burnout. It allows you to mentally shift from the demands of the office to the demands of home.

  » *Improved Mood and Patience:* A brief period of self-care can help improve your mood, making you more patient and responsive when interacting with your partner and baby.

  » *Balancing Self-Care with Family Care:* By taking care of yourself first, you ensure you're in the right headspace to fully engage with your family, leading to more positive and meaningful interactions.

- *Strategies for a Successful Soft-Landing:*

  » *Set a Time Limit:* Decide how much time you need to decompress and stick to it. Setting a time limit ensures that your break doesn't encroach too much on family time, whether it's 10 minutes of meditation, a quick shower, or a short walk.

  » *Create a Transition Ritual:* Develop a simple ritual that helps you unwind and signal the end of the workday. This could be listening to a favorite song, practicing deep breathing, or enjoying a cup of tea.

  » *Communicate with Your Partner:* Let your partner know about your need for a brief break and agree on a plan that works for both of you. This ensures they feel supported and that your transition into family time is smooth.

Balancing "Me," "We," and "Us" Time

Regardless of whether you prefer a hard-landing or soft-landing approach, it's important to find a balance between "me" time, "we" (couple) time, and "us" (family) time (refer back to Chapter 24A for more explanation). Each of these areas is crucial for your overall well-being and the health of your relationships.

1. *Me Time:*

    » *Importance*: Taking time for yourself is essential for maintaining your mental and emotional health. It helps you recharge and manage the stresses of both work and parenting.

    » *How to Incorporate*: Even if it's just a few minutes a day, find moments to do something you enjoy, whether it's reading, exercising, or simply sitting in silence. Communicate your need for this time to your partner so that it can be built into your routine.

2. *We (Couple) Time:*

    » *Importance:* Maintaining a strong connection with your partner is key to a healthy relationship and a supportive parenting environment. It's easy to let your relationship take a backseat but making time for each other is essential.

    » *How to Incorporate*: Schedule regular date nights, even if they're at home after the baby goes to bed. Use this time to reconnect, talk about things other than the baby, and enjoy each other's company.

3. *Us (Parenting) Time:*

  » *Importance:* Parenting is a shared responsibility, and spending quality time with your baby is vital for their development and for strengthening your bond.

  » *How to Incorporate:* Engage in activities that involve both parents and the baby, such as feeding, bathing, or playing. These shared experiences not only support your baby's growth but also reinforce your partnership as co-parents.

Finding What Works for You

Every family is different, and there's no one-size-fits-all approach to transitioning from work to home life. Whether you prefer a hard landing or a soft landing, the key is to find a routine that works for you, your partner, and your baby. Be flexible and willing to adjust your approach as needed. What works one week might need tweaking the next, especially as your baby grows and your work demands change.

The transition from work to home is a critical part of your day, and how you navigate it can greatly impact your evening and overall well-being. Whether you choose a hard-landing approach, jumping straight into family life, or a soft-landing approach, taking time to decompress, the goal is to create a routine that allows you to be fully present for your partner and child(ren). By balancing "me," "we," and "us" time and communicating openly with your partner, you can make this transition smoother and more fulfilling, ensuring that your home remains a place of love, support, and connection, even amid the busy demands of parenthood.

Is it Really 50-50?

Photo credit: JSB-co, Unsplash.com

When couples transition to parenthood, the notion of balancing home and family commitments often surfaces with the hope of achieving a 50-50 split. The idea seems simple: share household chores, child-rearing, and career responsibilities equally. However, many couples find that achieving this balance is more elusive than expected. In fact, if one partner feels they're contributing more than 50%, say 60% or even 70%, it might reflect a reality closer to 50-50.

This perception gap occurs because the mental load—the invisible work of managing schedules, planning meals, and remembering key dates—often feels more significant than the physical tasks themselves. Research shows that women, even in dual-income households, often bear the brunt of this mental load. A study by Pew Research found that 52% of mothers report taking on more household responsibilities compared to only 12% of fathers. Conversely, 20% of fathers feel they contribute more than their partners believe they do.

This misalignment in perception is a common challenge and can lead to frustration or resentment. In heterosexual couples, research indicates that women, on average, perform more hours of unpaid household labor each week, even when both partners work full-time. Men, meanwhile, often underestimate the time spent on these tasks by their partners. These disparities aren't intentional but reveal a need for clearer communication and shared responsibility in managing family life.

The Reality of "Equal" Effort

The truth is, no partnership operates on a perfect 50-50 scale every day. Life's demands fluctuate—there may be seasons when one partner needs to take on more at home while the other focuses on a career project, or vice versa. This is normal and healthy in the long run, as long as the division feels fair to both parties.

But how do you know when it's fair? The key is regular, honest conversations about the workload. Many couples (particularly new parents) assume their contributions are evenly distributed, only to realize their partner's experience is very different. If left unspoken, these differences can lead to an imbalance where one person feels they are giving far more than their share.

Recognizing the Mental Load

The mental load is an important part of this equation. It's not just about who does the laundry or bathes the baby—it's about who carries the emotional burden of managing it all. Who plans the doctor's appointments? Who keeps track of school events, grocery lists, and extended family obligations? This emotional labor is often unseen but can be just as exhausting as the physical work.

In striving for balance, recognizing and redistributing the mental load is essential. If one partner manages most of life's logistics while the other only completes tasks handed to them, the 50-50 split is an illusion. For true balance, both partners need to be invested in both the execution and the planning.

A Reality Check for Couples

If you're feeling the strain, take a moment to evaluate how responsibilities are divided. Ask yourselves the following:

- *Who regularly initiates conversations about daily tasks or routines?*

- *How are major decisions (like financial planning or children's activities) typically made?*

- *Does one partner feel like they're always managing schedules or household needs?*

- *How often do you check in with each other about how the workload is feeling?*

These conversations can provide clarity and a more realistic picture of the balance in your household. Remember, balance doesn't mean both partners do identical tasks; it means both feel equally supported and valued in their contributions.

A High-Level Checklist: Evaluating Your Division of Responsibilities

After reflecting on the reality of your workload, use this checklist to assess how evenly responsibilities are divided in your household:

1. *Household chores*: Who typically handles cleaning, laundry, dishes, and general maintenance? Is this task shared, rotated, or delegated to one person?

2. *Childcare duties*: Who is responsible for feeding, bedtime routines, diaper changes, school drop-offs, and attending events? Is this division equal, or does one partner handle more day-to-day tasks?

3. *Emotional labor*: Who carries the mental load of planning and organizing schedules, coordinating activities, and managing the household's emotional well-being?

4. *Work-life balance*: Do both partners feel they can balance work commitments with family life? If one partner is more career-focused, how does the other's role shift to accommodate that?

5. *Health and self-care*: Are both partners ensuring time for self-care, exercise, and rest, or is one person sacrificing their own well-being for family needs?

6. *Financial management*: Who takes the lead on budgeting, paying bills, and managing savings? Is this responsibility shared or assigned to one partner?

7. *Extended family responsibilities*: How do you divide the communication and support roles with extended family, like in-laws or aging parents?

A More Detailed Checklist: Evaluating Your Division of Responsibilities

For those who are more detail-oriented, here is some space for you to jot down your thoughts about your division of responsibilities, and any tension points. On the following pages there are more specific checklists for consideration. It separates home, family, and financial responsibilities and classifies them into typically daily, weekly, monthly, and annual activities. Think of it as a "starter list" and add your own specifics to come to a common understanding of task division.

____

____

____

____

____

____

____

____

____

____

____

HOME RESPONSIBILITIES

	Mom	Dad
DAILY		
Cleaning up after meals	☐	☐
Clutter control & clean-up	☐	☐
Preparing and cooking meals	☐	☐
?	☐	☐
WEEKLY		
Cleaning:		
Changing bed linens and cleaning baby items (bottles, toys)	☐	☐
Cleaning bathrooms and kitchen	☐	☐
Dusting surfaces	☐	☐
Laundry (clothing, bedding, towels) and possibly ironing	☐	☐
Vacuuming and mopping floors	☐	☐
?	☐	☐
Grocery Shopping:		
Making a shopping list based on weekly meal planning	☐	☐
Planning weekly meals	☐	☐
Purchasing groceries, baby supplies, and household necessities	☐	☐
?	☐	☐
Maintenance:		
Checking and changing out light bulbs or basic fixes	☐	☐
Mowing lawn, watering flowers, shovelling snow	☐	☐
Taking out trash, recycling, and diaper pail	☐	☐
Watering indoor plants.	☐	☐
?	☐	☐
Services Management:		
Identifying, hiring, on-boarding, managing housekeeping/housekeeper services	☐	☐
?	☐	☐
MONTHLY		
Deep Cleaning:		
Cleaning and organizing baby gear (high chairs, playpens)	☐	☐
Cleaning out the fridge and pantry	☐	☐
Organizing closets, including baby clothes that no longer fit	☐	☐
?	☐	☐
Maintenance:		
Car service and inspections	☐	☐
Checking HVAC filters or calling for any needed repairs	☐	☐
?	☐	☐
ANNUALLY		
Deep Cleaning:		
Seasonal decluttering (attic, garage, basement) and decorating	☐	☐
Yard maintenance, washing windows	☐	☐
?	☐	☐
Home Safety:		
Checking home security systems and perimeter security	☐	☐
Testing and changing batteries in smoke/carbon monoxide detectors & fire extinguishers	☐	☐
?	☐	☐
Long-Term Maintenance:		
Reviewing home insurance policies or warranties on major items	☐	☐
Scheduling home improvement projects (painting, garden work)	☐	☐
Servicing major appliances	☐	☐
?	☐	☐
???		
?	☐	☐
?	☐	☐
?	☐	☐

FAMILY RESPONSIBILITIES

	Mom	Dad
DAILY		
Feeding baby	☐	☐
Diapering baby	☐	☐
Bathing baby	☐	☐
Putting baby to sleep	☐	☐
Daycare / school / social activities; packing lunches/baby food, managing homework	☐	☐
Petcare – feeding, litter, walking, appointments	☐	☐
?	☐	☐
WEEKLY		
Child Care:		
Managing baby's feeding and sleep schedule	☐	☐
Coordinating playdates or family activities	☐	☐
Manging nanny/daycare/sitters	☐	☐
?	☐	☐
Laundry and Baby Care:		
Baby laundry (clothes, bibs, swaddles)	☐	☐
Washing baby bottles and sanitizing feeding equipment	☐	☐
?	☐	☐
MONTHLY		
Child Care and Education:		
Checking in with daycare or babysitters on schedules.	☐	☐
Reviewing and planning early learning activities (reading, toys, etc.)	☐	☐
?	☐	☐
Health Appointments:		
Paediatrician visits - routine well visits, immunizations	☐	☐
Scheduling any follow-ups for both baby and parents (dentist, therapist)	☐	☐
?	☐	☐
Social Calendar:		
Planning date nights, fun activities	☐	☐
Managing family visits - scheduling and airport pick-ups	☐	☐
Managing birthdays, parties and special events	☐	☐
?	☐	☐
ANNUALLY		
Health and Well-being:		
Scheduling annual health check-ups for parents and children	☐	☐
Renewing health insurance or assessing coverage	☐	☐
?	☐	☐
Family Traditions and Vacations:		
Planning family vacations or holiday gatherings	☐	☐
Updating family traditions, such as birthdays and milestone celebrations	☐	☐
?	☐	☐
???		
?	☐	☐
?	☐	☐
?	☐	☐

FINANCIAL RESPONSIBILITIES

	Mom	Dad
MONTHLY		
Bills and Budgeting:		
Paying caregivers	☐	☐
Reviewing, reconciling and paying household bills (utilities, subscriptions)	☐	☐
Reviewing and adjusting budget for groceries, childcare, and other expenses	☐	☐
Transferring funds to savings accounts (college savings or rainy-day funds)	☐	☐
?	☐	☐
ANNUALLY		
Financial Planning:		
Reviewing long-term financial goals (retirement, college fund)	☐	☐
Updating life insurance choices and sign-ups	☐	☐
Updating wills, life insurance, and beneficiary information.	☐	☐
?	☐	☐
Taxes:		
Researching strategies for efficiency	☐	☐
Processing and paying	☐	☐
?	☐	☐
???		
?	☐	☐
?	☐	☐
?	☐	☐

Moving Forward with Intention

Achieving true balance is less about rigidly adhering to a 50-50 split and more about creating an ongoing dialogue about fairness. Each couple's needs are unique, and roles will evolve over time. By using these checklists and maintaining open, honest communication, you can ensure that both partners feel supported in managing home and family life together.

Balancing responsibilities is an ongoing process that requires effort from both sides. It's not about perfection but about ensuring that no one feels they're carrying more than their fair share for too long. The goal is to create a partnership where both partners feel heard, valued, and supported—whether the split looks like 50-50, 60-40, or something else altogether.

Sustaining It

Hopefully, you have been through all the exploration and preparation and should be well on your path to successful reentry into the world of work and career.

Let me leave you with a final reminder. Life evolves, journeys migrate, things change, and shit happens.

Just as you would take stock of your career through annual performance reviews, so might you review your life journey and progress. So, as you reenter the workforce as a new parent, may I suggest you put a note to self on the calendar to stop, evaluate, and adjust how life is moving along.

Truly, we are each the "CEO of me" and both "Co-CEOs of Family, Inc" (see Chapter 31D for more insight), and it's worth pausing to reflect on it. Just do it now. Get it on the calendar for a month or two out: *"A meeting with me."*

Photo credit: Manasvita S, Unsplash.com

Ready for Round 2?

Photo credit: Curated Lifestyle, Unsplash.com

Seriously?! *Round 2?*

Okay, I know—just hearing those words might make you want to toss this book across the room (preferably into something soft, like a pillow). Especially if you're currently deep in the trenches of expectant parenthood, asking yourself, "*Will this pregnancy ever end?*" or "*Will my baby ever figure out that nighttime is for sleeping and not hosting a rave?*" I hear you. Loud and clear.

Going through the whirlwind again—sleepless nights, diaper blowouts, and a love so overwhelming it feels like your heart might explode—might seem like the *last thing* you want to think about right now. I get it. You're knee-deep in spit-up and nursery rhymes, and the mere suggestion of doing this all over again feels like madness. Maybe you›re thinking, "*Who in their right mind would sign up for a sequel?*"

But before you dive under your blanket and vow never to emerge until your kid is off to college, hear me out. Life has a funny way of surprising us. While navigating the glorious chaos of parenthood, it might seem like the *wrong* time to think about the future—let alone the possibility of another little one. And it's totally okay if the mere thought makes you want to crawl into the fetal position with a cup of coffee and a Netflix marathon.

Maybe you're in the "*One and done, thank you very much!*" camp. Or perhaps you're taking a more "*Let's survive this first one, and then we'll talk*" approach. There's also the "*Who the heck knows what the future holds*" crowd—because predicting the future when your present involves negotiating nap schedules like a high-stakes United Nations peace treaty feels impossible. (And sometimes more difficult.)

But here's the thing: as you wade through this wild ride of parenting, it might be worth giving a teeny-tiny, passing thought to the bigger picture. No pressure. Seriously. Maybe you'll decide that one kiddo is the perfect number for your family, or maybe—just maybe—a little voice inside (not the one coming from the baby monitor, the other one) will quietly whisper, "You know, you *might* want to do this again someday..."

Now, if the mere mention of "Round 2" makes you want to throw something (ideally something soft), don't worry—I'm not here to push you off the cliff. This is about gently peeking at what the future *might* look like without diving headfirst into the deep end. Just a casual glance. No commitment required.

And if this talk of Round 2 has you eyeing the nearest diaper pail with the intent to hurl this book straight into it—hey, I won't take it personally! Just remember: this journey is yours to navigate. Whether it's a one-time rollercoaster ride or the beginning of a bigger, wilder, and more love-filled adventure than you ever imagined, you get to decide the route.

So, there it is. Just a thought. I'm ducking for cover now.

Inspirational Quotes and Words of Wisdom

Photo credit: Marek Studzinski, Unsplash.com

A. INSPIRATIONAL QUOTES FOR NEW DADS

- *"A father is neither an anchor to hold us back, nor a sail to take us there, but a guiding light whose love shows us the way."* – Origin unclear

- *"Anyone can be a father, but it takes someone special to be a dad."* – Wade Boggs

- *"The best thing a father can do for his children is to love their mother."* – John Wooden

- *"It is not flesh and blood, but the heart which makes us fathers and sons."* – Johann Friedrich von Schiller

- *"Dads are most ordinary men turned by love into heroes, adventurers, storytellers, and singers of songs."* – Pam Brown

- *"Being a good father is like shaving. No matter how good you shaved today, you have to do it again tomorrow."*
  – Reed Markham

- *"A father's smile has been known to light up a child's entire day."* – Susan Gale

- *"There is no greater thing you can do with your life and your work than follow your passions—in a way that serves the world and you."* – Richard Branson

- *"Fathering is not something perfect men do, but something that perfects the man."* – Frank Pittman

- *"A father doesn't tell you that he loves you. He shows you."*
  – Dimitri the Stoneheart

B. WORDS OF WISDOM FOR NEW DADS

- *"You're not just raising a child; you're also raising yourself as a parent."*
  Fatherhood is a journey of growth for both you and your child. Embrace the personal development that comes with being a dad.

- *"Embrace the chaos."*
  The early days of fatherhood can be unpredictable and messy, but the most meaningful moments are within the chaos.

- *"It's okay not to have all the answers."*
  Parenthood is a learning experience, and figuring things out as you go is perfectly fine. Give yourself permission to make mistakes and learn from them.

- *"Be present, not perfect."*
  Your child doesn't need a perfect dad; they need a present one. Focus on being there for the small moments—they're often the ones that matter most.

- *"Don't forget to take care of yourself."*
  While getting caught up in caring for your newborn and supporting your partner is easy, self-care is crucial. A well-rested and healthy dad is better equipped to handle the challenges of parenthood.

- *"Set realistic expectations."*
  Parenthood will test your patience and endurance. Set realistic expectations for yourself and your partner, and don't be afraid to adjust them as you go.

- *"Cherish the early days—they go by fast."*
  The sleepless nights and endless diaper changes may seem overwhelming, but these early days are fleeting. Try to savor the small moments of bonding, as they'll soon be memories.

- *"Your presence is the greatest gift you can give your child."*
  Whether it's reading a bedtime story, taking a walk, or simply being there when they need you, your time and attention are invaluable.

- *"Remember, you're a role model."*
  Your child will look to you as an example of how to treat others, how to handle challenges, and how to love. Strive to be the best version of yourself.

- *"Patience is your best friend."*
  Parenthood requires patience in abundance. Whether it's dealing with sleepless nights, tantrums, or endless questions, remember that patience will help you navigate the ups and downs of fatherhood with grace.

C. INSPIRATIONAL QUOTES FOR NEW MOMS

- *"There is no way to be a perfect mother, and a million ways to be a good one."* – Jill Churchill

- *"Motherhood: All love begins and ends there."*
  – Robert Browning

- *"The most important work you will ever do will be within the walls of your own home."* – Harold B. Lee

- *"A mother's love is the fuel that enables a normal human being to do the impossible."* – Marion C. Garretty

- *"To the world you are a mother, but to your family, you are the world."* – Unknown

- *"Motherhood is the greatest thing and the hardest thing."*
  – Ricki Lake

- *"Mothers hold their children's hands for a short while, but their hearts forever."* – Unknown

- *"You are doing better than you think."* – Unknown

- *"The moment a child is born, the mother is also born."* – Bhagwan Shree Rajneesh

- *"The joy of motherhood comes in moments. There will be hard times and frustrating times, but amid the challenges, there are shining moments of joy and satisfaction."* – M. Russell Ballard

D. WORDS OF WISDOM FOR NEW MOMS

- *"Trust your instincts."*
  You know your baby better than anyone else. Trust your intuition when making decisions about your child's care and your own well-being.

- *"It's okay to ask for help."*
  Motherhood is demanding; you don't have to do it alone. Reach out to family, friends, or support groups when you need assistance or a break.

- *"Take it one day at a time."*
  The early days of motherhood can be overwhelming. Focus on getting through each day rather than worrying about everything at once.

- *"Self-care is not selfish."*
  Taking care of yourself is crucial to being the best mom you can be. Make time for rest, relaxation, and activities that rejuvenate you.

- *"Celebrate the small victories."*
  Whether it's successfully breastfeeding, getting the baby to sleep, or just making it through a tough day, acknowledge and celebrate the small wins—they add up.

- *"You are allowed to have bad days."*
  Every mom has days where things don't go as planned, and that's okay. It doesn't mean you're failing; it just means you're human.

- *"Your love is enough."*
  No matter how challenging things get, your love for your child is the most important thing you can offer. It's more than enough.

- *"Remember, you're doing the best you can."*
  Motherhood is a learning process, and there will be ups and downs. Be gentle with yourself and remember that you're doing your best, and that's all anyone can ask for.

- *"Find joy in the little things."*
  The tiny moments of connection with your baby—like their first smile or the warmth of their tiny hand—can bring immense joy and remind you why this journey is so special.

- *"You are stronger than you think."*
  Motherhood will test you in ways you never expected, but it will also reveal a strength you didn't know you had. Embrace it and know that you can handle whatever comes your way.

E. WORDS OF WISDOM FROM MY CLIENTS

I asked my Maternity Magic and Parental Pivot coaching clients to share a sentence or two about their most critical insight in managing the transition to parenthood as it related to working in fast-paced environments.

Here's what they had to say:

- *"Many of us are achievement-oriented, which makes it hard to 'just be,' but try not to put too much pressure on yourself to accomplish a lot of personal stuff during your parental leave. If the only thing you're able to do is spend quality time with your new baby during this time, that's amazing!"*

- *"Pumping and working is harder than being pregnant and working. Seriously consider how the decision to stop (breastfeeding) coincides with the decision to start (working)."*

- *"I think the biggest thing I learned (other than how to power nap) was how to try not to be a perfectionist."*

- *"I was actually kind of surprised that they (the company) agreed to everything I asked for. And so far, so good. It's really working for us."*

- *"I was well aware of the emotional/hormonal impact of being pregnant (like the hormonal changes of becoming a teen), but I was unaware of how my hormones would change, and my feelings would just sort of put themselves out there when I first returned to work. It's OK to cry. Just go find that 'wellness room.'"*

- *"I thought I'd be tired, but that's an understatement. I was exhausted. And so was my wife. Being new parents was not always the nirvana we thought it would be. But it's so worth it!"*

- *"Work used to be my everything. Now, it's just one thing. And it's not to say that my dedication to work shrank. Rather that the pie grew, and I now have a more balanced set of priorities and a much richer life."*

- *"I learned the importance of taking time for myself. For just me. Rather than spending every last minute with (my daughter) to soak in those last moments, I am glad I took a week to get myself together before going back to work."*

- *"I didn't realize I was actually, fundamentally, a control freak. Until my totally uncontrollable, unpredictable son came along. Don't even plan on getting out the door on time anymore. Or at least build in an extra 30 minutes that you never seemed to need before."*

- *"I was pretty good at carving out 'me' time, but not so good at carving out 'us' (wife) time. Sometimes, we just have to stop and cuddle and remember why we wanted this in the first place."*

- *"Don't let moms (or mothers-in-law) stay too (too) long!!!"*

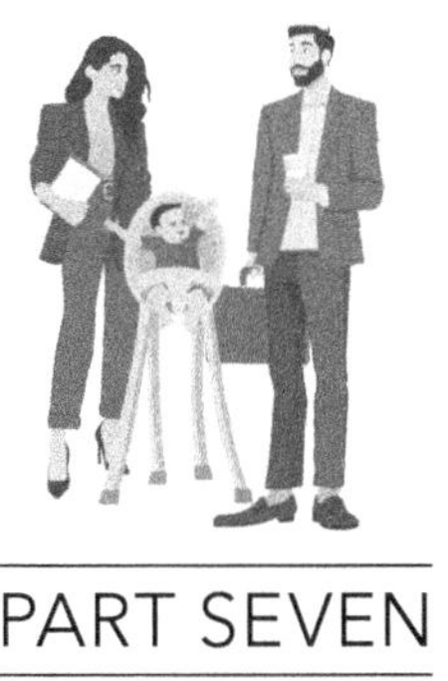

PART SEVEN

OBSTACLE BUSTING

Just when you thought you had it all figured out, life throws you a curveball—or several. In this section, we're diving into the nitty-gritty of overcoming the obstacles that inevitably pop up when plans meet reality. Whether it's dealing with those pesky internal voices that love to sabotage your progress, navigating the emotional rollercoaster of parenthood, or simply learning to calm your mind amidst the chaos, this part is all about equipping you with the tools to keep moving forward.

Expect to challenge your thinking, get cozy with your emotions, and pick up some practical techniques for keeping calm and centered—even when the going gets tough. We're busting through the barriers, one by one, so you can emerge stronger, wiser, and more resilient. Let's get started on turning those obstacles into steppingstones!

The chapters here will cover:

43. Plans Are Not Reality and Minds Are Not Rational

44. Techniques for Calming (You)

45. When Things Are Really Tough

Plans Are Not Reality and Minds Are Not Rational

This chapter delves into the often-chaotic intersection of our emotions, thoughts, and perceptions.

We begin by exploring how to identify and understand our **Emotions**, crucial for navigating the complexities of life. Then, we confront the critical voices in our head—our **Saboteurs**—that can undermine our confidence and decision-making. These Saboteurs can be tamed by unleashing our **Sages**— those calming, positive, rational voices in our heads.

From there, we'll tackle those pesky **ANTS (Automatic Negative Thoughts)** and **FEARs (Future Events Appearing Real)** that often cloud our judgment, offering strategies to recognize and manage them.

We'll also explore the concept of **Open vs. Closed Mindsets**, guiding you to adopt a more flexible and growth-oriented approach.

Finally, we'll introduce the idea of **Distinctions that Reframe**, a powerful tool to help you view situations through a new lens, transforming challenges into opportunities.

By the end of this chapter, you'll be better equipped to navigate the unpredictable terrain of life with a more balanced and resilient mindset.

A. Emotions: Name Them to Tame Them

B. Saboteurs and Sages

C. Ants

D. FEAR

E. Open vs. Closed Minds

F. Distinctions that Reframe

A. EMOTIONS: NAME THEM TO TAME THEM

Emotions—those unpredictable, often inconvenient guests that show up unannounced and crash on your couch. Sometimes, they bring a gift, like joy or excitement, and other times, they arrive with a suitcase full of stress. But whether they're welcome or not, these emotional visitors are here to stay, and it's up to you to manage them before they take over the house.

The secret to keeping your emotions from running wild? Name them. That's right—just like calling out a friend's name in a crowded room, identifying your emotions can help you find some order in the chaos. It's like playing a game of emotional hide-and-seek: *"I spy with my little eye… something that feels like anxiety!"* Once you've spotted it, you're already on your way to taking back control.

Most of us tend to shove our emotions into the *"I'll deal with this later"* drawer while focusing on more pressing matters. But there's real value in pausing for a moment and asking yourself, *"How am I really feeling right now?"* Not just the superficial *"fine"* we toss around but instead digging a little deeper. This simple check-in can do wonders for your mental well-being. It's like giving your brain a much-needed reset.

Enter the *Feelings Wheel*—your personal cheat sheet for decoding emotions. This handy tool helps you move beyond the usual suspects like *"happy," "sad,"* or *"angry"* and delve into the specific flavors of what you're feeling. Are you really just *"angry,"* or is it more *"frustrated"* or *"betrayed"*? Are you *"happy,"* or is it more like *"content"* or *"proud"*? The more accurately you can name your emotions, the better you'll manage them.

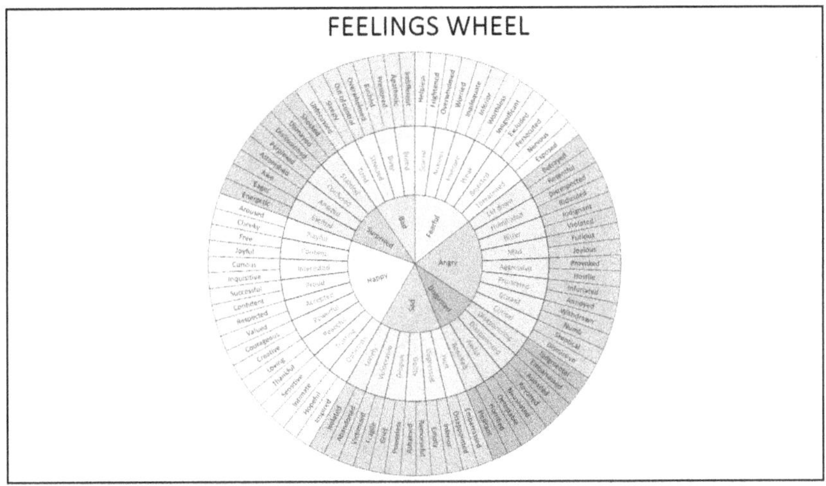

Credit: Google search attributes to Geoffrey Roberts

Once you've named what you're feeling, you can start to manage it rather than letting it manage you. It's like saying, *"Okay, frustration, I see you, but you're not steering this ship today."* This simple act of naming can be a powerful way to keep your emotions in check and prevent them from turning your day upside down.

So, next time you're feeling a bit off, take a moment to check in with yourself. Pull out the Feelings Wheel, identify what's happening inside, and watch how this small act can make a big difference. After all, you've got enough on your plate without letting your emotions run the show.

B. SABOTEURS AND SAGES

"You have been criticizing yourself for years, and it hasn't worked. Try approving of yourself and see what happens. Self-criticism only serves to undermine your confidence and well-being. By choosing self-approval and kindness, you can transform your self-perception and unlock your true potential."
—Louise Hay, American motivational author and founder of Hay House

The basic idea here is to become aware of our *"Saboteurs"* and tame them by unleashing our *"Sages."* There's a lot of depth to this research and thinking. If you want the details, there's a great book titled *Positive Intelligence* by Shirzad Chamine. At the time of writing, the hard copy of this book was wickedly expensive (perhaps they ran out of books?), but the e-versions were reasonably priced and readily available.

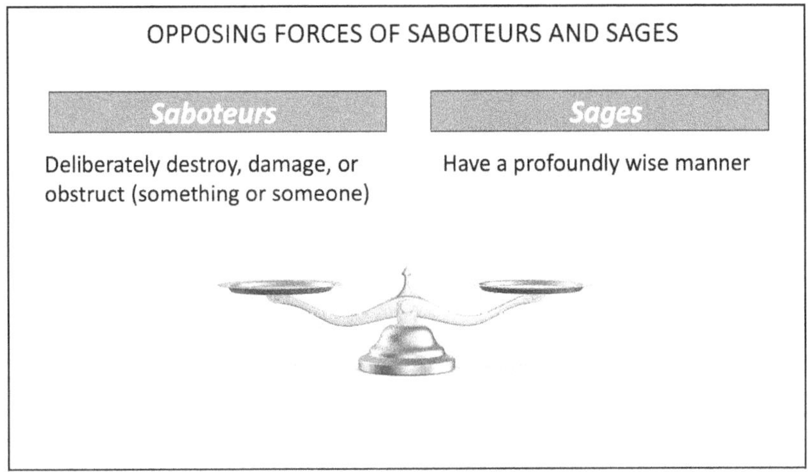

Recent advances in functional MRI (fMRI) have enabled us (well, technically, other people) to pinpoint the regions of the brain involved in producing thoughts and feelings and identify the neural functions involved with what can be called Saboteurs and Sages.

The Saboteurs: Live in the brainstem, limbic system, and parts of the left brain, generating negative emotions while you handle life's challenges. They produce much of our stress, anxiety, self-doubt, anger, shame, guilt, frustration, and negative mind chatter! They present in ten forms:

- Judge (this one is universal—we all have one)

- Avoider

- Controller

- Hyper-achiever

- Hyper-rational

- Hyper-vigilant

- Pleaser

- Restless

- Stickler

- Victim

The nine "*Accomplice Saboteurs*" (beyond the Judge) above are all present in us at some times. It's just that some of them might be more brutally vocal within different people and circumstances.

The Sages: Live in the middle prefrontal cortex "*empathy circuitry*" and parts of the right brain, generating positive emotions while handling life's challenges. Activating this region releases endorphins, which support feelings of empathy, compassion, gratitude, curiosity, joy of creativity, and calm, clear-headed, laser-focused action. They present in five forms:

- Activate

- Empathize

- Explore

- Innovate

- Navigate

There's a free online self-evaluation that helps highlight which of your Saboteurs might be loudest (courtesy of Shirzad Chamine, PositiveIntelligence.com). It can add another layer of insight into who we are and how we're wired, and that is worth exploring. I think you will be amazed by becoming aware of where all that incessant self-chatter is coming from throughout the day.

Meanwhile, here's my take on each of the Saboteurs. We all have all of them in varying degrees of obnoxious loudness. If you watch for them, you will recognize them talking in your head—incessantly, loudly, and rudely. If our best friend spoke to us as our Saboteurs do, you'd likely never speak with them again. If our romantic partners spoke to us as our Saboteurs do, you'd dump or divorce them. Seriously.

Flip through the one-page descriptions of each of the Saboteurs, and rate each for yourself on a scale of 1–10 to identify the ones that attack you the most strongly and most often. These are the voices we must become acutely aware of and tame, particularly as they cast doubt on your return-to-work decision and approach.

Pick one or two to pay attention to in the coming days, and don't let them get to you and sap your confidence!

Let's start with The Judge, our universal Saboteur.

 Saboteur: The Judge ___/ 10

Characteristics

- <u>Self</u>: Badgers self for past mistakes or current shortcomings

- <u>Others</u>: Focuses on what is wrong with others rather than appreciating the good things about them. Gets into inferior/superior comparisons.

- <u>Circumstances</u>: Insists a circumstance or outcome is "bad" rather than seeing it as a gift and opportunity

Thoughts

- *"What is wrong with me?"*

- *"What is wrong with you?"*

- *"What is wrong with this?"*

Feelings

- All of our guilt, regret, shame, and disappointment

- Much of our anxiety and anger

Justification Lies

- "Without pushing you, you'll get lazy."
- "Without punishing you for mistakes, you won't learn."
- "Without scaring you about bad outcomes you won't work hard to prevent them."
- "Without judging others, you'll lose objectivity and not protect your self-interest."
- "Without making you feel bad, you won't change."

Impact (on self and others)

- Guilt, regret, shame, disappointment, anxiety, and anger

- Relationship conflicts

Adapted from: *Positive Intelligence*, Shirzad Chamine

And now let's take a peek at the 9 Accomplice Saboteurs! Recognize these in yourself?

 ## Saboteur: The Avoider

___ / 10

Characteristics

- Avoids conflict
- Says "yes" when not desired
- Downplays problems
- Deflects to others

- Has difficulty saying "no"
- Passive-aggressive behaviors
- Loses self in comforting routines and habits
- Procrastinates

Thoughts

- *"This is just too unpleasant."*
- *"Maybe if I let it go it will take care of itself."*
- *"I'll hurt someone's feelings and I'd rather not."*
- *"I don't like conflict."*
- *"I've found balance and I don't want to mess with it."*
- *"I don't want to create a scene."*

Feelings

- Tries to remain even keeled
- Feels anxiety about the avoidance or procrastination
- Fears interruption of hard-earned peace of mind

Justification Lies

- *"It's good to spare others' feelings."*
- *"No good comes out of conflict."*
- *"If you can't say something nice, say nothing at all."*
- *"It's good to be flexible."*
- *"Someone needs to be the peacemaker."*
- *"You catch 'em better with sugar."*

Impact (on self and others)

- What's avoided doesn't go away. It festers.
- Relationships are superficial through conflict avoidance.
- Others' trust is eroded because it's unclear when negative information is withheld.
- Authenticity erodes by denying conflicts and negativities.

Adapted from: *Positive Intelligence*, Shirzad Chamine

Saboteur: The Controller

`__ / 10`

Characteristics

- Strong need to control and take charge
- Connects through competition, challenge, physicality, or conflict
- Willful, confrontational straight talker
- Comes alive when doing the impossible
- Stimulated by and connects through conflict
- Intimidates others
- In-your-face communication interpreted as anger or criticism

Thoughts

- *"I am either in control or out of control."*
- *"If I work hard enough, I can and should control the situation to go my way."*
- *"Others want and need me to take control."*
- *"No one tells me what to do."*

Feelings

- Anxious when something not going their way
- Angry and intimidating when others don't follow
- Impatient with others' feelings and different styles
- Does feel hurt and rejected, though rarely admits to it

Justification Lies

- *"Without me, you can't get much done."*
- *"You need to push people."*
- *"If I don't control, I will be controlled."*
- *"I am trying to get the job done for all our sakes."*

Impact (on self and others)

- Gets temporary results
- Generates anxiety in others who feel controlled, resentful, manipulated, and unable to tap into their own value
- Generates anxiety in self as most things are ultimately not controllable

Adapted from: *Positive Intelligence*, Shirzad Chamine

Saboteur: The Hyper-achiever

_ / 10

HYPER-ACHIEVER

Dependent on constant performance and achievement for self-respect and self-validation.

Highly focused on external success, leading to workaholic tendencies and loss of touch with deeper emotional and relationship needs.

Characteristics

- Competitive
- Image- and status-conscious
- Good at covering up insecurities and projecting a positive image
- Adapts personality to fit what impresses others
- Goal-oriented, workaholic tendencies
- More drawn to perfecting public image than introspection
- Can be self-promoting
- Keeps people at a safe distance

Thoughts

- _"I must be the best at what I do."_
- _"If I can't be outstanding, don't bother trying."_
- _"I must be efficient and effective."_
- _"Emotions get in the way of performance."_
- _"Focus on thinking and action."_
- _"I can be anything I want to be."_
- _"I am worthy and successful because others think so."_

Feelings

- Doesn't like to dwell on feelings too long
- Sometimes feels empty and depressed inside
- Needs to feel successful
- Feels worthy mainly through accomplishment
- May fear intimacy and vulnerability as closeness might reveal imperfections

Justification Lies

- _"Life is about achieving and perfecting results."_
- _"Portraying a great image is what helps me get results."_
- _"Feelings are just a distraction and don't achieve much."_

Impact (on self and others)

- Peace and happiness are short-lived in brief celebrations of achievement.
- Self-acceptance is continuously dependent on the next success.
- Loses touch with deeper feelings and self
- Has difficulty connecting intimately with others
- Can pull others into the lopsided performance vortex

Adapted from: _Positive Intelligence_, Shirzad Chamine

Saboteur: The Hyper-rational

_ / 10

HYPER-RATIONAL

Intense and exclusive focus on the rational processing of everything, including relationships.

Can be perceived as cold, distant, and intellectually arrogant.

Characteristics

- Intense and active mind
- Can come across as intellectually arrogant or secretive
- Private, doesn't let many people into deeper feelings

- Mostly shows feelings through passion for ideas
- Prefers to watch and analyze from a distance
- Can lose track of time due to intense concentration
- Strong penchant for skepticism and debate

Thoughts

- *"The rational mind is where it's at."*
- *"Feelings are distracting and irrelevant."*
- *"Many people are irrational and sloppy thinkers."*
- *"Needs and emotions of others distract me."*
- *"I need to shut out intrusions."*
- *"Knowledge, understanding, and insight are the most valuable."*

Feelings

- Frustrated with others being emotional and irrational
- Anxious about preserving personal time, energy, and resources against intrusion
- Can feels different, alone, or misunderstood
- Is often skeptical or cynical

Justification Lies

- *"A rational mind is the best mind."*
- *"I have to protect myself from other people's wasteful intrusion."*
- *"Other people's messy emotions and needs slow my work down."*

Impact (on self and others)

- Limits the depth and flexibility of relationships
- Spends time analyzing rather than experiencing feelings and life
- Intimidates less analytically minded people

Adapted from: *Positive Intelligence*, Shirzad Chamine

Saboteur: The Hyper-vigilant

__ / 10

Characteristics

- Always anxious, with chronic doubts about self and others
- Extraordinary sensitivity to danger signals
- Constant expectation of mishap or danger
- Suspicious of what others are up to
- Expectation that others will mess up
- May seek reassurance and guidance in procedures, rules, authorities, and institutions

Thoughts

- *"When is the other shoe going to drop?"*
- *"If I make a mistake, everyone will jump down my throat."*
- *"I want to trust people, but I am suspicious of their motives."*
- *"I need to know the rules, even if I don't always follow them."*

Feelings

- Skeptical
- Sometimes cynical
- Often anxious
- Always highly vigilant

Justification Lies

- *"Life is full of dangers."*
- *"If I don't look out for danger, who will?"*
- *"Someone will get hurt if I don't watch out for them."*

Impact (on self and others)

- Burns vital energy that could otherwise be put to great use
- Loses credibility with "the boy who cried wolf" phenomenon
- Others feel drained by the intensity of the nervous energy, and may avoid interaction.

Adapted from: *Positive Intelligence*, Shirzad Chamine

Saboteur: The Pleaser

__ / 10

PLEASER

Indirectly attempts to gain acceptance and affection by helping, pleasing, rescuing, or flattering others.

Loses sight of own needs and becomes resentful as a result.

Characteristics

- Strong need to be liked
- Earns being liked by helping, pleasing, rescuing, or flattering others
- Needs frequent reassurance of the acceptance and affection of others
- Doesn't express own needs openly and directly
- Indirectly expresses own needs by making people feel obligated to reciprocate

Thoughts

- "A good person puts the needs of others ahead of their own."
- "People can be so selfish and ungrateful when they don't notice or care about what I've done."
- "I give to others too much, but not to myself."
- "I can get anyone to like me."
- "If I don't help rescue them, no one else will."

Feelings

- Expressing own needs directly feels selfish
- Worried that insisting on own ideas will drive others away
- Resents being taken for granted, but has difficulty expressing it

Justification Lies

- "I don't do this for myself, I do it for others."
- "I help others selflessly and don't expect anything in return."
- "The world would be better if everyone behaved like me."

Impact (on self and others)

- Can jeopardize taking care of one's own needs (emotional, physical, or financial)
- Can lead to resentment and burnout
- Others can develop dependence instead of learning to take care of themselves.
- Others can feel obligated, guilty, or manipulated.

Adapted from: *Positive Intelligence*, Shirzad Chamine

Saboteur: The Restless   __ / 10

RESTLESS

Constantly in search of greater excitement in the next activity and constantly busy.

Rarely at peace or content with the current activity.

Characteristics

- Easily distracted
- Can get scattered
- Stays busy, juggling tasks and plans
- Seeks excitement and variety, not comfort and safety
- Bounces (escapes) from unpleasant feelings very quickly
- Seeks constant new stimulation

Thoughts

- *"This isn't very fulfilling."*
- *"The next thing has got to be more exciting."*
- *"Negative feelings suck so I move on to the next thing."*
- *"No one seems to be able to keep up with me."*

Feelings

- Impatient with what's happening in the present
- Wonders what's next
- Fears missing out on more worthwhile experiences
- Feels restless and wants more options
- Worries that focus on a negative feeling would make it grow and become overwhelming

Justification Lies

- *"Life is too short, and should be lived fully."*
- *"I don't want to miss out – FOMO!"*

Impact (on self and others)

- Anxiety-based escape from being present is underneath a surface of fun and excitement.
- Avoids real and lasting focus on the issues and relationships that truly matter
- Others have a hard time keeping up with the frenzy and chaos, and are unable to build a sustainable relationship.

Adapted from: *Positive Intelligence*, Shirzad Chamine

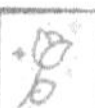 ## Saboteur: The Stickler

__ / 10

STICKLER

Perfection and a need for order and organization taken too far.

Characteristics

- Perfectionist, punctual, methodical
- Highly critical of self and others
- Can be irritable, tense, opinionated, sarcastic

- Strong need for self-control and self-restraint
- Works overtime to make up for others' sloppiness or laziness
- Is highly sensitive to criticism

Thoughts

- "I know the right way."
- "If you can't do it well, don't do it at all."
- "Others have really lax standards."
- "I need to be more organized and methodical than others so that things get done."
- "I hate mistakes."
- "I hate wasting time."

Feelings

- Constant disappointment and frustration with self and others for not living up to high standards
- Anxious that others will mess up the balance and order
- Sarcastic, with self-righteous overtones
- Suppressed anger and frustration

Justification Lies

- "It's a personal obligation."
- "It's up to me to fix the messes I encounter."
- "Perfectionism is good."
- "When things are good, I feel better about myself"
- "There's usually a clear right and wrong way and I know how it should be done."
- "I've got to do the right thing."

Impact (on self and others)

- Causes rigidity and reduces flexibility in interacting with change and the diverse styles of others
- Is a source of ongoing anxiety and frustration
- Causes resentment, anxiety, self-doubt, and resignation in others who feel continually criticized
- Others resign themselves to the fact that no matter how hard they try, the Stickler will not be pleased.

Adapted from: *Positive Intelligence*, Shirzad Chamine

Saboteur: The Victim

__ / 10

Characteristics

- If criticized or misunderstood, tends to withdraw, pout and sulk
- Fairly dramatic and temperamental
- When things get tough, wants to crumble and give up

- Represses rage, resulting in depression, apathy, or constant fatigue
- Unconsciously attracted to having difficulties
- Gets attention by having emotional problems, or being temperamental and sullen

Thoughts

- *"No one understands me."*
- *"Poor me. Terrible things always happen to me."*
- *"I might be uniquely disadvantaged."*
- *"I am what I feel."*
- *"I wish someone would rescue me from this mess."*

Feelings

- Tends to brood over negative feelings for a long time
- Feels alone and lonely, even around family and friends
- Experiences feelings of melancholy and abandonment
- Dwells on envy and negative comparisons

Justification Lies

- *"At least when I act this way, I get some of the love and attention I deserve."*
- *"Sadness is noble and sophisticated. It shows exceptional depth, insight, and sensitivity."*
- *"Bad things always happen to me, and I have to cope with it."*

Impact (on self and others)

- Vitality wasted by focus on internal processing and brooding
- Backfires by pushing people away
- Others feel frustrated, helpless, or guilty that they can only put Band-Aids on the Victim's pain.
- Others give up on a two-way relationship and walk away.

Adapted from: *Positive Intelligence*, Shirzad Chamine

Now sum it up for yourself, become aware, and tame those top Saboteurs!

<table>
<tr><td colspan="2">WHICH OF YOUR SABOTEURS ARE YOUR BIGGEST ENEMY TO TAME?</td></tr>
<tr><td><u>Saboteur</u></td><td><u>Your Self-Score</u></td></tr>
<tr><td>JUDGE</td><td>______</td></tr>
<tr><td>Avoider</td><td>______</td></tr>
<tr><td>Controller</td><td>______</td></tr>
<tr><td>Hyper-achiever</td><td>______</td></tr>
<tr><td>Hyper-rational</td><td>______</td></tr>
<tr><td>Hyper-vigilant</td><td>______</td></tr>
<tr><td>Pleaser</td><td>______</td></tr>
<tr><td>Restless</td><td>______</td></tr>
<tr><td>Stickler</td><td>______</td></tr>
<tr><td>Victim</td><td>______</td></tr>
</table>

C. ANTS

Photo credit: Peter F. Wolf, Unsplash.com

You know those tiny, pesky ants that appear out of nowhere, marching in a single file line across your kitchen counter? Well, in the world of our thoughts, we have a similar kind of nuisance: ANTs, or Automatic Negative Thoughts. These mental critters are just as annoying as the real ones, except instead of raiding your sugar bowl, they raid your peace of mind.

Just like real ants, these thoughts have a way of creeping into your brain, often uninvited and usually at the worst possible moments. They love to whisper all sorts of doomsday scenarios in your ear—*"You're going to mess this up," "Everyone will think you're a failure,"* or *"This is never going to work."* Before you know it, they've built an entire ant hill of anxiety in your mind.

But most of these ANTs are based on pure fiction, not fact. They're sneaky little liars; the best way to deal with them is to call them out. Picture yourself with a mental magnifying glass, focusing on these tiny intruders and asking a few key questions to squash them before they can do any real damage:

- *Is this fact or fiction?* Because we all know ants love to spread fake news.

- *What's the evidence?* Are there any crumbs of truth here, or is it just fluff?

- *What data runs counter to this?* Time to play detective—what clues show this thought isn't as solid as it seems?

- *How might someone else see this?* Because sometimes, our perspective is a bit too zoomed in, like staring at an ant up close.

- *What advice would I give a person in the same situation?* It's always easier to see the solution when it's not your own problem, right?

- *What are possibly more realistic and optimistic thoughts?* In other words, where's the silver lining, even if it's tiny?

The truth is most ANTs are harmless if we spot them early and challenge them head-on. And even if some of them have a tiny bit of truth, they're usually not as scary as they first appear. So, next time you notice those mental ants scurrying around, grab that metaphorical magnifying glass, get curious, and start asking questions. You might just find they're not so big and bad after all—which brings me to the next acronym—FEAR.

D. FEAR

Photo credit: Melody P, Unsplash.com

Ah, FEAR—an acronym that's so spot-on it might just deserve a permanent place on your wrist as a reminder (but let's hold off on the tattoos for now). FEAR stands for:

FEAR:
Future
Events
Appearing
Real!

Those pesky scenarios our brains love to invent that seem terrifying but are, in reality, just figments of our overactive imaginations.

Picture this: you're sitting peacefully, minding your own business, when suddenly your brain decides it's time to project you into a future disaster. You're not just imagining missing a deadline at work; you're seeing yourself jobless, living in a cardboard box under the freeway, with nothing but a sad harmonica to keep you company. It's amazing how quickly we can go from *"mildly concerned"* to *"total catastrophe."*

But here's the kicker—these terrifying future events? They're not real. They're just fears, illusions our minds conjure up when we start thinking too far ahead. The truth is, we can't change the past (no matter how many times we replay that awkward moment in our heads), and we definitely can't predict the future (if we could, we'd all be billionaires by now). What we do have is the present moment; in most cases, it's not all that bad. Unless you're currently being chased by a bear, in which case, feel free to panic.

For the rest of us, when FEAR starts creeping in, it's time to hit the pause button. Engage your rational brain, take a deep breath, and check in with reality. What's actually happening right now? Probably nothing as dire as your brain is suggesting will happen.

As you prepare to return to work—or face any other big, life-changing event—you'll need to keep this in mind. Those worst-case scenarios your brain is serving up are just that—scenarios. Not reality. Here are my top 5 ways to keep FEAR in check:

In Life:

1. *Practice Mindfulness:* Ground yourself in the present moment. Focus on what's happening right now, not what might happen down the road.

2. *Check Reality*: Ask yourself, "Is this fear based on facts, or is it just a story I'm telling myself?"

3. *Stay Flexible*: Remember that life is unpredictable, and that's okay. Adaptability is your best friend.

4. *Seek Perspective*: Talk to someone you trust. They can help you see things more clearly when you're too close to the problem.

5. *Breathe:* Seriously. Deep breaths can work wonders in calming those anxious thoughts.

In Work:

1. *Prioritize and Compartmentalize:* Break down your tasks into manageable steps. Focus on what you can do today, not everything that needs to be done by the end of the year.

2. *Communicate:* Don't let fear paralyze you. Reach out to your team, mentor, or boss when you feel overwhelmed.

3. *Stay Positive:* Replace those negative thoughts with more balanced, optimistic ones. What's the best that could happen?

4. *Reflect on Successes*: Remind yourself of past accomplishments. You've tackled challenges before, and you'll do it again.

5. *Take Action:* Even small steps forward can help you feel more in control and less fearful of the future.

You'll need a strong dose of this advice as you imagine returning to work! Here is some space to jot down your top FEAR thoughts:

In life:

____

____

____

____

____

____

In work:

____

____

____

____

____

____

E. OPEN VS. CLOSED MINDS

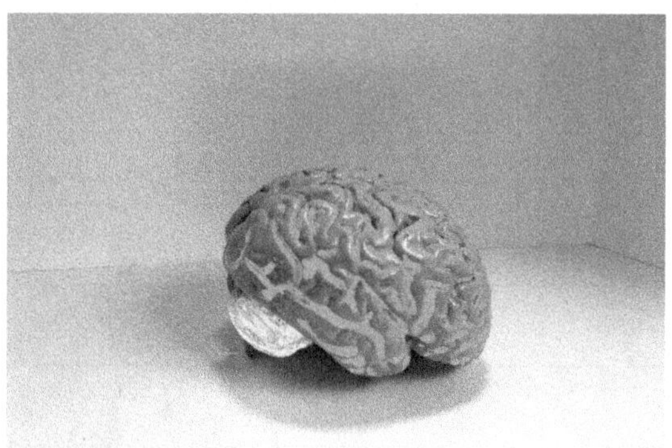

Photo credit: Natasha Connell, Unsplash.com

How we approach challenges, effort, and feedback can vary greatly depending on whether we have an open or closed mindset. The graphic below illustrates the key differences between these two mindsets, providing a helpful framework for self-reflection, especially as you prepare for a significant transition like returning to work.

CLOSED VS. OPEN MINDS		
	Closed	*Open*
Growth:	Static	Developing
Attitude:	Knower	Learner
Challenges:	Avoid	Embrace
Obstacles:	Give up	Persist
Effort:	Wasteful	Path to mastery
Criticism:	Ignore	Learn from
Comparisons:	Feel threatened	Find inspiration and lessons
Development:	Deterministic	Free will

With a *closed mindset,* we might find ourselves stuck believing that our abilities and intelligence are static. This often leads to avoiding challenges, giving up easily when obstacles arise, and feeling threatened by the success of others. It's a mindset that craves certainty and resists change, making us more likely to stick with what we know rather than stepping into the unknown.

On the other hand, an *open mindset* thrives on the idea that we can grow, learn, and improve. Challenges are embraced as opportunities to develop, and setbacks are seen as part of the journey toward mastery. Instead of fearing criticism, we learn from it. This mindset fosters resilience, curiosity, and a willingness to try new things—even if it means making mistakes along the way.

As you prepare to return to work after your leave, it's important to recognize that your mindset can significantly influence your experience. An open mindset can transform the challenges of re-entry into opportunities for growth, helping you navigate new responsibilities with confidence and flexibility.

Whether adapting to a new routine, learning to balance work and parenting, or finding new ways to connect with colleagues, approaching your return to work with an open mindset can make the transition smoother and more fulfilling.

So, as you think about your next steps, consider your current mindset. Are you ready to embrace the journey ahead with an open mind, or do you find yourself clinging to the comfort of what's familiar? The choice is yours and can make all the difference in how you experience this new chapter in your life.

F. DISTINCTIONS THAT REFRAME

Words matter—a lot. The words we use, even just in our own heads, have the power to shape our perceptions and, ultimately, our reality. Sometimes, all it takes is a slight shift in how we frame things to see a world of difference in how we feel and act.

Consider this as a mental makeover. Below are examples of distinctions that can reframe our perspectives and, in doing so, our experiences. By making small shifts in the language we use (particularly within ourselves), we can unlock new ways of thinking and empower ourselves to approach challenges with a fresh mindset.

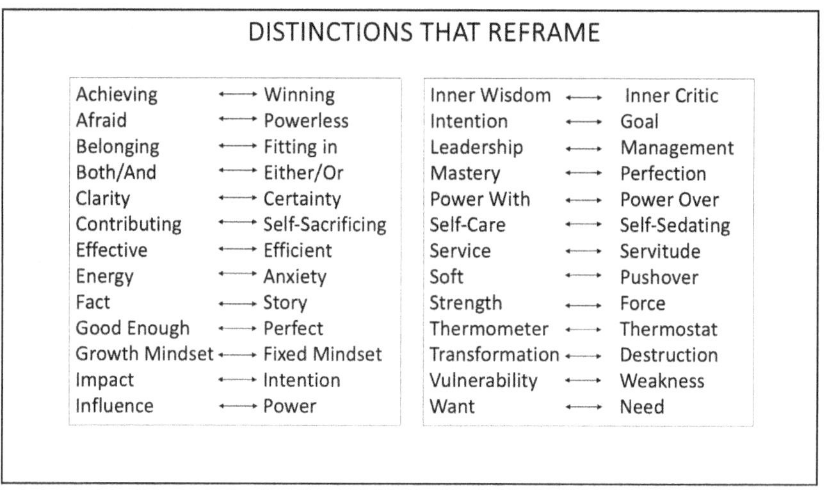

This kind of reframing isn't just a neat trick—it's a powerful tool you can use to navigate your return to work and all the transitions that come with it. I encourage you to review the distinctions above and circle the words or phrases in each pairing that resonate most with your current thoughts. Then, take a moment to challenge yourself. What if you could reframe just one or two of these? What might shift for you?

Remember, it's not about radically changing who you are—it's about fine-tuning the lens through which you see the world. A small tweak here or there can make a world of difference in your journey back to work and in life.

Techniques for Calming (You)

In the whirlwind of parenting and daily life, finding moments of calm and reconnecting with yourself can be challenging, yet essential. This chapter highlights a few of the many practices that can help you strengthen the mind-body connection and tune into your internal wisdom. Over the years, I've gathered 54 such practices that I selectively share with my clients, each offering a unique way to cultivate inner peace and resilience.

I initially considered including a large selection of these techniques here because I truly believe in their power and know that different practices resonate with different people. But I also recognize that too much information can be overwhelming, especially when you're already navigating the complexities of parenthood. So, I've carefully chosen a few techniques that I believe can make a significant impact.

If you're skeptical about self-calming practices, I encourage you to commit to trying just a couple in the coming week. You might be surprised by how a small shift in your routine can lead to a profound sense of calm and clarity. These practices, from **Grounding** to **Yoga and Meditation** to **Listening to your Heart** to **Settle Your Glitter** and **Absorbing the beauty Around You**, are simple yet powerful tools to help you find balance amidst the chaos of life. So, take a deep breath, open your mind, and explore these techniques with curiosity and openness—you might just find the one that resonates with you.

    A. Grounding

    B. Meditation and Yoga

    C. Inviting Your Somatic Wisdom

    D. Listening to Your Heart

    E. Settle Your Glitter

    F. Absorbing the Beauty Around You

A. GROUNDING

Photo credit: Melissa Askew, Unsplash.com

Back in the days of the caveman and our life on the savanna, we evolved to be highly aware of our surroundings and monitor for danger. When presented with a threat, we shifted to high alert and released stress hormones to accelerate our impending fight-or-flight reactions. The brainstem is wired to do this unconsciously, even today.

Well, we don't live in caves anymore (at least most of us don't, the wi-fi would suck, and electricity would be hard to wire up), yet we still possess this instinct. While lions may not roam our streets, we are still wired for reaction to inputs. In today's busy world, there are way more "alert inputs" than humans used to have when quietly picking berries in peaceful meadows.

We are bombarded with "stressors" today. Incessantly. As a result, our minds tell our bodies to tense up and get prepared for action. And our tensed-up, fragmented, reactive bodies let our minds know that so we can be prepared for danger. Then, our minds tell our bodies to tense up further. The infinite cycle reinforces itself.

Without even being aware of it, our tensed-up bodies, in a state of high alert, are keeping us on edge and distract us from being fully present in the now. There's a whole bunch of literature on what stress hormones do to our health and longevity (and I'll leave it for others to explain). I'll just say it's not pretty.

To break the mind-body stress cycle and be fully present in the moment, you can do a simple two-minute technique to release pressure and become more fully present. It's called "Grounding." Here's how it works:

- Sit up comfortably on your chair (or stand, if you prefer), arms relaxed with hands on your lap (or at your sides) and unclenched.

- Close your eyes (well, after reading all the directions here!).

- Take *five slow, deep cleansing breaths* to clear your mind, counting each one. Pause.

- Then, *scan and release tension in your body,* starting at the very top of your head and working all the way down your body, naming the parts. Scalp, temples, cheeks, mouth, tongue, jaw, neck, collarbone, etc. Keep going down to the tips of your toes. When you reach your toes, take one more deep cleansing breath. Pause.

- Next, take a *slow (slow!) and luxurious neck roll* in one direction and then in the other. Notice anything? Almost everyone reports stiffness or soreness and sometimes even crackling or popping sounds. That's stress-tension release.

- Last, *stretch your arms and hands way up above your head,* towards the ceiling. Bend your face towards the sky. Stretch far. Maybe take a yawn. Clasp your hands together way above your head and gently *stretch to the left and right.* Breathe.

- Finally, when you are ready, gently *open your eyes, returning to your present space.*

- *Aaaahhhhh.* Feel better?

Notice how different you feel and how it affects calming and focusing your mind on the present moment. This can be done at any time. It only takes two minutes. Some people start and/or end their days with it; others find it useful before meetings or when switching activities. Whatever works for you.

Can you commit to trying it out a couple of times a day, say, for the next week? Nothing to lose if it doesn't do much for you other than 14 minutes of your life.

B. MEDITATION AND YOGA

Photo credit: Getty Images, Unsplash.com

Let's talk about meditation and yoga, shall we? I know, I know—half of you are already devotees, hitting the mat with enthusiasm, while the other half are rolling your eyes so hard they might just stay that way. But hear me out!

Yoga:

For those of you who are *not* exactly on the yoga train yet, I totally get it. The thought of cramming in a session at the gym, breathing in the communal hot air, and contorting yourself into what can only be described as "human pretzel mode" might not be appealing. And who wants to risk toppling over in downward dog, anyway?

But here's a little idea that might just change your mind: a free app called *FitOn*. This nifty tool lets you customize your yoga and meditation practice to fit your needs—no studio required. Want something easy? Set the difficulty to 1. Short on time? Go for a 10-minute session (or double up if you're feeling wild!). They even offer two-minute "work workouts" you can do right at your desk. Seriously, how much easier could it get? If you have any secret inkling to give it a try in the privacy of your home, here's what the app looks like (it's purple):

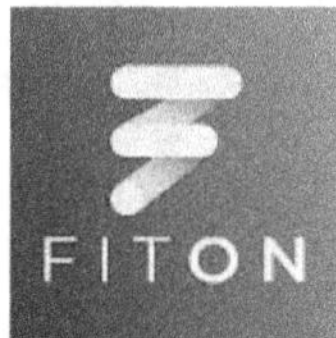

Meditation:

For those who scoff at meditation, let's look at some numbers. Practiced meditation can lead to some pretty awesome benefits:

- **76%** reported better general wellness

- **60%** felt they had more energy

- **50%** noticed sharper memory and focus

- **29%** reduced their anxiety

- **22%** reduced their stress

- **18%** reduced their depression

Not too shabby, right? So, if you can carve out even 10–20 minutes a day (especially before bed), give it a try. There are plenty of apps out there that make meditation easy, enjoyable, and effective.

Now, I'm not here to preach—okay, maybe just a little. But if you've ever had even the faintest urge to give yoga or meditation a shot, why not try it in the privacy of your own home? No judgment, no sweaty strangers, just you and your mat (or office chair).

C. INVITING YOUR SOMATIC WISDOM

Photo credit: Niloufar Nemati, Unsplash.com

So, when did you last take a moment to listen to your body? I'm not talking about those times when your stomach growls to remind you it's time for lunch, or when your back yells at you after a long day hunched over a desk. I'm talking about a real, intentional pause to tap into the wisdom that your body quietly holds.

Most of us treat our bodies like silent servants, always there, doing their job, until something goes wrong. But here's the thing: Your body is constantly sending you signals, little whispers of insight that can guide you if you just take a moment to listen.

So, here's a simple invitation: take two five-minute time-outs each day to tune into what your body has to say. The first could be right when you wake up—before your feet hit the ground. Yes, that might mean setting your alarm five minutes earlier, but trust me, it's worth it. The second can be whenever it works best for you—before lunch, after dinner, during your nightly tooth-brushing ritual (because I'm sure we all brush our teeth twice a day, right?).

Here's how it works:

- Sit or stand comfortably, feet grounded, arms relaxed.

- Start by taking five deep breaths—nice and slow.

- Then, mentally scan your body from head to toe. Name each part as you go and ask yourself, *"How does this part feel today?"* Notice any tension, discomfort, or ease. Relax each area as you move on.

When you're done, if you're into journaling, take 30 seconds to jot down any insights. Maybe you'll notice something new—like the fact that you've been holding your tongue against the roof of your mouth (a surprisingly common discovery). Or maybe you'll realize just how tense your shoulders are, all geared up to face the day's battles.

Some of you might be thinking, *"This sounds a bit out there for me,"* and might be tempted to skip to the next section. But give it a try for a few days. You might be surprised by what your body says when you listen.

D. LISTENING TO YOUR HEART

Photo credit : Michelle Dot, Unsplash.com

In our daily grind, we're often laser-focused on checking off to-dos and using our brains to navigate the chaos. We might even carve out time for our bodies, squeezing in that run or yoga session. But when did you last pause to listen to your *heart*? Not in the metaphorical, poetic sense, nor in the Apple Watch sense, but literally asking it (your heart) what it desires and what it needs to feel nourished and whole. Chances are, that moment doesn't come around very often—if ever.

So, here's a gentle nudge to change that. I invite you to dedicate just 15 minutes to listening to your heart each evening. Consider it a mini retreat, a chance to step away from the noise of the day and tune into what truly matters to you. Set a reminder before your sleep app tells you it's bedtime and be dogmatic about sticking to this ritual for a couple of weeks.

Here's how to do it: Start by setting the mood. Light a candle, put on some soothing music—Spa Radio, Enya, or whatever melts away your stress—and set a gentle 15-minute timer.

Now, find that cozy chair by your bed, wrap yourself in a warm blanket, and bask in the soft glow of the candlelight. Begin with a deep breath and a quick five-minute body scan (yes, that same one from "Inviting Your Somatic Wisdom" in the prior section). Feel every part of your body, acknowledge any tension, and let it go.

And then, just sit. Quietly. Ask your heart, *"What do I want for me going forward?"* Keep returning to that question. Whatever comes up, let it be. No judging, no overthinking—just pure, unfiltered listening. Thank each thought, whether it feels right or not, and let it sit with you or float away like a wisp of smoke. If a to-do list tries to crash the party, gently escort it out of your mind, letting those distractions drift by like clouds on a breezy day.

If you keep a journal, jot down any insights for later reflection. It's a simple practice, but one that can reveal profound truths about what you need, want, and hope for in your journey ahead.

E. SETTLE YOUR GLITTER

Photo credit: Getty Images, Unsplash.com

Parenthood is filled with moments of pure joy but comes with its fair share of challenges, especially in the early days. Sleep deprivation, constant demands, and the overwhelming responsibility of caring for a newborn can sometimes push even the most patient and composed parents to their limits. In these moments, it's easy to react impulsively—whether it's lashing out, losing your temper, or making hasty decisions. But what if there were a simple, effective way to pause, regroup, and respond more calmly? Enter the concept of "Settle Your Glitter."

"Settle Your Glitter" is often taught to kindergarten children to help them manage their emotions. The idea is simple: when faced with a situation that stirs up strong feelings, imagine your emotions as glitter swirling inside a snow globe. Instead of reacting immediately, you take a moment to still the snow globe and watch the glitter settle. As the glitter slowly falls to the bottom, so do your emotions, allowing you to respond from a place of calm rather than reactivity. This concept can be incredibly valuable for new parents navigating the stresses of early parenthood.

Why "Settle Your Glitter" Works

The science behind "Settle Your Glitter" lies in mindfulness. Mindfulness is the practice of being fully present in the moment, acknowledging your emotions without immediately reacting to them. By taking a moment to pause and let the "glitter" of your emotions settle, you create a space between the situation and your response. This space allows you to choose a more measured, thoughtful reaction rather than one driven by stress or frustration.

For new parents, this technique can be a lifesaver. Here's how it can help:

- *Reducing Stress and Overwhelm:*
  When you're running on little sleep, and your baby is crying for what feels like the hundredth time that night, it's easy to feel overwhelmed. Instead of reacting out of frustration, "Settle Your Glitter" gives you a moment to breathe, acknowledge your stress, and let it pass before taking action.

- *Improving Communication:*
  Sleep deprivation and the demands of parenting can lead to miscommunication and tension between partners. Taking a moment to "settle your glitter" before responding to a heated conversation makes you more likely to communicate calmly and clearly, reducing the likelihood of conflict.

- *Modeling Calmness for Your Baby:*
  Babies are incredibly sensitive to their parents' emotions. When you react calmly, even in stressful situations, you're modeling emotional regulation for your child, which can positively impact their own emotional development.

How to Practice "Settle Your Glitter"

Incorporating "Settle Your Glitter" into your daily routine doesn't require much—just a little mindfulness and a few moments of your time. Here's how you can do it:

1. *Recognize the Trigger:*

   The first step is to recognize when you're feeling triggered or overwhelmed. This could be anything from your baby's persistent crying to an unexpected mess to feeling overwhelmed by your to-do list. The key is to notice the moment when your emotions start to spike.

2. *Pause and Breathe:*

   Once you've recognized the trigger, pause for a moment. Take a deep breath in, hold it for a couple of seconds, and then slowly exhale. This simple act of breathing helps to calm your nervous system and brings your focus back to the present moment.

3. *Visualize the Glitter Settling:*

   Imagine your emotions as glitter swirling inside a snow globe. Picture yourself shaking the globe, and then watch as the glitter slowly settles to the bottom. As the glitter falls, allow your emotions to settle as well, creating a sense of calm.

4. *Choose Your Response:*

   After the glitter has settled, take a moment to consider how you want to respond to the situation. What's the best course of action? How can you address the situation calmly and effectively? By creating this space between the trigger and your response, you're more likely to choose a reaction you won't regret later.

5. *Practice Regularly:*
   Like any skill, "Settle Your Glitter" becomes more effective with practice. The more you use this technique, the easier it will become to access that sense of calm, even in the most challenging moments of parenthood.

Making "Settle Your Glitter" a Family Practice

"Settle Your Glitter" isn't just for parents—it's a valuable technique you can teach your children as they grow. By making it a regular part of your family's approach to handling emotions, you're helping to build a foundation of emotional intelligence and resilience.

- *Use a Real Snow Globe:* Consider keeping a real snow globe in your home as a visual reminder to "settle your glitter." When emotions run high, you or your child can physically shake the globe and watch the glitter settle as a calming exercise. They even make plastic snow globes, just in case someone's impulse is to throw it across the room in the moment.

- *Create a Calm-Down Corner:* Designate a space in your home where anyone can go to "settle their glitter." This might include the snow globe, comfortable seating, and other calming tools like books or soft toys. It's a safe space for anyone in the family to take a moment and regroup.

Parenthood is full of moments that can test your patience and emotional resilience. But by practicing "Settle Your Glitter," you can create the space needed to respond calmly and thoughtfully, even in the most challenging situations. This simple yet powerful technique helps you manage your emotions, improve communication, and model calmness for your child. So, the next time you feel the urge to react impulsively, remember to shake that snow globe in your mind, watch the glitter settle, and approach the situation with the calm and clarity you and your family deserve.

F. ABSORBING THE BEAUTY AROUND YOU

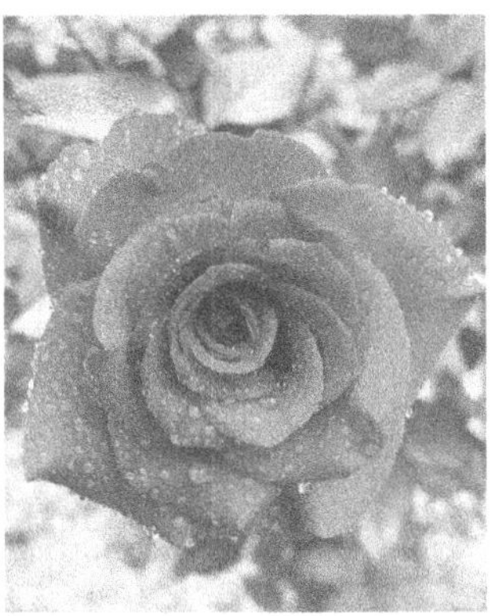

Photo credit: Rose Arkadiy, Unsplash.com

You know how Nike says, "*Just do it*"? Well, my version is, "*Just take a walk.*" Schedule it in your calendar like an important meeting because this walk is not about getting somewhere—it's about fully experiencing what's already around you. But here's the catch: this isn't your typical stroll. This is a walk where you engage all five of your senses—fully, completely, and with zero distractions.

First, *look*. Observe the colors around you—the vibrant greens of the trees, the delicate hues of flowers, or even the different shades of gray in the concrete. Notice the details, like the texture of the bark on a tree or the way the sunlight dances through the leaves. Take in the faces of people passing by, not to judge or analyze, but simply to notice and appreciate the diversity of expressions and features.

Next, *listen*. Tune into the symphony of sounds surrounding you. Maybe it's the rustling of leaves, the distant hum of traffic, birds chirping in the trees, or the crunch of gravel underfoot. Let the sounds wash over you without labeling them as good or bad—just let them be.

Now, focus on *smell*. Breathe in deeply, noticing the fresh scent of grass, the earthy aroma after a rain, or even the faint perfume of flowers as you pass by. Smell has a unique way of grounding us in the present, so let each inhale remind you of where you are right now.

Don't forget to *feel*. How does the ground feel beneath your feet? Is it solid pavement, soft grass, or something else? What about the air—does it have a crisp chill or a warm embrace? Pay attention to how your body feels as you walk. Are your muscles relaxed or tense? Notice the subtle sensations on your skin, like a gentle breeze or the warmth of the sun.

And finally, *taste*. You might not be tasting during your walk, but maybe there's a lingering flavor from your last meal or a hint of salt from the sea air. Taste is often the most overlooked sense in these experiences, but it's just as important. If you happen to walk by a bakery, let the smell almost translate into a taste. Let your mouth water at the aroma of fresh bread or coffee.

This walk is about more than just clearing your mind; it's about filling it with the richness of the world around you. When your thoughts wander—as they inevitably will—gently guide them back to your senses. Let go of any internal chatter and just absorb everything around you.

When you're done, take a moment to reflect. How do you feel now? How has your mind cleared, your heart lightened, and your body relaxed? Jot down anything notable in your journal—whether it's a cool observation or just a feeling you want to remember. And make this a habit. A walk like this, a couple of times a week, can be a powerful reset button, giving you the space to appreciate the beauty of the world—and yourself—more fully.

When Things Are Really Tough

When life gets tough, it's easy to feel alone, spiraling, and barely holding it together. The pressure, the uncertainty, and the sheer exhaustion can make everything feel overwhelming, especially when juggling the demands of work, family, and your own well-being. This chapter is here to remind you that while you can't control everything, you can influence how you navigate through these tough times.

We'll start by exploring the concept of "**Choosing Narratives**." Whether you feel like a hamster on a treadmill, a juggler trying to keep too many balls in the air, or even a tightrope walker trying not to fall off, it's essential to recognize the story you're telling yourself and understand that you have the power to rewrite it. Your narrative shapes your reality, so let's shift from just surviving to thriving.

Then, we'll dive into the ancient Japanese art of "**Kintsugi,**" which beautifully illustrates how brokenness can lead to a stronger, more resilient self. Just like pottery that's mended with gold, your cracks and breaks are part of your unique story. Embrace them and see how they've made you who you are today—stronger, wiser, and more beautiful in your imperfections.

Through these concepts, this chapter aims to help you find strength and peace, even when things seem impossibly tough. You'll learn to reframe your challenges, find meaning in the struggle, and emerge with a deeper sense of self and resilience.

In this chapter we'll explore:

A. Choosing Narratives

B. Kintsugi

A. CHOOSING NARRATIVES

Everyone has a "*Current Narrative*"—the way we *are* in our current environment, what we're *experiencing*, and how we're *being*.

These narratives vary all over the board. The most common Current Narratives I hear from parents returning from parental leaves are:

- "*The Hamster on a Treadmill.*" Keeps going and going on the treadmill of life, exhausting themself while going the distance, day after day after day.

- "*The Rubik's Cube.*" Trying to figure out how all the pieces fit together and can be organized; they are constantly putting the puzzle together.

- *"Superwoman/Superman."* Attempting to do all things for all people, with great time pressure and expectations. Superpowers on the outside.

Photo credit: Miguel Bruna, Unsplash.com

- *"The Tightrope Walker."* Aspires to stay on top of things and not fall off their precarious balance.

Photo credit: Aleksandr Kadykov, Unsplash.com

- *"The Juggler."* Challenges themself to keep all the balls in the air and not let one drop.

Photo credit: Alexey Turenkov, Unsplash.com

- *"The Guarded Heart under Attack."* Feels trapped and attacked from all angles, looking for a route to escape and waiting for the next lightning bolt to hit.

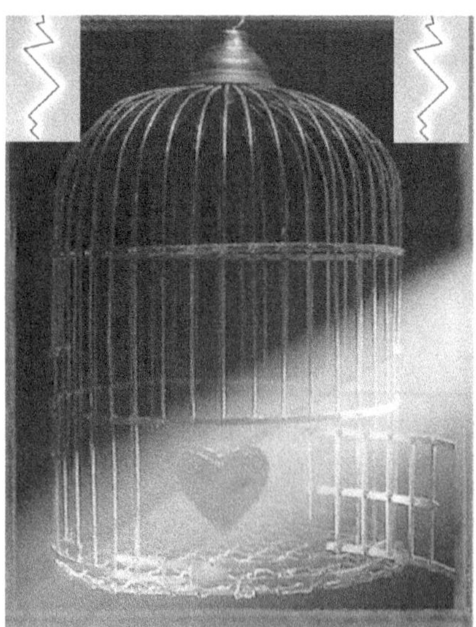

Do any of these resonate with you? Do you have an image with some words that sum up your life? Ask yourself, "*it's like what (image, picture, analogy)?*" (note: the question is NOT "*what's it like?*"). Pause and think about it—name it, picture it. Check out www.Unsplash.com for some free images to download for inspiration.

Not exactly a pretty picture for those who have gone blindly into this major life transition! Of course, new parents may find current narratives much more appealing. However, these themes are surprisingly common when I meet with my clients. You may not identify with any of the above narratives and may be able to describe your own Current Narrative if you dig deep. But one thing's for sure—whatever your narrative is, it's only going to intensify if it hasn't already.

In writing this book, my hope is that you can migrate toward a deeper narrative. One in which you are more calm, balanced, focused, wise, and sage. This picture captures it for me. I call it "*The Wise Grounded Woman.*"

Source: New Ventures West

B. KINTSUGI

金継ぎ

(For those of you who can read Japanese, I do hope that these symbols translate to what I am told they are, or someone is having a great joke on me.)

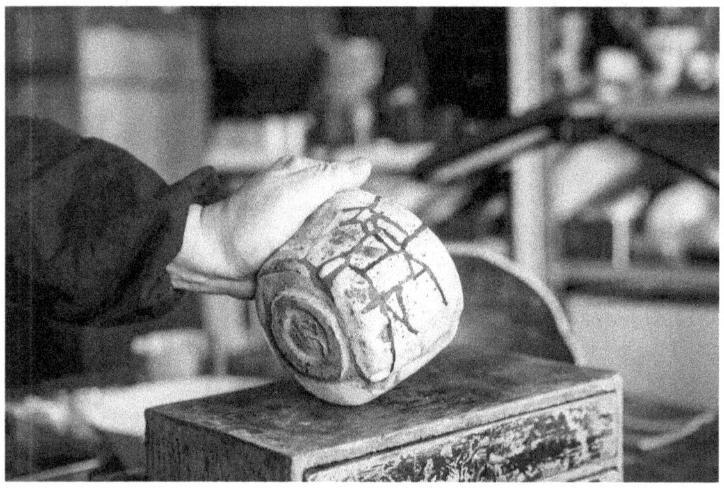

Photo credit: Motoki Tonn, Unsplash.com

Kintsugi, or 金継ぎ, translates to *"golden joinery"* in Japanese. It's a centuries-old art form that involves repairing broken pottery by mending the cracks with lacquer mixed with powdered gold, silver, or platinum. The idea isn't just to fix the broken object but to highlight the breaks, making the mended object even more beautiful and unique than it was before. The philosophy behind Kintsugi is that breakage and repair are part of the history of an object, not something to disguise.

This concept applies beautifully to our own lives. As we move forward, striving toward our goals and dreams, it's essential to look back and reflect on where we've been and how our past experiences—especially the tough ones—have shaped us. Life's challenges and setbacks, the things that broke us or left us feeling less than whole, are like those cracks in the pottery. But instead of hiding these cracks, we can fill them with our own "gold," turning our scars into something that adds value to who we are.

To embrace this idea, take some time for a personal reflection exercise. Find a quiet, comfortable spot—maybe light a candle, play some soft music, and grab your journal. Start by listing some of the hardest experiences you've gone through. These might be times of loss, failure, or deep disappointment—moments that left you feeling fragmented. Ask yourself: "*What were the toughest parts of my life?*" Write down a handful or even a dozen. Write them down without judgment.

Include even those experiences you would rather not have happened. Pause. Take some deep breaths.

Notes to self:

____

____

____

____

____

____

____

Once you've done that, think about how these experiences have contributed to the person you are today. Ask yourself: *"How did it contribute to who I am today?"* and *"What did I learn from it?"* and *"How did this experience make me stronger, wiser, or more compassionate?"* and *"What hidden gifts came out of this tough time?"*

Jot down your thoughts and take some time to sit with them. Consider where you might even find gratitude for these experiences, as difficult as they may have been. Our past creates who we are today and who we might become in our future.

Just as Kintsugi turns broken pieces into something more beautiful, reflecting on and embracing your own cracks can reveal a more resilient and unique version of yourself.

Notes to self:

APPENDIX

1. Other Personality Assessments

    A. Clifton Strengths

    B. MBTI – Myers Briggs

    C. DiSC

2. Adult Development

    A. Ways of Being

    B. Six Streams of Competence

3. Digging Deep

    A. Childhood Essence

    B. Your Legacy

    C. Message from Your Older, Wiser Self

Other Personality Assessments

There's no shortage of "self-assessment" tools—each with its own approach, validity, and cost. My go-to tool is the Enneagram, which I've found invaluable in understanding the growth paths of my clients. That's why it's front and center, as Chapter 1 in this book.

You might wonder why we're diving into self-assessment in a book focused on parental transitions. The reason is simple: expecting a baby or preparing to return to work is a pivotal time to reflect on who you are, where you've been, and how you want to grow moving forward. It's a golden opportunity for self-awareness.

In addition to the Enneagram, I see value in other personality assessments like the MBTI (**Myers-Briggs Type Indicator**), DiSC, **and Clifton Strengths**. Each tool offers unique insights and can be incredibly useful in your personal and professional life. Whether you're looking for something simple and straightforward or a more in-depth exploration, these assessments provide different perspectives that can help you understand yourself better.

This appendix offers a bird's-eye view of three additional assessments—each widely used and well-validated. Whether you're new to these tools or looking to explore them further, this section provides an overview to help you decide how they might fit into your personal diagnostic toolkit. If you're intrigued, there's plenty of literature out there for a deeper dive into any of these assessments.

In this appendix, we'll explore:

A. Clifton Strengths

B. MBTI – Myers Briggs

C. DiSC

A. CLIFTON STRENGTHS

Clifton Strengths (formerly known as Strengths Finder) focuses on identifying and amplifying your innate talents rather than attempting to "fix" weaknesses. This strengths-based approach is a refreshing perspective that emphasizes building on who you already are.

Clifton Strengths (owned by Gallup, created and developed by Don Clifton) identifies 34 distinct themes representing the most common talents. Each theme is detailed in a dedicated chapter within the accompanying book, providing insights into how these strengths manifest in your life and work.

It identifies a diverse list of 34 Themes (or most common talents) and has a chapter describing each one:

34 CLIFTON STRENGTHS

Achiever	Activator	Adaptability
Analytical	Arranger	Belief
Command	Communication	Competition
Connectedness	Consistency	Context
Deliberative	Developer	Discipline
Empathy	Focus	Futuristic
Harmony	Ideation	Includer
Individualization	Input	Intellection
Learner	Maximizer	Positivity
Relator	Responsibility	Restorative
Self-Assurance	Significance	Strategic

WOO! *(You'll have to take the test to decipher that one for yourself.)*

How to Access and Utilize Your CliftonStrengths

The **Clifton Strengths 2.0** book, available on Amazon, includes an access code for the online assessment. In just 15 minutes, you'll receive a personalized report that ranks your strengths and offers strategies for maximizing them.

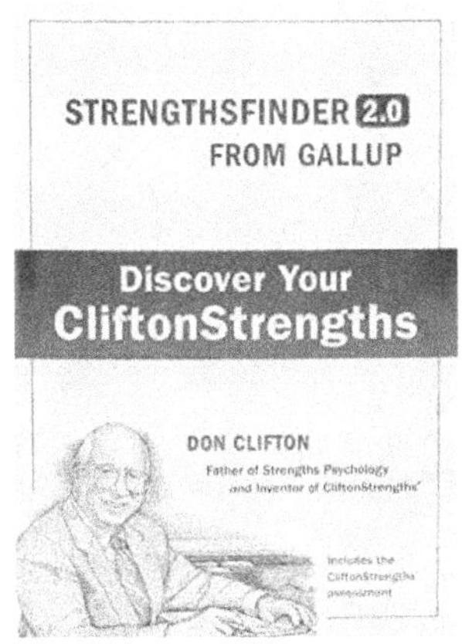

Strengthsfinder 2.0 from Gallup: Discover Your Clifton Strengths

Practical Application During Parental Leave

Taking the Clifton Strengths assessment can be particularly enlightening as you prepare for parental leave and your eventual return to work. Reflect on these key questions:

1. *What are your top strengths to leverage?*
   Identify your top five strengths and consider how they've served you in your career and personal life.

2. *How have you been leveraging them?*
   Reflect on the ways you've already put these strengths to use. Are there areas where they've made a significant difference?

3. *How are you going to leverage them going forward?*
   As you transition back to work, consider how you can continue to apply your strengths. This is your opportunity to strategically align your strengths with your evolving career goals and personal life.

My Top 5 Clifton Strengths:

1. ____

2. ____

3. ____

4. ____

5. ____

My Notes on How to Leverage them (Past and Future):

____

____

____

____

____

____

____

Remember, your strengths are your superpowers—use them wisely and often!

B. MBTI (MYERS-BRIGGS)

If you've been around the corporate world for a while, you've likely encountered and probably even taken the "Myers-Briggs" (aka "MBTI" or Myers-Briggs Type Indicator) assessment at some point.

It identifies 16 "Types" derived from four forces, each of which has two pairs (E vs. I, S vs. N, T vs. F, and J vs. P).

1. *Source of Energy*: Extraversion or Introversion

2. *Information-Gathering Function*: Sensing or iNtuition

3. *Decision-Making Function*: Thinking or Feeling

4. *Lifestyle Orientation:* Judging or Perceiving

While it can be highly useful in understanding our behaviors and those of others, it can be challenging to keep track of and understand all 16 types (other than my own ENTJ type, which, of course, I find most interesting and worthy of deep study).

So, in my sometimes-simplistic mind, I've developed a couple of overview/cheat sheet summaries, which are largely modified from a wonderful book, *Type Talk* by Otto Kroeger and Janet M. Thuesen.

If you don't already know your four-letter type, an online assessment is available at www.mbtionline.com. It's approved by the Myers-Briggs Foundation, and at the time of this writing, it is $49.95 for the assessment and read-out report. It takes less than an hour and can be quite insightful and helpful in identifying behavioral tendencies.

Here's the highest-level summary of the way I think about MBTI (largely derived from the *Type Talk* book mentioned above).

<table>
<tr><td colspan="3" align="center">MYERS-BRIGGS KEY DIMENSIONS</td></tr>
<tr><td>E or I?</td><td>Extraversion
• Focus on the outer world.
• Energy by interacting with people and/or doing things.</td><td>Introversion
• Focus on the inner world.
• Energy through reflecting on ideas, information, and/or concepts.</td></tr>
<tr><td>S or N?</td><td>Sensing
• Notice and trust facts, details, and present realities.</td><td>Intuition
• Attend to and trust interrelationships, theories, and future possibilities.</td></tr>
<tr><td>T or F?</td><td>Thinking
• Make decisions using logical analysis to achieve objectivity.</td><td>Feeling
• Make decisions using personality-centered values to achieve harmony.</td></tr>
<tr><td>J or P?</td><td>Judging
• Tend to be organized and orderly and to make decisions quickly.</td><td>Perceiving
• Tend to be flexible and adaptable and to keep options open for as long as possible.</td></tr>
</table>

And here's a bit more color around each dimension (again, largely derived from *Type Talk*).

<table>
<tr><td colspan="3" align="center"><u>Source of Energy</u>
Extraverts vs. Introverts</td></tr>
<tr><td align="center">E
Extraversion</td><td></td><td align="center">I
Introversion</td></tr>
<tr><td align="center">Sociability</td><td align="center">⟵⟶</td><td align="center">Territoriality</td></tr>
<tr><td align="center">Interaction</td><td align="center">⟵⟶</td><td align="center">Concentration</td></tr>
<tr><td align="center">External</td><td align="center">⟵⟶</td><td align="center">Internal</td></tr>
<tr><td align="center">Breadth</td><td align="center">⟵⟶</td><td align="center">Depth</td></tr>
<tr><td align="center">Extensive</td><td align="center">⟵⟶</td><td align="center">Intensive</td></tr>
<tr><td align="center">Multiple relationships</td><td align="center">⟵⟶</td><td align="center">Limited relationships</td></tr>
<tr><td align="center">Energy expenditure</td><td align="center">⟵⟶</td><td align="center">Energy conservation</td></tr>
<tr><td align="center">External events</td><td align="center">⟵⟶</td><td align="center">Internal reactions</td></tr>
<tr><td align="center">Gregarious</td><td align="center">⟵⟶</td><td align="center">Reflective</td></tr>
<tr><td align="center">Speak, then think</td><td align="center">⟵⟶</td><td align="center">Think, then speak</td></tr>
</table>

<table>
<tr><td colspan="3" align="center"><u>Information-Gathering Function</u>
Sensors vs iNtuitives</td></tr>
<tr><td align="center">S
Sensing</td><td></td><td align="center">N
Intuition</td></tr>
<tr><td align="center">Sequential</td><td align="center">⟵⟶</td><td align="center">Random</td></tr>
<tr><td align="center">Present</td><td align="center">⟵⟶</td><td align="center">Future</td></tr>
<tr><td align="center">Realistic</td><td align="center">⟵⟶</td><td align="center">Conceptual</td></tr>
<tr><td align="center">Perspiration</td><td align="center">⟵⟶</td><td align="center">Inspiration</td></tr>
<tr><td align="center">Actual</td><td align="center">⟵⟶</td><td align="center">Theoretical</td></tr>
<tr><td align="center">Down-to-earth</td><td align="center">⟵⟶</td><td align="center">Head-in-clouds</td></tr>
<tr><td align="center">Fact</td><td align="center">⟵⟶</td><td align="center">Fantasy</td></tr>
<tr><td align="center">Practicality</td><td align="center">⟵⟶</td><td align="center">Ingenuity</td></tr>
<tr><td align="center">Specific</td><td align="center">⟵⟶</td><td align="center">General</td></tr>
</table>

Decision-Making Function
Thinkers *vs.* **Feelers**

T Thinking		F Feeling
Objective	⟷	Subjective
Firm-minded	⟷	Fair-hearted
Laws	⟷	Circumstances
Firmness	⟷	Persuasion
Just	⟷	Humane
Clarity	⟷	Harmony
Critique	⟷	Appreciate
Policy	⟷	Social values
Detached	⟷	Involved

Lifestyle Orientation
Judgers *vs.* **Perceivers**

J Judging		P Perceiving
Resolved	⟷	Pending
Decided	⟷	Wait and see
Fixed	⟷	Flexible
Control	⟷	Adapt
Closure	⟷	Openness
Planned	⟷	Open-ended
Structure	⟷	Flow
Definite	⟷	Tentative
Scheduled	⟷	Spontaneous
Deadline	⟷	What deadline?

Finally, pulling it all together, here's the matrix of all 16 types and some high-level descriptors about how each type might stereotypically present itself.

MYERS-BRIGGS 16 TYPES				
		S		N	
		T	F	T	F
I	J	ISTJ "Doing what should be done"	ISFJ "A high sense of duty"	INTJ "Everything has room for improvement"	INFJ "An inspiration to others"
	P	ISTP "Ready to try anything once"	ISFP "Sees much but shares little"	INTP "A love of problem-solving"	INFP "Performing noble service to aid society"
E	J	ESTJ "Life's administrators"	ESFJ "Hosts and hostesses of the world"	ENTJ "Life's natural leaders"	ENFJ "Smooth-talking persuaders"
	P	ESTP "The ultimate realists"	ESFP "You only go around once in life"	ENTP "One exciting challenge after another"	ENFP "Giving life an extra squeeze"

Enjoy and explore. Read about yourself, read about others. Then tuck it in your tool kit of information about yourself and your interactions with other Types.

My Myers-Briggs Type Indicator (MBTI):

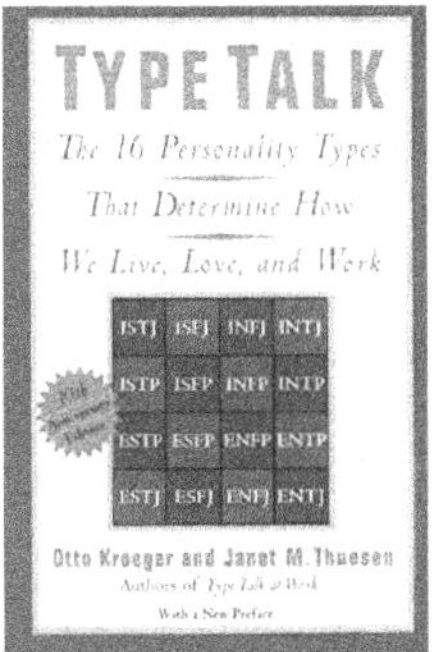

Here's a great book that goes into more detail, available on Amazon.

C. DISC

Now that we've waded into the Enneagram (see Chapter 1), Clifton Strengths, and Myers-Briggs, let me share my fourth (and final!) favored assessment tool—DiSC. (Yes, the "i" is not capitalized, and my curious mind had to know why. It turns out they couldn't get the trademark for DISC, so they went with DiSC.

DiSC is commonly explored with working teams to help reveal and simplify the dynamics of team interactions. There are four primary Styles (green, yellow, red, blue), and at times a secondary Style for each individual. A team often plots each member's "dot" on the circle in the appropriate location and explores team dynamics.

Take a look at the overview below and see if you can "plot" your dot on the circle. Many people can easily recognize their Style. If you are struggling to "plot the dot," you can, of course, take an online assessment. It becomes even more interesting if you have your whole team take the assessment, which produces an often-feisty debate about appropriate team dynamics. There are plenty of good books about DiSC out there to explore.

For you, for now (as you ponder your approach to leaving and returning to work), tuck it into your personal knowledge tool kit.

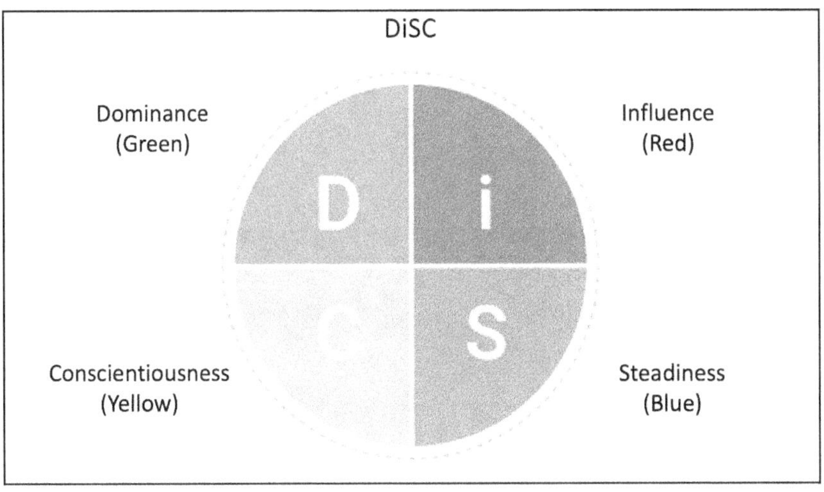

DiSC OVERVIEW

<u>DOMINANCE (Green)</u>	<u>iNFLUENCE (Red)</u>
Results **Action** **Challenge** *Motivators*: Power, authority, success, competition, and winning *Values*: Competency, concrete results, personal freedom *Style*: Driven, direct, decisive, strong-willed, self-confident, daring, determined, fast-paced *Fears*: Loss of control, being taken advantage of, vulnerability	**Enthusiasm** **Action** **Collaboration** *Motivators*: Social recognition, group activities, relationships *Values*: Coaching & counseling, freedom of expression, individuality *Style*: Charming, collaborative, energizing, trusting, enthusiastic, impulsive, optimistic, persuasive *Fears*: Social rejection, disapproval, loss of influence, being ignored
<u>CONSCIENTIOUSNESS (Yellow)</u>	<u>STEADINESS (Blue)</u>
Accuracy **Stability** **Challenge** *Motivators*: Opportunities to gain knowledge, showing their expertise, quality work *Values*: Quality, accuracy, challenge *Style*: Cautious, systematic, private, objective, analytical, diplomatic, accurate, reserved *Fears*: Criticism, unclear methods, being wrong	**Support** **Stability** **Collaboration** *Motivators*: Cooperation, opportunities to help, sincere appreciation *Values*: Loyalty, helping others, security *Style*: Calm, patient, predictable, deliberate, stable, warm, passive, loyal *Fears*: Loss of stability or harmony, change, offending others

My DiSC Type:

Primary:

____

Secondary:

____

Adult Development

A. WAYS OF BEING

I bet you've already picked up books on infant, baby, and toddler development. These will be followed by a multitude of books on raising teenagers and adolescents. (Good luck with that. You'll need strength and patience, but they do come out the other side, and miraculously, you will regain your status as an intelligent person—again, a topic for another book.)

But have you ever read a book about the states of *adult* development? I sure hadn't until I got into coaching and executive advisory. And I wish I had because it's so blatantly obvious (and reassuring to know that one's path is "normal"). It's amazing that leaders, who tend to rely heavily on information and analysis, were not given this information way earlier in life. It should be a core high school curriculum course!

If you haven't heard about this, read on. There are apparently ten levels of adult developmental "Ways of Being." But I'll focus on the first five because a nearly infinitesimal number of people are scattered over the remaining five upper levels. I envision those people as monks living in a monastery, enlightening and growing them-selves to higher levels of consciousness. In case you are interested, those upper levels are: *6. Freedom from Assessment, 7. Freedom from Meaninglessness, 8. Freedom from Narcissism, 9. Freedom from Suffering,* and *10. Freedom from Death.* I don't know about you, but I'm nowhere near those upper levels, at least for now and probably forever.

So, back to us mortal humans…

The ten developmental "Ways of Being" describe an adult development journey. I will paraphrase and adapt liberally here from the writings of James Flaherty in his book *Integral Coaching.* (If you're so inclined, the book has some deep and interesting thinking in it.)

Here are highlights and caveats about our adult development:

- Development moves in one direction only and unfolds in a particular natural order.

- It's not inevitable; it requires our active participation.

- Most of us don't listen until there's a (midlife) crisis.

- The levels build on each other, and no one is permanently at one level.

- We can be at different levels for different dimensions within our lives.

- Higher ("deeper") does not mean better.

- We can only be in the life that we have at this moment.

Now, what are these first five levels?

1.   Addressing Immediate Concerns

2. Balance

3. Conversations

4. Power

5. Vocation

Here's a description of each of the levels:

1. *Addressing Immediate Concerns*
    The most constrained level, when the world seems to be on fire. No learning, no preparation, no reserves. We're doing our best to keep our heads above water, save the people we care about, and get to safety. This is survival mode.

2. *Balance*
    We're just so busy we don't have time to do anything. Every moment is jammed with multiple tasks; booked and over-booked. It's hard to separate our likes from what is healthy. We are loath to give up anything. We believe we are indispensable. High activity is disguised as a sense of meaning. We may brag about the number of hours we work, often with a gnawing fear that we're not so important. We're keeping all the juggling balls in the air.

3. *Conversations*
    We're becoming more proficient in speaking and listening, and we're able to see other people's views as just as valid as our own. We're willing to refrain from attacking others with different views but still do not see them as equal. We have discovered asking for what we want and negotiating what is requested of us. We are open and curious about what others know and have the capacity to speak and listen from multiple

perspectives without being unduly attached to any one of them. We learn to listen and catch on that the world is not just based on facts.

4. *Power*

   Power in this context means having what we intend to happen in the world actually happen in a way that unifies us and contributes to others. It means attending to the kind of person we are becoming and living in the world that consequently opens. It is not about force, but it can turn into it. The human world is eternally fluid, shaped by how we speak and listen to it. We become present, focused, patient, resilient, creative, and steady in our sense of worth. We've overcome procrastination, settling, and justifying. We look courageously and dispassionately at ourselves and our lives, asking, *"How do I do this?"* rather than *"Can I do this?"* It is still about getting what we want for ourselves.

5. *Vocation*

   This step up is a large one that most people never make. In this level, life is not about what I want, but rather about what life wants from me. It's about listening to the call of life, *Vocation*. Vocation is not a job or a matter of willpower. Many people "visit" a stage of Vocation. It's a transformation because it's a complete reorientation of our world. We quiet ourselves so we can hear our inner call and wait to respond to whatever unfolds in front of us. Fear is much diminished, and we take on deeper trust in life as it unfolds. We find a place of profound meaning and belonging. Do not confuse this with fame, status, wealth, or even "making a difference." We are true to our intention and aligned with the best expressions of wisdom, compassion, integrity, and well-being. The essence of Vocation is surrender and the death of our self-importance and mechanisms of defense. So few reach this level because we're too attached to what we like and haven't found out how to trust. The evolution of our Vocation is not usually a dramatic one.

With that little educational detour about adult development wrapped up, what do you do with your newfound knowledge? I'd like to suggest that you pause and reflect on where you are across different parts of your life. Where have you been, when? Where is your growth edge?

One thing's for sure: The baby's arrival can draw you to the "Balance" or even "Addressing Immediate Concerns" stages like a magnet. Consider yourself forewarned!

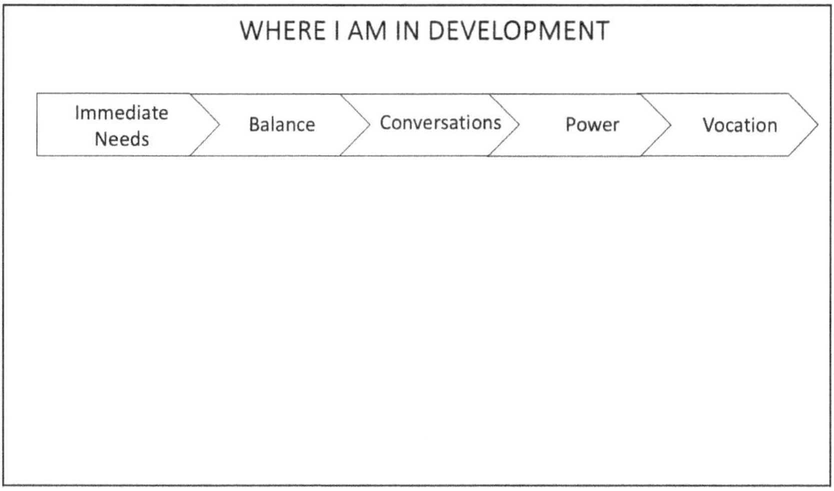

WHERE I AM IN DEVELOPMENT

Immediate Needs > Balance > Conversations > Power > Vocation

Here is some space to jot down your thoughts:

____

____

____

____

____

____

B. SIX STREAMS OF COMPETENCE

Here's one last educational framework for thinking about where you are in your life. This section is adapted from materials shared in my Integral Coaching Certification with New Ventures West (an excellent school and community if you are considering becoming a coach).

This framework has "Streams of Competence" that independently and interdependently shape us. They are Cognitive, Emotional, Somatic, Relational, Spiritual, and Integrating. Unlike the "Ways of Being" we just reviewed, there is no order or hierarchy—they are simply different aspects (or pillars) of ourselves, and each can be at a different stage of development.

Cognitive

The ability to make observations in a particular field of activity and then to synthesize them into a coherent understanding. "Understanding" means seeing possibilities for action, making accurate predictions, and foreseeing potential breakdowns. *It's about taking a logical approach.*

Emotional

The ability to discern your own emotional states, what you are feeling at this moment, what the background emotional tone of your life is, what emotions are present when you experience difficulties, and other observations. Also, the ability to discern the emotional state of others, even when they themselves may be oblivious to it or denying it. This includes staying present and available to relationship and in communication amid strong emotional events (yours or others'). *It's about knowing the range of emotions and expanding the language.*

Somatic

The ability to observe what is happening in your body, e.g., feeling energized, tired, heavy, open, or tight. It's being able to tap into the wisdom of your body, which may have a different insight into what's happening than your intellect or emotions. *This is not about whether you go to the gym 24/7 but how you embody it.*

Relational

The ability to initiate and sustain mutually satisfying relationships. This includes being able to listen deeply and communicate profoundly with a wide variety of individuals and groups. It also includes the ability to compromise, see the world from different viewpoints, and be supportive of others' intentions; the ability to set aside one's desires for the sake of the relationship while maintaining a sense of your worth and dignity. *It's about being open to new networks of support and allowing multiple perspectives.*

Spiritual

The ability to create a life dedicated to the benefit of everyone, not only for the advantage of yourself, your family, company, or clan. This means the competence to initiate and sustain practices that strengthen your bond to the wide web of life connecting all people, all living systems, all things. This also includes developing yourself as an active member in communities dedicated to compassion, wisdom, and service to others. *It's about how we can trust the universe or web of life; it's NOT about organized religion, per se.*

Integrating

The ability to eliminate all the ways you compartmentalize your life so that your commitments, learning, and values are present in all your words, thoughts, actions, and relationships. It requires that you confront what you've been denying, avoiding, and justifying and that you be open to continuous learning and input from others. *It's about being the same person in all parts of life, integrating postures, values, and masculine & feminine sides.*

Again, having read this, sit back and reflect on yourself. Where are you in each of the streams? Which are more or less developed for you? Which might challenge you after the arrival of the baby and its dramatic shift in your universe?

6 STREAMS OF COMPETENCE

Cognitive	Emotional	Somatic
Relational	Spiritual	Integrating

Here is some space to jot down your thoughts:

Digging Deep

In this Chapter, we will journey inward and explore the deeper layers of your soul. Parenthood is a transformative experience, and it's often in these moments of significant life change that we reflect more deeply on who we are, where we've been, and where we're headed. The exercises in this chapter are designed to help you reconnect with your core essence, reflect on the legacy you wish to leave, and gain wisdom from a future version of yourself.

First, we'll begin with "**Childhood Essence**," an exercise that invites you to revisit your pure, unfiltered self as a child—the passions, dreams, and joys that made you who you are before the world layered on expectations. Rediscovering this essence can help you bring a sense of authenticity and joy into your parenting journey.

Next, in "**Your Legacy**," we'll explore the impact you want to have on the world and your family. This isn't just about career achievements or material success; it's about the values, lessons, and love you want to pass on to your children and the mark you want to leave behind.

Finally, we'll tap into your wisdom with a "**Message From Your Older, Wiser Self**." This exercise will guide you to imagine your future self, looking back on the life you've lived. What advice would they give you? What would they tell you to focus on, cherish, or let go of? Listening to this inner sage can provide clarity and guidance as you navigate the challenges and joys of parenthood.

These exercises are meant to be introspective and personal, allowing you to dig deep, reflect, and find strength and direction as you move forward in your journey as a parent.

    A. Childhood Essence

    B. Your Legacy

    C. Message From Your Older, Wiser Self

A. CHILDHOOD ESSENCE

Photo credit: My parents!

Begin by finding a photo of yourself when you were younger (ahem, much younger). Something that captures that innocence, playfulness, and happiness of you as a small child. Above is the photo I use for myself:

Start by Grounding yourself and becoming fully present (see Chapter 44A if you've forgotten). Find a quiet spot with soft light, a comfy seat, and no interruptions. Make sure you have paper and pen(s). This exercise will take about 15 minutes.

Look deeply into the eyes of that child. Look into her essence and soul. Complete the sentence *"I am …"* multiple times and jot down the words that come to mind. Look for the positive.

Avoid the temptation to become too analytical or rational, and just let your thoughts flow. Avoid surfacing any negative thoughts or resentments. This is all about the magical powers of your younger self. Take 5–10 minutes to explore deeply.

Now go look at yourself in the mirror. Stare deep into your eyes. What do you see? Is that essence still there? Let me be clear here: we're not looking in the mirror to critique ourselves, comment on our wrinkly happy-lines eyes, or note the spinach in our teeth. Take five minutes to celebrate the power and essence of you. Just you. See how the current now still has the essence of the you then, though sometimes it is hidden well beneath our seasoned exterior.

I realize that this exercise seems odd on paper (and that you might think I'm a bit woo-woo crazy), but please just try it. My clients tell me it's an enlightening experience. I found it so revealing that I now keep a copy of that photo on my desk to remind me who *"I am …"*

B. YOUR LEGACY

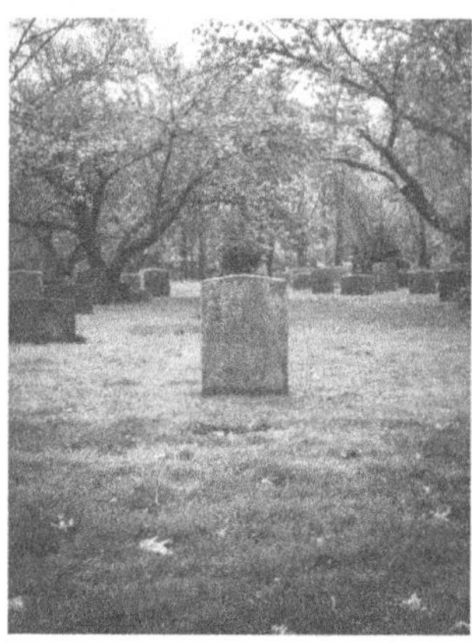

Photo credit: John Thomas, Unsplash.com

What do you want to be remembered for?

Stepping back to the longest-term perspective, many refer to the "Gravestone" exercise or the "Obituary" exercise or the "Funeral Commentary" exercise. All these (somewhat morbid) exercises look at your values, the principles you lived by, and how you made others feel. It can be a list of keywords or a simple statement (*"She was an incredible mother and wife"*).

If you haven't thought about it already, a good starting point is to consider what you want to be remembered for. Very few people identify the kinds of things that would go on such a list. It's often things at a much higher and enduring level, which can even be quite spiritual or cosmic.

Here's a spot for you to jot down your thoughts.

____

____

____

____

If you're stuck, here's something called the "Legacy Exercise" that might offer some inspiration. When we think about our legacy, we often think in grandiose terms like "generations to come" and "eternity."

Well, guess what? Your direct "legacy" is likely to span only a couple of generations. That realization helps us pull in our thinking somewhat.

To illustrate:

1. Think of your two parents. What were their names? What did they do?

   Mom:_______________________________________

   Dad:_______________________________________

   (Of course, this exercise becomes even more complex if you feel you have more than two "parents." In that case, add them here too.)

   Another mom:_______________________________

   Another dad: _______________________________

   Another parental figure:_____________________

2. Think of your four grandparents. What were their names?
    What did they do?

    Maternal Grandma:____

    Maternal Grandad: ____

    Paternal Grandma: ____

    Paternal Grandad: ____

3. Think of your eight great-grandparents. What were their
    names? What did they do?

    Maternal Grandma's Mom: ___________________________________

    Maternal Grandma's Dad: ___________________________________

    Maternal Grandad's Mom: ___________________________________

    Maternal Grandad's Dad: ___________________________________

    Paternal Grandma's Mom:____________________________________

    Paternal Grandma's Dad:____________________________________

    Paternal Grandad's Mom: ___________________________________

    Paternal Grandad's Dad: ___________________________________

1. Think of your 16 great-great-grandparents. What were their
    names? What did they do?

    Maternal Grandma's Mom's Mom: _____________________________

    Maternal Grandma's Mom's Dad: _____________________________

    Maternal Grandma's Dad's Mom: _____________________________

    Maternal Grandma's Dad's Dad: _____________________________

Maternal Grandad's Mom's Mom: _______________________

Maternal Grandad's Mom's Dad: _______________________

Maternal Grandad's Dad's Mom: _______________________

Maternal Grandad's Dad's Dad: _______________________

Paternal Grandma's Mom's Mom: _______________________

Paternal Grandma's Mom's Dad: _______________________

Paternal Grandma's Dad's Mom: _______________________

Paternal Grandma's Dad's Dad: _______________________

Paternal Grandad's Mom's Mom: _______________________

Paternal Grandad's Mom's Dad: _______________________

Paternal Grandad's Dad's Mom: _______________________

Paternal Grandad's Dad's Dad: _______________________

OK, now my head is spinning with all the combinations. And, at least for me, the "fill in the lines" are mostly blank, even if just trying to recall their names.

I won't even challenge you to list the names and occupations of your 32 great-great-great grandparents because unless you're heavily into ancestry and genealogy, you'll fall into the 99 percent of the population who can name none, or only one or maybe two.

My point is that we typically can't even remember our ancestors' names. Let alone their occupations or what they were all about. We might recall an anecdotal tale or vivid story passed down through the generations. Maybe even a broader set of "family values" or "family mottos"—though these are rarely attributable to a particular individual. So, the identifiable lasting impact you'll have is really only on the next couple of generations. Does that help you narrow down the scope of what you want to be remembered for?

Let's go back to the list you drafted at the beginning of this chapter and revise and build on it. Here's a fresh space to note down your updated draft of what you want to be remembered for. (This may be further refined as you ponder it).

Here's a space for you to jot down your thoughts about what you want to be remembered for:

____

____

____

____

____

____

C. MESSAGE FROM YOUR OLDER, WISER SELF

Source: The New York Public Library, Unsplash.com

If you are up for this final section, it can really add the icing to the cake. This exercise provides yet another lens of insight into where you are at this point in your journey.

Here's how it goes:

1. Start by Grounding yourself (see Chapter 44A).

2. With your eyes closed, go "inside" yourself, observing your being as you are today. Notice the smallest, most discrete functions of your body. How is your heart beating? How does your tummy feel? What is going on inside your very being? Get really granular and really small.

3. Then, pull yourself "up" and out of your body. Observe yourself and your body. Then, your environment. Then, your place on this earth. Then your dot on the earth from far above. Look at yourself from a much higher vantage point. Look down on yourself as a speck in the universe.

4. Now, pause and ask yourself:

   a. *"What's important for me to pay attention to?"*

   b. *"What's not important that I shouldn't worry about?"*

   c. *"What advice do I have about how to live my life?"*

4. After reflecting and absorbing what your higher, sage self has to say, slowly descend from the meta-view to the micro-view. Take your time and descend back into your body slowly and thoughtfully.

5. Take three deep cleansing breaths, and when you are ready, open your eyes and come back to reality.

6. Note down any advice that comes to mind. Here is some space for you to jot down your notes:

____

____

____

____

____

____

I realize this exercise is a bit woo-woo for some. But if they are curious enough to experiment with it, many clients share that it is a truly revealing experience that you can have from the comfort of your own home, without expectations, and in less than 15 minutes. I throw it out there for your playful self to experiment with!

PARTING THOUGHTS

PARTING THOUGHTS

Enjoy being, not doing
Take it easy
Forget perfect
Pursue what works for you
Find your voice to ask for what works for you
Make it work ... for now
Share your experiences and wisdom with the women
who follow

Have fun and enjoy the <u>now!</u>

If I can be of further service to you, please do reach out!

With love and support for you on your journey,

Anna

Key Topic References

About the Author

Anna Minto is an executive advisor focused on empowering executives to thrive in fast-paced environments. She is the founder of Transformational Change and You Are Possible, which provide coaching and executive advisory services, motivational workshops, and inspirational speaking. Her clients include executives from Fortune 500 companies and professional services firms.

She has an MBA with distinction from The Harvard Graduate School of Business, is recognized by the International Coaching Federation as a Professional Certified Coach, Integral Coach, and Enneagram Coach, and is certified in Infinite Possibilities and Harvard EdX Happiness. She spent 17 years with The Boston Consulting Group, including time as Managing Director and Partner.

— Contact —

ANNA MINTO

Executive Advisor & Collaborator,
Founder of Transformational Change & You Are Possible
aminto@TrChange.com • (214) 263-0234
linkedin.com/in/annaminto • YouArePossible.club
TrChange.com

Please reach out to me if I can be of service to you

www.ingramcontent.com/pod-product-compliance
Lightning Source LLC
Chambersburg PA
CBHW071442140726
47997CB00005B/1562